Philip Putnam spent school holidays toiling in London's second filthiest factory and controlling the valves in the Walthamstow Sewage Treatment Works. Perfect preparation for a long career as an advertising copywriter and creative director.

For my Father, James Putnam, who gave me his love of books.

Philip Putnam

NEVER PAT A BURNING DOG

AUSTIN MACAULEY PUBLISHERS™

LONDON * CAMBRIDGE * NEW YORK * SHARJAH

Copyright © Philip Putnam 2024

The right of Philip Putnam to be identified as author of this work has been asserted by the author in accordance with sections 77 and 78 of the Copyright, Designs and Patents Act 1988.

All rights reserved. No part of this publication may be reproduced, stored in a retrieval system, or transmitted in any form or by any means, electronic, mechanical, photocopying, recording, or otherwise, without the prior permission of the publishers.

Any person who commits any unauthorised act in relation to this publication may be liable to criminal prosecution and civil claims for damages.

This is a work of fiction. Names, characters, businesses, places, events, locales and incidents are either the products of the author's imagination or used in a fictitious manner. Any resemblance to actual persons, living or dead, or actual events is purely coincidental.

A CIP catalogue record for this title is available from the British Library.

ISBN 9781035822768 (Paperback)
ISBN 9781035822775 (ePub e-book)

www.austinmacauley.com

First Published 2024
Austin Macauley Publishers Ltd®
1 Canada Square
Canary Wharf
London
E14 5AA

Chapter 1

A short sturdy man in his mid-sixties, brown hair greying, grin enduring, pauses at the kerb in Soho, London. Looking up, he observes, 'a lone cloud sidles nervously across a wan, spring sky. No, Freddy,' he admonishes himself, 'not good enough, stick to advertising.'

Crossing the street, he nimbly sidesteps an onrushing white van, pauses ritually outside an office building, runs his sleeve across a worn brass plate inscribed Grimshaw and Welbeck Advertising, and enters.

Receptionist Grace Selby withdraws her Doc Martens boots under an old, scrubbed pine table, closes her copy of Smash Hits and sits up, smiling. Today, she wears an old school uniform she has obviously outgrown. Tie awry, her white blouse strains unsuccessfully to contain an uplift bra.

'Morning Mr Grimshaw, good weekend?'

'Good morning, Grace, yes, we had a lovely weekend in the country.'

Freddy assesses Grace's outfit, rolls his eyes theatrically and slowly shakes his head.

'A St Trinian's Day, is it?'

Grace looks up at him, puzzled, 'If you say so, Mr G.'

'Before your time, Grace. And Grace, please call me Freddy.'

Grace wrinkles her nose. 'You say that every morning, boss man,' she replies affectionately as he hurries off.

Michael Michaels, Account Director, bustles in.

'Morning, Mr Michaels.'

'Good morning, Grace.'

Beady-eyed, snub-nosed, pouty-lipped, face a perpetually shiny pink, he's known to younger staff members as Mr Piggy. Michaels checks his wristwatch, raising his wrist and a bulging briefcase to confirm to a casual observer he's on time and takes work home. Grace, who tends to view all men as overgrown schoolboys, suspects Michaels' pompous manner caps a well of deep insecurity.

'Ah, Grace I gather from your outfit there's a Reader Pet Foods client meeting today?'

'Yes, Mr Sergeant's coming in, dirty old bugger.'

'I'm not sure we should describe our clients in such a manner Grace, or that extra stimulus is required to persuade them to buy our creative work. I take it this is one of Arbuthnott's ideas?'

Grace leans forward conspiratorially. 'Anything to sell an ad, Phil says.' Michaels steps back smartly to avoid the view down her blouse.

'Er, Grace, anyone else in yet?'

'Freddy, I mean Mr Grimshaw. And Phil and Ralph are in the boardroom,' she carefully counts them off on her fingers, 'with Jonno and Paul. For Braithwaite's beer.'

Michael Michaels nods.

'Grace, Freddy has determined we call each other by our first names.'

Grace, noting Michael's discomfiture, flicks her long, raven hair and smiles her innocent smile.

'Seems silly to say Michael twice, Mr Michaels.'

In the boardroom Ralph Bertram, account director for Braithwaite's Beer switches off the projector and with it his presentation.

'Yes, Mr Braithwaite, it is nostalgic, but in a forward-looking kind of way.'

That's so lame, did I really say that?

He glances at art director, Philip Arbuthnott and copywriter Paul Johnstone. Head bowed, Phil stares moodily at a notepad covered in doodles. Paul gazes indifferently out of the window at a pair of pigeons scrabbling on the window ledge. They fly off to claim their perch on the raddled head of Cibber's statue of Charles the 2nd in Soho Square.

And with them flies away a weekend's work, thinks Paul, sourly.

George Braithwaite rises slowly to his feet.

'Thank you, Ralph, but no thanks.'

George, great grandson of the brewery's founder, understands the power of a large client over a small agency. He demonstrates this by indicating the impressive expanse of the black granite boardroom table.

'The clients of this agency paid for this table and what do we get for it?'

He turns to Paul and Phil. 'Last Friday you, Paul, and you Philip presented me with an idea that involved officers of the Light Brigade and their part in the famous charge of one hundred and thirty years ago. Light Brigade, India Light Ale, a tenuous link.'

He looks beadily around the table.

'If I remember your script correctly,' George assumes his sour beer expression, 'a couple of the officers pull out of the charge early to get to the mess tent and partake of my family's brew before anybody else returns from that gallant, yet vainglorious action. Cannons to the left of them, cannons to the right of them,' his voice rises, 'and Braithwaite's Light Ale in the mess tent?'

His nostrils flare, dark runnels in a cratered nose, fast losing the battle with the brewery's product.

'Such cowardice not only denigrates the bravery of the British Army but my family's proud history of participation in several wars.'

Paul slowly turns his head to take in his client. *Get on with it, you old fart.*

George Braithwaite sonorously continues. 'And I do believe the Charge of the Light Brigade could be counted as a failure, a military catastrophe. More than that, it says Braithwaite's is a beer for losers.

'Then this week the brewery, having kindly given you the weekend to come up with another idea,' he pauses for emphasis, 'now you wallow in nostalgia by taking us back to the depression era, hardly an economic triumph, to demonstrate that even in Britain's darkest days a Braithwaite's Light Ale could be relied upon to lift the spirits. No, gentlemen, I'm sorry, but no.'

He looks slowly at each of the agency members before levering his tall, angular figure back into one of the agency's Danish modern tub chairs. As Paul, the future novelist notes, *beady eyes, beaked nose, mane of black hair receding from a widow's peak, his dark suit settled around him, a crow folding its wings.*

Ralph turns to stare fixedly at Phil, willing him not to say anything. Paul stirs his languid form. 'Mr Braithwaite, if I may?'

Phil shakes his dense mass of black, unkempt hair and interrupts. 'Excuse me, Paul. Mr Braithwaite, eh oop. Eh oop is what we say up north, where you and I and your family's beers come from.

'With respect, Mr Braithwaite, in't depression my grandfather used to say our family lived in shoebox after we ate the shoes, but even in those dark days, my family could still laugh even when we didn't have a pot to piss in, if you'll excuse my language. We had now't, and my Grandad, bless him, loved a Braithwaite's Light Ale, and that's what this new idea is based on, true beer values.'

It's an unusually long speech for Knotty, as he's known. Braithwaite's Marketing Department's latest recruit, Jenny Brownlow, not long out of university, chooses this moment to contribute. Paul thinks back to an Italian film he saw at the Hampstead Everyman, of the other woman in a marital triangle, her beautiful, calculating face with its sharp planes framed by long, black hair, her expensive designer suit.

'Unfortunately, Phil, the idea addresses the wrong demographic. This is the 1980s. Brass bands are hardly now and the muffler and flat hat are so old hat.'

Jenny pauses to get her breath and let the agency savour her wordplay. 'This is now. New age. The '80s is not 50 odd years ago. What our qual research indicates is that the young, urbane Gen I is most likely to be our next Braithwaite's user.'

Paul, seeing Phil's face darken, places a foot on one of his art director's and presses, warningly. Jenny looks disdainfully at the creative team.

'We know our target audiences' tastes; we think our Light Ale could well be the next trendy accessory. Put that old brown bottle next to your brand new, candy coloured Apple personal computer and both ends of the spectrum are met, the old and the new; yin and yang. It shows the user fully understands all the good things on offer today. The juxtaposition with the latest in contemporary technology brings Braithwaite's up to date. This is the sort of thing I believe we're looking for.'

'Jenny,' Paul gently interposes, 'Jenny, Light Ale is something of a traditional product and Phil—'

Ignoring the pressure on his foot, Phil lurches awkwardly to his feet and leans across the table towards Jenny, who shrinks back in her chair from the wild eyed, black bearded Northerner with his well worn Smiths T-shirt.

'Excuse me for being meself, Jenny, but frankly, what can focus groups of 20-year-old vinny Rose wine sipping urban ponces teach us about what real blokes drink? Last time I looked, flat 'ats were in trendy Covent Garden clothes shops along with mufflers, and frock and froots, folk rock and folk roots from my part of the world, the north, Braithwaite's Brewery country, still get a lot of airplay.'

Managing to free his foot from under Paul's, Phil straightens. 'Sorry Jenny, sorry, my apologies, didn't mean to get in your face.'

'Phil, Phil we all of us know, and appreciate, how passionately you feel about your ideas.' Jon, call me Jonno Noonan, the agency's creative director has sat through the meeting without commenting.

He tickles at the parting in his immaculately trimmed hair with crooked forefinger before tapping reflectively on his jaw. 'Mr Braithwaite, Jenny, while I let Paul and Knotty run with their idea and I know they spent most of the weekend in the office finessing it. I took the opportunity to read Jenny's research, and while I sympathise fully with Paul and Phil's direction I must say, Jenny, I agree with your more contemporary view of the position of Light Ale in society today, and late last night had a thought of my own.'

Phil looks up. *Thank you, your chubbiness.* Jonno smooths the papers in front of him as if the idea is actually there. Paul unscrews his fountain pen, leans across and writes on Phil's note pad, "We'll fix the fat fucker."

Phil borrows the pen and writes, "You owe me a fiver."

'If you can give me a couple of hours to finesse the script,' Jonno continues smoothly, 'it involves both live action, and special effects that are, uniquely, available to G and W,' he adds for Mr Braithwaite's benefit.

'It'll look very new, of now. And, given my contacts I think I can pull some strings, that's guitar strings,' Paul manages to control a wince, 'and talk to the D'Ciples about an original track. They're a new, London band, as you'd know, Jenny, going to be very big.'

Jonno places his hand against his breastbone to confirm his sincerity.

'I think we can hit slap bang in the middle of the bullseye of your Gen I target audience. Once you've approved the script, you'll come to the recording session and shoot of course, you and Mr B?'

George Braithwaite's eyes narrow at the familiarity. He then visibly relaxes, unfolding his arms from their defensive position across his chest. Jenny unfolds hers too, having unconsciously mimicked her boss.

'Sounds good Jon, eh Ralph, Ralph, you still with us?'

Ralph is looking wistfully out of the window with his familiar 'I Wish I Were Somewhere Else' expression. George Braithwaite eyes him as being "a few pints short of a round" a phrase he often uses to describe the brewery workforce.

'I feel comfortable, and I can see Jenny's comfortable with that. I knew you chaps would pull the fat out of the fire, nothing like a bit of pressure to stoke the flames of inspiration, eh? We look forward to vetting a script, don't we Jenny? Tomorrow, mmm?'

Hands are shaken and the meeting breaks up. Phil and Paul walk straight out of the office, pausing only to talk to Jonno's PA, Jane 'Perfect' Saunders.

'We'll be in Boardroom Five, Perfect.'

'Remind me?'

'Four is Riley's, five is Locanda, six is the Feathers.'

'Going to join us?' asks Phil hopefully.

'Knotty, are you talking to me or my tits?'

'He's talking to all three of you I think, Perfect,' observes Paul. 'Come on you, drinkies.'

Chapter 2

Paul and Phil climb the narrow stairs of the old Frith Street building and settle down amid Locanda's much put upon furniture and fading green flock wallpaper.

'Fettucine al Fredo for you Phil and same for you, Paul? And a carafe of the house vino?'

'The white to start with, please Maria.'

'Perfetta, Paolo.'

The two creatives sit there for a moment. Paul pulls a crumpled five-pound note from his pocket and pushes it towards Phil, who pushes it back.

'Don't bother, I knew that fat fucker would do that, obvious when he kept quiet through the meeting, does it every time, not normally with us, though.'

Phil affects a plummy public-school accent, 'Actually, I've had an idea all of my own, Mr B, you will be coming to the recording session, Jenny, won't you?'

They lapse into silence, as Maria puts a carafe on the table, and pours them a large tumbler each. Black hair pulled into a tight bun, white blouse and voluminous skirt, strong forearms and cheek bones, proprietor Maria is the nonna on the label of a Passata bottle.

Words are unnecessary. Jonno's a creative director who will, at the 11th hour, suddenly have an idea that corresponds exactly with what the client has articulated he wants, irrespective of what Jonno has approved for presentation. Phil had made the cynical bet that he'd do just that.

'Knotty, the problem with Jonno is that he can't tell the difference between what clients' want and what they actually need.'

Maria approaches the table with bread and olives.

'Here you go, boys. No good to drink that stuff on an empty stomach. Oh, boys, you left this Friday.'

She pulls a torn and crumpled piece of the butcher's paper that serves as tablecloths from her copious apron pocket. As a piece of forensic evidence, it charts the progress of a long Friday lunch, covered as it is in wine stains, coffee cup rings, Phil's scribbled layouts and Paul's writing in descending stages of legibility.

'Maria, the mother we never had, you're a saint. These, these are ideas that any other agency would give its eye teeth for. Words beyond value.'

Paul gives it a cursory look, crumples it and stuffs it into a pocket. Paul and Phil are rather old fashioned in their approach to work, invariably having their best ideas in boardrooms four, five and six.

'Phil,' Paul sips his wine, 'you have to stop doing it.'

'Doing what?'

'Directing any conversation with a woman at her chest. You even do it with Maria and she's old enough to be your mother. Were you deprived of breast milk as a child? Did you not suckle?'

Phil tops up their glasses.

'I'm shy, you Southern shite, shy. The moment I look into a girl's eyes, I completely lose it. There's now't I can do, my eyes just sort of dip down. Especially when I talk to Perfect.'

'Mate, listen, it doesn't help us when we're trying to sell an idea. You know the first rule.'

'Aye, Paul's first rule,' says Phil caustically, 'buy me, buy my idea.'

Paul exhales. 'Phil, it's like that stroke you pull with Grace and the school uniform, it's crude. Crass.'

'Mebbe, but Grace isn't silly, there's more going on there than you think. A canny one, Grace is. She knew the moment Sergeant first came in what he was about. She mentioned it to me, we talked about it, school uniform was her idea, and Sergeant buys it every time.'

'Maybe he'd buy the work anyway? He's not a fool.'

'Mebbe, mebbe.'

Paul exhales, sips his wine, and looks fixedly at his art director.

'Phil, sheep shagger extraordinaire, back to my previous point about you and the fair sex.'

Paul puts down his glass, sits back, sighs, 'alright, get on with it.'

'Phil, my point is all about respect. Oh, forget it, you know that. Just learn not to stare fixedly at the chest of every female you talk to. And calling them all love and darling in that Yorkshire patois doesn't go down too well.'

'I think love is more East London.'

'Touché.'

They were silent for some moments. What by unspoken agreement they wouldn't admit is that Jonno had hauled the agency out of a hole. It was unlikely Braithwaite's would ever buy one of Paul and Phil's ideas, and though the boys heartily resented it, they knew that if the business were to go, they would too, before they'd had time to build a joint reputation.

Paul and Phil had only been teamed for a few months. Phil, dark of complexion, physically dysfunctional—his body parts follow each other around in a random, shambling, bear like manner—is fresh from a small agency in Manchester, keen to make his name in the big smoke, keen to take "the short walk" to the podium at award functions.

He's determinedly blue collar working class, disarmingly blunt with "a chip on each shoulder" as Jonno said when introducing him to Paul.

'Aye, fried in lard, not duck fat,' Phil had added, proudly.

Phil thinks of Paul as "white bread lower middle class". Paul is an East Londoner, clever and advertising street wise. Spare, slightly stooped, diffident of attitude and expression, with long, sandy hair, thin, aristocratic nose, long jawed, face prematurely lined. Paul looks now exactly as he will at 60, a mildly successful novelist.

He's capable of great acts of kindness and nasty personal comments that border on spite. His stylish clothes and calculated looks are an unconscious reaction to a white collar, working class, background. His father earned less than many manual workers and struggled to support Paul when he won a scholarship to a minor public school, which Paul conspicuously failed to repay through any application to study.

Jonno had cannily put Paul and Phil together, "wine and cheese", something Phil grudgingly conceded. Phil won't give Jonno an inch yet Paul, ever the realist, knows exactly where Jonno is coming from.

It's Sunday, day of the ritual pint in Paul's local, The Engineer.

'Phil, in Jonno's defence, it is a case of picking the right client to buy clever creative work and until Jonno was hired, the agency had been leaking clients. Surely you know about Crash Cranshaw?'

Phil had put his pint down and shrugged. 'I know a bit.'

'Years back, when Marcus Welby left us, Freddy made a big mistake. Marcus was the master of giving clients what they wanted. But Freddy had seen how really creative agencies were picking up the sort of clients who wanted clever, intelligent advertising.'

'Bit thin on the ground.'

'Still are. Anyway, Freddy saw the work that Banford's were doing at the time.'

'Great. It's what got me interested in advertising when I were a student.'

'I wasn't aware they had any sheep dip accounts.'

'I shall ignore that with the contempt it deserves.'

'Anyway, Charlie Cranshaw was winning them a lot of awards.'

'Didn't know his real name.'

'The Crash thing came later. Charlie was totally uncompromising. You must have seen pictures of him. Like something stale out of the morgue. Thin, lined faced, like a cadaver. Mouth was always set in a contemptuous sneer. That was when he wasn't bellowing with mad laughter.'

'Get on with it. Wasn't he the one who was always saying he'd "kill for an ad"?'

'That's him. So, Freddy promised lots of dosh and big clients. The problem was most of the clients then had a set way of working and the last thing they wanted was clever, funny ads. They were research mad. Every press campaign and TV script went in front of a panel of consumers.'

Phil nodded and raised a finger to make a point.

'Opinions are like arseholes. Everyone's got one, and all you get is shite.'

'Exactly, my bard of the moors. Pass over that packet of crisps.'

Paul snaffles a handful and reflectively sips his pint.

'So, by the time Crash has worked out he wouldn't be making many award winning ads at Grimshaw and Welby, most of the big clients have upped and taken their business elsewhere. That's when the account guys started calling him Crash 'n' Burn. Which got shortened to Crash. And by the time Charlie left, there was a new saying in London advertising.'

Phil interjects. 'Question. How do you create a small agency?'

Paul. 'Answer, put Crash Cranshaw in charge of a large one.'

They sit there for a moment, as the late afternoon sun creeps across the bar. Paul ponders on his pint. How many novelists, he wonders, have expressed the imagery of light playing on a glass of beer? Phil rouses him from his reverie.

'Who gave Perfect her nickname? No' that she's not perfect.'

'Crash.'

'So, he did leave something lasting.'

'Yep.'

'Really? He called her Perfect?'

'In a manner of speaking. There was a time we were affiliated to other agencies around the world and that year, the annual international conference circulated to London.

'The agency booked a large hotel conference room and at each break, PAs would come in with messages for their boss. One lunchtime, Jane bustles in and, looking around the room, spies Crash lounging in the far corner. "Crash, the car," she shouts. This gets the delegates' interest, and they all turn to look at her and Crash.'

Paul pauses for another sip.

'Jane announces to the room at large, "Crash, I put the Saab through the carwash, then I had to put it through again to get the sick off the side."

"Perfect," says Crash.'

Chapter 3

Paul is in Jonno's office. He's checked, Jonno is out and is about to put a tube of haemorrhoid ointment into Jonno's in-tray when Jonno wanders in. Paul quickly replaces his evil grin with a serious, concerned look and delicately lifts the tube into view.

'Jonno, I found this in the khazi. It is yours, isn't it? I saw you come out of the gents just before I went in. And I didn't think you'd want anyone else to find it.'

Jonno looks at Paul, expression guarded.

'Jonno, I couldn't help seeing your face when you sat down, very slowly, in that meeting yesterday.'

Paul grimaces theatrically. 'Oooch, the old Farmer Giles, you have my sympathy, I got the message immediately, had piles myself once. Not good, haemorrhoids are no joke, second assistant's disease and all that.'

'Second assistants?' Jonno looks puzzled.

'Film crew expression, you know, on location, sitting on cold stone walls out on the moors.'

Jonno shifts uncomfortably. His hand drifts towards his bottom to be quickly snatched away. 'Gotcha. Thanks Paul, I wondered where it had gone. You won't tell anyone?'

'Course not Jonno, chaps together, as a fellow sufferer—'

'Piles,' Jonno pronounces, 'are a pain in the neck.'

'That's brilliant,' says Paul admiringly, slipping around Jonno's corpulent form and out of the office, 'you should use that, Jonno.'

Jonno bestows him a beaming smile and a pat on the shoulder. 'I can still crack 'em, eh Paul?'

'I'm not sure crack is the word I'd use, Jonno.'

They share a laugh as Paul exits, well aware the line came from a famous small space newspaper advertisement of many, many, years ago.

Phil puts his feet up on his desk, leans back and screws his face into a disgusted expression.

'So, you saw Jonno coming out of the lavvy and reckoned the ointment must be his. And you picked the tube up, after he'd been smearing it up his fat bum. Errgh, errgh.'

Paul eyes him quizzically.

'Fuck no, Knotty, you northern git, I picked it up in some paper towels and threw the tube straight in the bin.'

'And then what, you went out and out of pure goodness of your heart, bought him a replacement tube?'

'Yes, my sheep shagging friend, I did. And then I bought a bottle of Tabasco sauce. I squeezed a bit of the pile ointment out to make the tube look used.' Paul mimes the action. 'Then I carefully dripped in the Tabasco, poked a paper clip in and wiggled it about to mix in the Tabasco, replaced the cap and returned the tube to Jonno.'

'You didn't?'

A wide, childish grin pushes its way across Paul's face. Phil shakes his head in admiration.

'You did,' he cackles, 'you cruel, nasty bastard, you did.'

'How are things with Jonno, Perfect? No, shouldn't ask.'

Paul and Phil sit protectively on each side of Jane at the bar of the Feathers, having their traditional Friday night drinks. Gracefully careworn, the Feathers is a Victorian pub that has weathered the ravings of the dissolute in its bars, nooks and snugs.

All scarred brown wood and bulging green velour banquettes, it retains the original bar screens with their pitted, etched glass panels, an uneven ceiling stained the sinister sickly amber of nicotine, the lights large milky globes on tarnished brass rods.

The only sign of modernity is the pristine green baize of the pool table in the back bar, recently replaced after an Irish dance demonstration by Brian 'Bitsa' Barnes, Grimshaw and Welby's studio manager.

Jonno has already left the pub after magnanimously buying a round. 'Just the one with the troops then home to wiffy and the sprogs, right. Oh, and make those G and Ts large ones eh, Jimmy.'

Jane knows that the exact sum will appear among Jonno's monthly expenses as "Drinks with client". She turns to the boys. 'Jonno was a bit odd, yesterday.'

Paul and Phil feign slight interest.

'Odder than usual? Go on, love.'

Jane puts her glass down and moves her stool so she can talk to both of them.

'Well, he got me to go along with him to the meeting at Friendship Industries to take notes. It was a lovely afternoon, so we decided to walk some of the way back. Well, walk until we saw a taxi. You know Jonno.'

'So, he waddles along Ken High Street with you,' suggests Paul, 'pausing only to pop into Harrods and inhale the Food Hall.'

Paul makes a loud sucking noise. Jane gives him a shut up look and continues. 'Well, we get to Hyde Park Corner and Jonno stops at the kerb. He looks at me, hands me his briefcase and runs into about five lanes of rush hour traffic, screaming aaah, aaah.'

'Aaah,' echoes Paul.

'He's hopping up and down, waving his arms up and down and grabbing at his bottom.'

Jane semaphores her arms up and down.

'He nearly caused a major pile up. It was not a good look. He staggered back to the kerb and bent over to get his breath. His face was so red, I thought it was going to burst.'

'Go on, Perfect, go on.'

Perfect looks concerned. Phil carefully puts his pint down and coughs, trying to hide his mirth. Paul's holding the edge of the bar with both hands, rocking on his stool and making strange, strangled noises.

'It's not funny. I'm going, are you alright Jonno, are you alright? His face is bright red, eyes streaming, poor bloke.'

'What was the matter?'

'Don't know. He just squirmed about looking uncomfortable and said, "just getting the meeting out of my system, Perfect, clients can be a real pain in the butt".'

Paul and Phil burst into loud, uncontrollable laughter.

'You two really are a couple of unsympathetic pricks. Get me another drink. In fact, get all three of me another drink, please Knotty.'

Next Monday, Paul and Jonno pass each other in the corridor.

'How are the, er?' Paul inclines his head downward.

'Paul, that ointment, it really works, it's like they're being cauterised. It's like having a red hot poker stuck right—'

'Yeah Jonno, I know, been there. I'd increase the treatment, more ointment, make the little bunches of blackberry buggers really cringe.'

They share an understanding nod, Paul biting his tongue as Jonno turns self-importantly into his office.

'See you at work-in-progress.'

Paul sees Perfect looking at him questioningly. He gives her a reassuring grin and retreats up the corridor.

Friday night again and Paul, Perfect and Phil are at the bar of the Feathers.

It has become a habit. They have a round together while reflecting on the week before splintering off into the heaving mass of drinkers from the various ad agencies and film production companies concentrated in the area. Paul turns to Perfect, gives her a solemn look and states, gravely, 'Perfect, I put Tabasco in Jonno's pile cream.'

Paul times the statement to coincide with Phil putting his pint to his lips and is rewarded by a gout of best bitter down Phil's T-shirt as he chokes and splutters with laughter.

'What?' enquires a bemused Perfect, 'who? Piles?'

'Perfect, Jonno has haemorrhoids, he left a tube of pile ointment in the gents, so I borrowed it and spiced it up a bit.'

Phil is now convulsed with helpless, shrieking laughter, causing heads to turn in the pub. Paul looks at Perfect's aghast expression and bursts into laughter.

'C'mon, joke Joyce, Perfect.'

'You did what? Tabasco? Put chilli pepper in a medicinal cream? But that's,' she looks at Paul, then Phil with contempt, 'you cruel, heartless bastards.'

Jane steps down from her stool, picks up her handbag and treats them to a withering look.

'You're both,' she shakes her head, 'not funny.' Before stomping off into the crowd.

'What did I say?' enquires Paul, wide eyed, as the two get down from their stools and embrace, clapping each other on the back, slopping yet more beer on the sticky carpet.

Chapter 4

At Monday's work-in-progress meeting, Jonno speaks enthusiastically to the other creative department members while pointedly ignoring Paul and Phil.

'Alright, Jonno?' enquires Phil, yawning and drawing a hand through his straggly black locks as his hangover bites home.

Johnno looks at Phil and Paul with a cold, hurt expression, then addresses his remarks to the other two creative teams. Rod Grant and Jim Wells, the junior team, look at him bright eyed. Fresh out of ad school, they're keen to make their mark.

Roddy models himself on Paul, smart casual, whereas Jimmy favours a tattered sweater, torn jeans and scruffy sneakers. They share none of Paul and Phil's weary cynicism, nor that of Cynthia Jacques and Claire Mullen.

As G and W's female team, they're justly entitled to their defensive suspicion of the machinations of a business where creative departments tend to be dominated and run by males. Hugely talented, vastly underrated, the two Cs are chalk and cheese, but looks are no clue to personality.

Short, pretty, pert-nosed, rosebud-lipped, fluffy blonde-haired, preppy Cynthia is the one with the acid tongue and short temper. Ms Macon Blanc, as she's known in The Feathers, is a source of constant complaints to Jonno from account service.

'Nigel, you really are a fuckwit,' she'll quietly annunciate, flicking a blonde lock from her forehead as she tears into the junior account executive's carefully written report detailing a client's changes to an ad. She'll literally tear into it, scattering pieces of paper on the carpet.

'Fuck knuckle, fuck head,' as her disconcertingly blue eyes bore into his.

'Cyn, Cyn, cool it. Don't shoot the messenger.' Claire would swing her cowgirl boots off the desk and turn to the poor AE.

With her cropped black hair, dark eyes and complexion, Chinese Destiny symbol tattooed on her neck and heavily muscled arms and shoulders under her tight black T-shirt, "Big Claire" is a daunting figure, until you know her.

The voice of reason, the agency go-to when you're down, a complete contrast to her volatile firebrand of a writer. Putting her arm around Nigel's shoulder, Claire will guide him out of the office, 'Nige, it'll be OK, you'll have the revisions by tomorrow night. Just let us get our heads around them and try and salvage something from the client's dross.'

'Cyn,' she'll say, returning to the office, 'please don't do that. Nigel's an easy target. It's Michaels who rolls over for the client, something for Jonno to sort out, not us.'

Nigel's boss Michael is loved by his clients. His accounts are the agency's cash cows, they keep Grimshaw and Welby's bottom line intact. Michaels comes from an agency background of packaged goods, toiletries and washing powder clients who invariably favour a style of ad that's hardly changed in 50-years.

As Freddy explains to his creative teams in the Feathers one Friday, 'when I was a young writer, a scribe, in the crude, dismissive, sexist London and New York agency world of the 50s, a washing powder brief was known as a 2CIK. They demanded two impeccably turned out housewives gushing about how white their sheets and bright their coloureds were after using a certain washing powder.'

'2CIK?' puzzles Roddy.

'If you'll all excuse my language,' Freddy says with obvious distaste, 'two cunts in a kitchen. It shows a total lack of respect for women. If I ever hear a client, or agency member ever use the expression, they'll be sacked on the spot.'

'So, what's changed?' Paul shrugs, 'sadly, it's a formula, if that's the word. Like misogyny, it exists and persists.'

'Righto,' says Jonno, 'where were we? I've signed off the Orange Grove brief,' he stretches and flourishes it casually. Paul, yawning, extends an arm to take it. 'And decided to give it to Roddy and Jimmy. Client asked if he could have a team with a bright, sparky, youthful approach.'

Before Paul and Phil can react, as they had written the last campaign, Jonno slaps it in front of his surprised young team and continues. 'And, Claire, Cyn, at last Friendship has decided to go for broke. They want the big brand spot, a print ad first maybe, a promotion, then the blockbuster, blanket TV rollout. I reckon I can get you a real production budget of 300,000 quid. Not bad, eh? That should help the agency's *bottom* line.'

He turns to his senior team.

'Paul, John Hardman and Angela Ainsworth asked me to thank you and Phil for the amazing job you did on radio last year. Really took the brand through the S-bend of public acceptance and into the mainstream.'

Paul looks pained at Jonno's mangled brand jargon, then resumes the impassive expression he saves for meetings that aren't going well.

'No one writes TV like you, Paul, but I've decided to give this one to the girls. Sounds obvious, I know, women and household cleaners, but this isn't a Jonno decision, oh no. When I told client at Fiorelli's the other night we had a female team, you should try Fiorelli's Paul, really well upholstered chairs there, very comfortable restaurant, sophisticated, not a *bum note*, bit hard on the *back pocket* though,' he pauses and smiles, maliciously, 'Hardman said one word, fantastic.'

Paul looks hard at Phil, who has kept a straight face all through Jonno's laboured attempt at humorous metaphors. Paul's expression signals, "don't react, don't give him the pleasure". Jonno continues on his cheerfully malevolent way.

'It'll give you guys a chance to finish the Grantham Industries promotions and brochures. Phil, there's an extra task, they want you to go up to their fishmeal processing plant in Hull and get some shots for the agricultural division. They sell it as fertiliser, as you know.'

Jonno is relishing the moment.

'I know it's not the ideal time of year with snow around and that East wind blowing in off the North Sea. At least it'll dull the smell of rotting fish. But being a Northerner, Philip, you'll be used to that sort of thing. Paul, you can stay down here and give Roddy and Jimmy a hand. OK,' he stood, decisively.

'OK I've got that recording with the D'Ciples then dinner with Jenny and Braithwaite after. Might take them to Fiorelli's, its Soho's *hot spot*, eh, Paul?'

After the meeting, Cynthia rounds on Phil and Paul.

'What the fuck did you two tossers do to deserve that?'

Claire merely looks at the pair and slowly shakes her head.

Chapter 5

Paul and Phil corner Perfect as she leaves the office at lunchtime.

'You told him, didn't you?'

'Guys, I had to. I caught him in his office this morning, blowing up this cushion, like a big red doughnut.'

Paul's accusing face collapses into a giggle.

'He said he'd pulled a gluteus maximus muscle at squash.'

Phil is trying not to laugh. 'Go on.'

'Then he went to the loo, and I was worried when he came back, he shut his office door, so I knocked, went in and he was crying.'

'Crying?' For a moment, Paul looks concerned.

'Well, I thought he was, but actually it was just his eyes watering, and he'd gone red. Redder than his red blow-up cushion. I thought he might do himself some real damage if he used any more of that cream. Really hurt himself.'

Perfect manages to look apologetic and reproachful at the same time.

'So, I sort of had to ask him if he had piles and was using a cream. Couldn't stop myself. Just blurted it out. Then I suggested that if he was, he mustn't use too much. And he got all suspicious and asked why on earth would I assume something like that?'

'And?'

'And I said the cushion gave it away and then I told him about the Tabasco, I had to, and his face went all hurt like a little boy, and then this horrible, twisted look came across his face.'

'That'll be the ointment,' Phil gasps, prompting another fit of giggles.

Jane continues, 'Then Jonno went all serious and he said, "I'll get those bastards. And then I'll get them again".'

For a moment, Phil and Paul's laughter is stilled. Jonno has a reputation around town for his practical jokes, his "wind ups". Paul and Phil haven't been on the receiving end, so far.

'Sorry, guys.'

The pair shrug and let her past. Phil looks at Jane's retreating back. 'I'd walk twenty miles barefoot through broken glass just to stand in her shite.'

'Yeh, yeh, a delightful image. Charming.' Paul puts his hand on his mate's shoulder. 'Get those sheepskin boots off, you Northern charmer and start walking.'

Phil turns from his layout pad. 'What makes Jonno so keen on windups?'

'He once told me it was all about camaraderie, shared fun, "togetherness among the troops, Paul".'

Phil is sceptical. 'Yeh?'

'Actually, he explained when he was a junior, finding his place at his first agency, he had this sunspot, melanoma thingy on his nose he had to have burnt off in hospital. Left a huge crater on his snozz and this big scab developed.'

'Oof, painful. And not a good look either.'

'Exactly. Jonno said he felt really self-conscious, didn't want to show his face in the agency. But he had to take the plaster off. Wanders in the next day and the receptionist says morning, Jonno, straight-faced. And she's got this cornflake stuck on her nose. And Jonno walks into the agency, it's a big one, and everyone's walking around with a cornflake on their nose like it's normal.'

'But mate, that's a nice wind up. Funny, but sympathetic. Unlike chilli up the arsehole.'

'Thank you, Phil.'

Paul has gone down to see his mum in the country. Phil sits between Cynthia and Claire in the Feathers.

'This Aussie white isn't bad,' comments Cynthia. She turns to Phil. 'It's really eating away at you, isn't it?'

Phil runs his hand through his hair.

'Merchant banker boyfriend, Porsche, you can't blame her. Why should she want to be seen with a low rent art director in a beaten up old Ford?'

Claire rattles her glass at Jimmy the barman, who goes to get her another bourbon and coke. 'And a pint for Knotty, and a large glass of Aussie thingy for Ms Macon Blanc here please, Jimmy.'

'I think you're underestimating Perfect, Phil. Porsche, eh. And she got into it with Mr Right and they drove off into the sunset did they?'

'Where did you get this from, Phil?'

'I heard Amy from accounts telling Samantha in the studio that Lois saw them on her way home. They clammed up when they saw me.'

'Well, everyone knows you're carrying a torch for Perfect, mooning around outside Jonno's office.'

Claire looks reflectively into her glass.

'Knotty, underneath that crude Northern exterior, you're a good guy. Want some advice from someone who'd like to meet a guy half as horrible as you?'

'Thanks, Claire.'

'No, seriously, Perfect has a brother. A sleazy, no count, fatted wallet investment banker arsehole called Julian who works in the city. And he drives a Porsche.'

'You're kidding.'

'No, I'm not kidding.'

Cyn looks at her colleague, wrinkling her eyebrows.

'Claire, just because he doesn't wear leathers and ride a chopper doesn't mean he's automatically a sleazy arsehole.

'He is, Cyn darling, I know, and I won't say how I know, and don't you ever tell anyone I told you Knotty, but Perfect has this mum she looks after. She's sick, she's agoraphobic.'

'Well, I don't like spiders either.'

'Don't be clever Knotty, doesn't suit you. You know it means panic attacks, scared to leave the house. She's been like it since Perfect's dad did a runner. So Perfect gave up her flat, moved in with her mum, schleps way down south every night, does the shopping, etc. and brother Julian doesn't lift a finger. Just bungs his mum a few quid when he pulls a massive bonus. And I didn't tell you this.'

Phil sits there, totally confused.

'Jeeze,' he says, pulling on his pint.

Claire leans back and runs a finger down Phil's chest. She then gently tousles his hair.

'Ah, lay off, Claire'.

'Phil, Knotty, how long have you been wearing that T-shirt?'

Phil shrugs, uncomfortably.

'You can afford to put on a fresh one every day. Or a new sweater with a bit of shape in it and a new leather jacket. And get your hair cut properly, there are hairdressers all over Soho, better still I'll take you to mine. Trim that beard, change your trainers occasionally.' She turns to appraise him properly. Phil bats her hand away as she pokes his stomach.

'Suck in that gut and get down to the gym more often.'

Cyn appraises him. 'Phil. Your shout, c'mon, get 'em in, lover boy.'

Chapter 6

Later in the week, Paul smoothens the ball of crumpled butcher's paper out on his desk.

'Did we have an idea?' enquires Phil.

'Can't remember. That Grappa's lighter fuel.'

They'd gone to Locanda on Monday lunchtime after work-in-progress. Jonno had continued with his campaign of giving them all the difficult briefs, but Monday morning, he was more Machiavellian than ever.

'Freddy has got us onto the McBrides pitch,' he announced.

'Wow,' his creative teams react in unison.

'McBrides, they're a biggie, number two in frozen foods, aren't they!' exclaims Claire.

'Yep,' replies Jonno, 'and they've bought several smaller brands. They're giving one out as a project to four or five agencies and the winning agency might snare the whole account.'

'Blimey, we'll be by far the smallest agency in the pitch, won't we?' asked Claire.

'Minnows,' Jonno confirms.

'Who else is on it that we know of?' asked Paul.

'Face, Broad and Green, and The Halo Group.'

Paul and Phil share an interested look. And Paul grimaces as he sees what's coming. *Oof,* he mutters as he lets out a breath. These were big, enormously well-resourced agencies who will throw several creative teams at the pitch, let alone planning and research. But none of them is particularly well regarded for their creative product.

'Paul and Phil, it's yours. You've got a week.'

It's a crafty move on Jonno's part, and Paul acknowledges it with a quick, wry smile. With Grimshaw and Welby probably only included in the pitch as a make weight, a wild card to see what a small shop can do when put up against the big boys, Paul knows he and Phil are on a hiding to nothing.

The agency would be hard pressed to carry the complete McBrides portfolio; unless of course, McBrides decides to split their business among several agencies. Paul knows Jonno could easily put all his teams on the pitch as most agencies traditionally do but can't afford to. And anyway, one pitch, one team is one of the few agency policy leftovers from Crash's time.

"It's nothing more than good sense; agencies are rarely reimbursed for pitches and pitches are often a lottery, you can lose the pitch for reasons that, when you see the winning agency's work, are totally fucking inexplicable."

For the pitch, McBrides have nominated a range of frozen meat and fruit pies. Aunt Nora's Pies.

After work in progress, Paul and Phil retire to Locanda to have some ideas.

'The name will have to go for a start,' states Phil.

'Yeah,' replies Paul, 'we get in the pitch and say that and their marketing bloke goes, sorry lads, Nora was the founder's aunt who took him in and brought him up when both his parents were tragically killed in a car crash when he was five and Nora's secret recipes have been locked in the company safe ever since. If that happens, we might as well pack up our PCs and go home.'

'Well, we can go the trad route, adjust the Braithwaite's beer idea, you know, "Everyone in't street wondered what the secret was of Nora's pie crust. The moment the smell of baking wafted from her kitchen window, they'd send young Jimmy round to look in and report how Nora got that crumbly, buttery—'

'Fettucine al Fredo for you, Paul, Fettucine al Fredo for you, Filippo.'

Soon the butcher's paper tablecloth is graced with Paul's copperplate and Phil's squiggles. Paul and Phil both like to get all the rubbish ideas down and out of their systems and wait for the big idea to come through. The page is covered with phrases; country kitchen, wood oven, fruits of the forests, fields and orchards, secret recipe, handed down by generations, roughly chopped wild strawberries.

There were even some suggested slogans. Tasty. Tasty, Auntie. Mighty tasty. Knead it, Nora and some meat references. Angus, Wagyu (crossed out), secret gravy ingredient, chunks, steak, lard, crust, (several times); Aunt Nora your recipe's safe with us, and references to Aunt Nora's sexual proclivities.

The result is now in front of them. A crumpled piece of butcher's paper covered with largely indecipherable scrawls, obscured by wine, coffee and a smear of raspberry coulis.

'I don't remember having dessert?'

'Must have done, before the grappa. And that hazelnut liqueur.'

'Nothing here,' announces Paul.

'Gee, you guys are clever, I like that.'

Perfect has slipped into the office and looks over their shoulders. She spins the paper around and points to the words at the edge of the tear.

'If you'd torn that an inch further up, you'd have lost it.'

Paul follows Perfect's pointing finger and reads the line to himself. He looks up, smile broadening, eyes alight.

'I said that right at the beginning of lunch, you know, Phil, when you asked where you got the pies and I said out of the supermarket freezer. I must have scribbled it down without thinking.'

His voice goes up an octave, as it always does when Paul gets excited.

'It's a whole campaign. Billboards, fridge magnets, the lot. A ten second reminder on TV every night because when you buy the pies, you put them in your home freezer. So, the line will work in the shop, in ads and in the home.'

Phil bends to look at the line and declaims it out loud. 'It's time to take Aunt Nora out of the freezer.' He reads it out again. 'It's time to take Aunt Nora out of the freezer. Mate, you've cracked it. You git, suppose we'd thrown it away?'

'That would have really torn it,' proffers Perfect.

Phil goes into his victory tap-dance.

'Let's keep on the secret recipe, crumbly pastry, pies like your Aunt Gladys could never make routes, and get Bitsa to work this up on the side. Keep the appetite appeal, use the other stuff as knockdowns in the pitch, and introduce the main idea at the last moment. With this one, we push the appetite appeal with the pie shots on the pack and in the ads.'

Paul turns to Perfect and envelops her in a hug.

'Perfect, please don't say anything to Jonno. Marry me. Or him.'

Phil goes bright red and turns away.

Paul crumples the paper into a ball and lobs it neatly into the wastebasket.

'Boardroom six, boys?' suggests Perfect.

Chapter 7

'Cracked it yet,' enquires Jonno, wandering into Paul and Phil's office. He slumps into a chair and gives an exaggerated, I'm cool, I'm not worried, not under pressure, yawn. 'I must say you boys are very relaxed.'

'Well, Jonno, boss, we really appreciate this opportunity. We're going the whole appetite appeal, secret recipe route, because I reckon that's what McBrides will be looking for.'

'Yes, Jonno,' Phil takes in a breath through his teeth, 'we're sitting on some really hot ones here.'

Phil keeps his face straight, Jonno's eyes narrow for a moment, but he lets it pass.

'It's the Advertising Effectiveness awards next Thursday, you two, the night before the pitch so I'm going to have to leave the last minute stuff to you. I'll probably take the girls along to represent the agency, seeing as you'll be tied up.'

'That's cool with us, chief, we're comfortable sitting that one out.'

Phil grins innocently at Jonno.

'When you're happy you've got something to show me,' Jonno pushes himself to his feet and wanders out.

'What's so funny, suddenly?' Paul looks quizzically at Phil, whose grin widens.

'Just thought of something.'

Paul shrugs. 'We won't be missing out on much if we don't go, just a mob of boring clients and agency execs all trying to look important. Anyway, there's no reason to hang around here tonight now, we've done the work, let's get a pint in on the way home.'

'No mate, I want to make sure I've got the Hull shoot set for the week after the pitch. I'm waiting for a call from Johnny Thornhill to do the piccies.'

'You can call him from the pub, get him round there.'

'Paul, no, I need the rough layouts in front of me, so I can discuss then with him. I can't afford to stuff this up, not the way Jonno is at the moment.'

'Suit yourself, I need to go to the supermarket on the way home, anyway. See you tomorrow.'

'Aye, I think I will suit myself.'

'Cyn, you look like a million dollars. That dress; you looking to race off a planner tonight? An MD? A researcher?'

Cynthia blushes, waiting for the turnaround, the joke, "light off in the wardrobe, was it? Can your mum do without the curtains?" but for once there's no put down. Paul's praise is genuine.

'Wait until you see Claire.'

It's the night of the Effectiveness Awards and the girls have changed in the office. A night when the ads aren't judged for creativity, but how much product they'd shifted, or how much they'd influenced brand perception. What's heartening, as Paul went to great pains to explain an unimpressed Michaels, was how often an attractive, really creative idea triggered winning sales figures: and an award.

'Might as well as tried to convince a breeze block wall,' Paul shrugged.

Phil enters waving a bottle, wine glasses hanging from his fingers.

'Cyn, look at you, fantastic. I talked Ralph into a bottle of white from his fridge. It'll be pizzas for us tonight, seeing as we'll be here till all hours putting the pitch together. Ralph must have changed his presentation slides three times already.'

'How's it hanging, boys?'

Claire appears around the door. She wears a simple black sheath dress, her hair gelled into spikes, her boots replaced by a pair of high heels. Her tattoo is hidden under a scarf. Paul appraises her, 'you look terrific.'

Claire feigns shock. 'You actually mean that, don't you?'

'He does and you do. Where's Jonno?' Asks Phil, 'I'm sure he'd like a glass.'

'He's gone to change.'

'Taking his time, isn't he? All he has to do is put his suit on.'

'He's a bit of a fashion maven,' says Cyn, 'likes to look the part when he's representing the agency.'

Jonno appears in Paul and Phil's office, two buttons of his jacket buttoned. He looks uncomfortable.

'What's with the jacket, Jonno?'

'Can't get the top button of my strides done up properly. Must have put on weight, all those dinners at Fiorelli's.' He looks at Paul.

'Just have to suck it in, Jonno'.

Phil steps back and inclines his head.

'You've got taller too, Jonno? Mind you, that's a fashionable look.'

Jonno's trousers don't break over his shoes. In fact, he's showing quite a bit of ankle.

'I noticed that,' said Jonno, 'really strange, reckon I'll have to put my jeans back on.'

'Jonno, you can't go to a dinner like this wearing jeans and a suit jacket, you'll look like an account director on a casual Friday.'

'No one will notice anyway, Jonno,' says Phil, sympathetically, 'It'll be pretty dark once you get into the hotel ballroom.'

Jonno looks unsure. 'I wanted to be on top of my game and now I'm going to feel off all evening.'

'C'mon mate, you'll be alright,' says Paul. 'Or you can stay here and have pizzas and I'll go.'

'No, no, you've got work to do, I'll be OK.'

'You can always tell them you're into a new look,' Phil smiles.

'Short pants with the top button undone, that Jenny bird might be there. She'll love it. Very Gen I Jenny.'

'Leave it, guys,' warns Claire. 'Pour us a drink and we'll be on our way. We want to get there while there's still some of the sponsor's champagne left.'

Left on their own, Paul picks up his phone.

'Got to make some calls, a few comments about Jonno's trousers tonight won't go amiss.'

'No, Paul, seeing his face was enough. He'll be uncomfortable all evening.'

'Not like you *not* to put the boot in.'

'Mate, it was enough just seeing his face.'

Paul shrugs and bends over his pad. Phil picks up his wine and starts giggling.

'What's so funny?'

'Just looking at him. He couldn't believe it. Putting on weight, getting taller.' Paul starts giggling again, spilling his wine.

'The short trousers were a bit odd. Maybe he was pulling them up too high?'

This drew another bout of giggles from Phil.

'Well, the alterations girl at the dry cleaners did think it was a bit strange when I asked her to take them up as well as take them in.'

'You what?' Paul's face slowly lights up.

'The other night when you went home and I worked late, I know where Perfect keeps Jonno's office keys, you know how the anal bugger locks it every night; he keeps a suit behind the door for meetings. So, I borrowed his strides for a day. He never noticed. Sneaked them back behind his door when Perfect went for lunch. Easy peasy.'

'Oh fantastic, fantastic.'

Paul picks up his phone. 'I'll give Scotty on Creative Mag a ring. He'll be there, takes all his own pics for the magazine. I'll ask him to get some extra ones of Jonno for agency PR. I'll tell him to make a couple of them full length. He'll do it for me.'

'It's a bit rotten of us,' says Phil, 'seeing how well Jonno went for the Nora idea.'

Paul grins. 'When we finally got round to showing it to him. But he'll back pedal if it doesn't go down too well in the pitch.'

At ten o'clock, Phil wearily takes his feet off his desk and puts his glass down.

'Paul, you go mate, I'm only waiting for the revised pack designs from the studio.'

'No, I can't leave it all to you. I'll need to check for typos, anyway.'

Phil chews on a piece of cold pizza crust.

'It's not as if there are many words to set. And I checked all the hard copy.'

'I could have made a ballsy earlier.'

'Paul, by the time they get to that part of the pitch, the clients' minds will be reeling anyway; how you can see four agencies in one day and be objective, I've no idea.'

Paul stands and stretches. 'T'was always the way, me old china. The only weak point of the pitch is how our line relates to the original brief. What this agency needs is a planner.'

It's something Paul pushes at every management meeting. Repeating his mantra ad infinitum, in most creative agencies the task of writing the strategy and brief is given to a planner, whose role is basically to see product and advertising from the consumers point of view so it can be played straight back to them via the idea.

'I don't think that's a problem, on the one hand our line's left field, yet absolutely right. It reminds consumers there's a treat in store.'

'And prompts them to take action, as Ralph will no doubt say. Anyway, bit late now.'

'Yeah, and the whole structure of the pitch is conventional, right to where we take the sudden left turn. It's a good line for the brand.'

'And contains a retail imperative.' Paul put on his serious, AE's voice, smoothing an imaginary tie.

'Phil, I think I might go home. Iron a shirt tonight, put the whistle on tomorrow, play the straight man, you can be the wild creative come down from the moors.'

'You'll take the piss once too often, my son,' replies Phil, affectionately.

Chapter 8

Freddy is unusually agitated as the agency team gathers in reception to greet the McBrides marketing department. This is a big opportunity.

'Tea, coffee ready, Grace?' he asks his receptionist, today very demurely dressed. 'Biscuits and cakies on the boardroom table, water? OK, OK.'

Paul and Phil stroll in. Catching the mood, they give each other a glance; no joking, for once.

'Remember, guys,' says Paul, 'a samurai only shows emotion once every three years. Where's Jonno?'

'He's not with us,' replies Ralph stiffly, 'food poisoning, I believe. Evidently, he wasn't looking too good after the awards last night, doesn't feel at all well. It'll be down to you and Phil.'

'Don't worry, guys,' says Freddy, 'streamlines it in a way, one less person talking. I'll cover Jonno's part as he was only introducing Paul and Phil. All you have to do is present the creative work.'

They all turn as Grace raises her eyebrows and nods towards the door. Through the glass wall, they can see an unfamiliar figure pushing at the door. Freddy's expression magically changes from pursed lips and lined brow to his usual grin and he hurries over, indicating the door should be pulled.

The man pulls hard, the door obligingly flies open and he staggers back, scattering his colleagues banked up behind him. Paul and Phil exchange glances, not the best way to start a presentation. Especially as Freddy then over compensates.

'You'll get used to that when we're working on your business and you're coming in regularly,' he suggests.

Displaying uncharacteristic nervousness, he extends a hand. 'Mr Brightwell?'

'Geoffrey Cummings,' says the man stiffly, 'Managing and Marketing Director. I believe we talked on the phone?'

'Geoff,' says Freddy, hurrying forward, 'Apologies, I've only communicated with Mr Brightwell. Freddy Grimshaw, MD. Welcome to our humble offices.'

'I find Geoff a little familiar, Fred,' the prospective client primly replies. 'I prefer Geoffrey.'

'Ooof,' goes Phil quietly.

'Yes, please call me Fred, everyone else does,' Freddy says, turning and looking poker faced at his team.

The presentation goes well. Up to a point. Ralph has tightly edited his strategy document and the five members of the McBrides marketing department all nod in the right places, smiling in recognition and agreement with some of Ralph's conclusions and suggestions.

Keeping the presentation flowing, Freddy quickly apologises for Jonno's absence, attributing it to urgent personal matters. Phil maintains a very restrained, serious expression throughout, attentive, not fidgeting. And, on being introduced is careful to couch his 'Thanks, Fred,' with just the right degree of deference.

In fact, all goes very well throughout the presentation of the "knock down" ideas. Paul and Phil assumed beforehand the three agencies that have already pitched that day will go hard on the convenience plus appetite appeal, and maybe emphasise the secret recipe aspect as well.

Phil explains and then dismisses the concepts as not even worthy of proper exploration. "Pies like your Aunt Gladys could never make" and "secret recipe" draw glances from the McBrides team, indicating, as Ralph suggests afterwards, that one or more of the other agencies took those routes.

The problem comes when Paul, having downplayed crumbly crusts and luscious fruits; loving, slow motion shots of chunks of beef being bathed in rich gravy, though these shots will undoubtedly find their way into the G and W work should they win the business, Paul then makes the sudden, startling, creative about face.

'All these ideas, good as they might be, are not pertinent, not relevant; impertinent if you like because they're exactly what your competitors' are doing,' he suggests vehemently, throwing the concept boards to one side and looking challengingly at each of the McBrides team in turn.

'I repeat, it's what all your rivals do. We must be different. What we need is a hard hitting retail line that'll set everyone back on their heels. Make it play off the appetite appeal shots.'

The agency members exchange Pavlovian nods of agreement.

'One that gets straight to the heart of the matter, whether our target market sees the McBrides call to action on a supermarket freezer, or on a magnet on the front of their fridge, on a poster, in a TV ad. An exhortation, an "It's time".'

'As Karl Marx suggested in his manifesto?'

'Oh yes, Mr Cummings, absolutely, you've got it,' agrees Phil, the irony entirely eluding him or purposely ignored.

'Oh yes, show 'em, Paul.'

Paul dutifully holds up a board. On it is lettered, It's time to get Aunt Nora out of the freezer.

The McBrides team read it, then again, word by word, looking at each other, puzzled, confused. Geoffrey Cunmmings says nothing, merely nods, very slowly.

'That's the agency recommendation, just,' he screws up his face, 'that?'

Freddy's on his feet in an instant.

'Geoffrey, as an agency we try to explore every avenue. If we made every decision easy for our clients, you'd surely think less of us. Yes, it's a complete volte face from the other work, yes it's a line that might polarise, but it attracts attention. It's an absolute call to action, in the supermarket and on the fridge at home. It's different we know, but G and W says, let your opposition yin and we'll yang, every time.'

Freddy then reverts to the speech he made every time he presented a Crash Cranshaw campaign. It gave the agency no room to manoeuvre and had resulted, invariably, in the idea being shot down in flames.

'But it is your recommended idea?'

Freddy looks around at his team. He could take the easy way out, say "we're divided, in its own way everything we've shown you has merit, some of us favour the other work, we like to give our clients choices". To his credit, he doesn't.

'Yes,' he says. 'Indubitably, yes.'

There's much shifting and sidelong glances among the McBride's team.

'Shall we adjourn to the ante room?'

The McBride's team at least stay long enough for a glass of wine.

'Find your peer level client, single them out, talk to them, get them onside, you might be working with them next week,' Freddy has instructed. 'And put some of that Sancerre in the fridge please, Grace.'

Agency and clients mingle after the pitch.

'You've had a long day.' Phil engages one of the McBrides marketing group in conversation.

'Frankly, I can't even remember which agency did what,' she says, tiredly. 'Sorry, Laura Greenlees. Paul Johnstone, isn't it? At least your approach is,' she raises her eyebrows, 'different. You're a necrophiliac, are you?'

It had been often said by others that Paul takes his work a trifle too seriously.

He reacts, affronted.

'No, no, on the contrary—'

'Joke, joke,' she emphasises, smiling, 'yes, it's been a long day.'

Geoffrey Cummings quickly, stiffly, excuses himself. 'You'll be hearing from us. I promise, a decision in a day or two. Good work, thank you all for all your efforts. I can see myself out.'

He pulls at the agency front door for a moment, remembers, nods stiffly, pushes it open and makes his way to the lift.

'He's a real bundle of fun,' Phil murmurs to Paul.

'Phil, you never know. I've seen clients laugh their way through a pitch, slap everyone on the back, and give the account to someone else. One like this can even come down to the agency that can afford to give the client the best deal.'

When all the clients have left, the agency gathers in the Feathers.

Nigel wanders in. 'How did it go? Cyn and Claire will be over in a moment.'

'You can never tell, can you?' states Paul.

'Cummings played golf with the Halo boys last week,' Ralph reports disconsolately.

'Charity day, old boy.' Freddy joins them. 'You draw lots to play. Luck of the draw. He'd have been well embarrassed. And annoyed. Could work in our favour.'

'I bet they let him win,' said Paul, downing half his pint in one go, 'that's better.'

'Phil?' Freddy puts his arm around the art director's shoulder, a natural, unforced gesture. 'You did well today. Never seen you in such fine form in front of a client, good work.'

'Thanks, Freddy. Did you notice that Laura's bazoomas? What a rack.'

Paul rounds on him. 'Phil, remember what we said?'

'C'mon. I said that purposely to wind you up. I knew how you'd react.'
'You meant it, you hairy Northern git.'
'Well, they are a bit special, aren't they?'

Chapter 9

When Jonno finally appeared the day after the pitch, eyes red rimmed and looking the worse for wear Claire followed him straight into his office and shut the door behind her. He went to speak, then thought better of it.

'Jonno,' she said, 'it's between you and I, no one else will ever know. I pulled your trousers from the fountain in front of the hotel and they're in the dry cleaners with your jacket.'

Jonno shuddered, appropriately shamefaced.

'Those trousers, they were killing me I had to take them off. What was I drinking?'

'The girls from White Page Media were feeding you Cock Sucking Cowboys. That was on top of all the jumping grape and beers you'd had earlier. God knows how I got a taxi to take you home in that state. I had to bung him an extra tenner to even let you get in the cab. Mind you, I told him I didn't think you had much left in you by then. God, you were sick, projectile vomited.'

Claire grimaced, expressively.

'I phoned Carol and warned her of the state you were in. She was very understanding, considering. I'm surprised she bothered to wait up for you, Jonno, but don't sweat it. We've all done it in our time. Nice boxer shorts, by the way. Loved the beach ball motif.'

Jonno pompously clears his throat.

'Thanks, Claire, just put the taxi on your expenses could you, charge it to client entertaining. Perfect will fix it.'

Claire raises her eyebrows and departs.

In the week after the pitch Jonno's unusually subdued, making regular visits to his creative teams, encouraging them, praising their work, making sensible suggestions. "Adding that five per cent" as he put it. In fact, behaving just as a good creative director should.

On the Friday he calls a meeting the boardroom "to rally the troops."

'It's been a week, Jonno, and not a word from McBrides.'

'Paul, if someone else had got it, the knockers would have been on the phone to us in an instant, crowing and putting the boot in and commenting sanctimoniously to the trade mags. The fact is, I talked to a couple of people and no one's any the wiser.'

'Doesn't it mean they're finding it hard to choose?' asked Jane.

'Perfect, you're the voice of positive thinking,' puts in Claire. 'But I agree it would be good to know. The guys bust a gut on that one, Jonno.' She sneaks him an evil grin.

Jonno gives her a glance and clears his throat. 'Paul, you've got to remember one thing. Cummings will speak to the agencies who lost, first, and they'll keep quiet. The winner's always the last to be told.'

Nigel wanders in. He self-consciously scratches among his locks of curly hair and clears his throat to get attention.

'I was just down the cafe. Heard something about the pitch.'

They all turn to him. 'Well, go on Nige, spit it out.'

'I've a friend in The Halo Group.'

'And?' Snaps Cyn.

'Leave it, Cyn,' Claire gently chides, 'go on, Nige.'

'Well, he said when McBrides sent the hard copies of the layouts back to the agency, they got Face's pitch instead of their own. And they checked; Broad and Green got Halo's work and Face got Broad and Green's stuff.'

'So, we were the only agency who got their own work back,' confirms Jonno.

'What that means is,' says Claire quickly, 'it means all the work was so similar, McBrides couldn't tell it apart. Apart from ours.'

They all stand, momentarily stilled.

'No, no, don't get your hopes up, they hated our line, you could see it on their faces,' warns Paul.

'It's time,' Freddy's voice booms down the agency corridor, 'It's time to get The Widow out of the freezer, the fridge.'

Heads appear around doors.

'Freddy, Freddy?'

Freddy stands there. 'We got it,' he announces quietly. Then louder, spinning to take in the whole agency. 'We got it. We've got the McBrides account.' His face lights up to a degree they haven't seen for some time. 'We got it. We got it. Bloody all of it, bloody all of it.'

'Freddy,' Ralph puts his hand on Freddy's arm, 'Freddy, do you mean all? All of all of it?'

Like a man transported by a life changing vision, Freddy turns his face to the ceiling, throws his arms out wide and sings. 'Every bloody frozen pea, every sprig of broccoli, every slice of apple pie, every piece of pizza pie,' he struggles to find a rhyme, 'every, oh alright, fish finger, green bean, broad bean, ice cream, meat pie, pie in the sky, here's mud in your eye,' his voice trails away, his smile broadens.

'Do McBrides make a pizza?' Enquires Nigel, thoughtfully.

'Does it matter?' shouts Bitsa, bursting from the studio, 'does it matter a blue buggery, nah? Let's get the Veuve down us, then it's the Feathers, you bastards, the Feathers and bring the petty cash tin. One thing I know about music, when it hits, you feel no pain,' he sings in a passable imitation of Bob Marley.

'Grace,' Freddy marches the troops through reception, 'we're closing the office. Patch the phones through to the pub and join us. That's an order.'

The agency bursts en masse into the Feathers. 'Jimmy, here's my credit card. Eight pints and six large G&Ts to start, please, and one for yourself.' Freddy turns from the bar. 'Right,' he instructs, 'let's get amongst it.'

'What did Cummings actually say, Freddy?'

'C'mon boss-man, give us the word by word.'

With attentive audience pressing forward, Freddy takes a long pull of his pint, 'OK, OK, my phone rings and Grace says, "I've a Geoffrey Cummings on the line, Mr G. I mean Freddy".

'So, I put down my cuppa Darjeeling and think, here it comes. Then I think, hang on it's 11:30 am, he's had time to ring three other agencies before us. Or at least one or two,' Freddy pauses to catch his breath and sip his pint. 'Then he comes on the line. "Fred, may I call you Freddy, Geoffrey Cummings on the line. I'd like to formally invite Grimshaw and Welby to be the agency of record for the entire McBrides brand and product portfolio".'

A ragged cheer and spilt beer greet his pronouncement.

'It means, it means, no, let's not be serious.'

Ralph ponders. 'Did he explain why it took so long?'

'Oh, yes, Ralph, yes, he said they looked through all the material the other agencies had proposed, and they looked through it again, and then he said, "I must be candid Freddy, a Priceline Supermarkets rep came into the office when I was considering the work one last time." He asked me how the pitch was going and whether we'd come to any decision? Your work caught his eye immediately and his reaction was overwhelmingly positive. "Goodness gracious who did that?" He asked. "Brilliant line, Mr Cummings, hard selling, I think Priceline could certainly negotiate a new deal with you based on that. I can see it all over your section of the freezer cabinet".

'Anyway, something like that. Then Cummings continues, "I started looking at your line differently, Freddy, I must admit. I'd promised to make a decision in a week, and that's what swung it, that rep's reaction, and they're always the bell weather, they're Johnny on the spot, sales wise".

'Then he continued, "I'm not sure us being your biggest client will be a negative, or a positive, but let's not worry about that now".'

Freddy looks around, wide eyed, breathless.

'My goodness, well, well done, well done, every one of you, I'm proud to be, you know.' A happy smile wallows across his face. 'I knew it would happen for us, one day. And a biggie like this is really going to get us noticed.'

Jonno appears at Phil and Paul's side. 'Guys, well done. As for the other thing,' he looks at them reproachfully then attempts a fond, fatherly, creative director's expression.

'Let's get shitfaced, Jonno, bottoms up, eh,' suggests Phil helpfully.

'Yes, let's hit the sauce, no, not the Louisiana hot, Jonno,' as Jonno turns, narrowing his eyes.

Later in the evening, Phil approaches Freddy whose red face and line of sweat under his peppered thatch betray the number of malt scotches consumed after the beer.

'Freddy, Freddy, that Priceline rep, the one Cummings was talking about, the one that made him change his mind,' Paul emphasises the words, 'he wasn't the same one I saw you talking to in reception the other week after the meeting with Claire and Cyn and the promotions people, was he? And wasn't it him you had cornered in the Feathers, later?'

For a telling moment, Freddy's eyes narrow and his eyelids flicker. He looks away from Paul before quickly composing himself.

'Paul, old son, you're not suggesting? Goodness gracious, no. As if I'd, I've no idea if he was even the same rep.' Freddy's struggling for words. 'No, as if I'd pull a stroke like that.' He gives Paul an awkward hug and forces a guffaw, 'good idea for the next pitch though, old chap, might use it. Need all the help we can get sometimes.'

Chapter 10

Next day in the office, Phil's head appears in Claire's line of vision. She looks up, startled.

'Jesus, Knotty,' she explodes, turning her Walkman off, 'that was like a 3 am repeat of The Creature from the Black Lagoon.'

'Sorry to startle you, love, I wondered how the other night went.'

'Messy,' Claire replies, non-committal. 'Ooh, could you give this to Perfect? It's the ticket for Jonno's suit. I dropped it into the dry cleaner's for him. Shit, I forgot to pick it up. It's been there all week.'

Phil's smile is calculating.

'Ah, yes, OK, can do; though tell you what, I'll pick it up for her. I've got to go that way, lunchtime.'

'Thanks, Knotty she'll appreciate that.' She looks up at Phil with an innocent expression and smiles back as he colours slightly.

'Now piss off, I've only got until Monday to explain the health benefits of natural organic cotton tampons.'

That afternoon Perfect appears at Paul and Phil's office door.

'Phil, did you pick up Jonno's suit?'

'Oh yes, no. Actually, no, it wasn't ready,' flustered, Phil attempts to look Jane in the eye, before looking down at his desk. 'No, I, it wasn't ready, er, needed a fly button replaced, he must have taken them off in a hurry. I'll pick it up tomorrow, Paul and I have to go that way.'

'That's good of you. I am a bit tied up tomorrow, promised to do something with the girls' lunchtime.'

Paul waits until Perfect is out of earshot before turning to Phil. 'What was that all about?'

'Claire asked me to pick up Jonno's suit, got a bit worse for wear at the awards. Apparently some chick vomited on him.'

'Oh yeah,' Paul guffaws.

'Anyway, he'd lost a button so I'm getting the alterations girl to let the waistband out a bit, and she's letting the strides back down again.'

'Knotty, Knotty, you might be pushing it just a bit too far.'

'Either of you guys got a belt you can lend Jonno?' Perfect enquires of the pair on Friday.

'I got the girl to ease the waistband a bit when she replaced the top button,' explains Phil.

'Thought it might make Jonno a bit more comfortable in the meeting. Maybe overcompensated a bit?'

'It was a nice thought, Knotty, but you also over estimated Jonno's height when you got the trousers let down. His legs look like one of those Chinese Shar Pei dogs with the folds of skin.'

'Here,' says Phil standing, 'he can borrow mine, it's the least I can do.'

Perfect raises her hand to restrain him.

'I don't really think the Hopi Indian look goes with Armani, thanks Knotty, all that silver and turquoise is probably a bit much for Jonno.'

'Suit yourself,' says Phil, looking around in vain for acknowledgement of his wordplay.

On his way to a meeting half an hour later, Jonno pauses at their door 'Bastard,' he says casually, coldly. 'Think you're funny, do you? Well, my wife doesn't. You're both bastards. You got the suit let out, Knotty, so it doesn't take a genius to work out who got it taken in, in the first place. So, it's down to you that I got out of order the other night. Now Carol's not talking to me, so watch it.' He stalks out.

'Oops, better pull our heads in.'

'I told you you'd overdone it, Knotty.'

Chapter 11

The East wind howls down the street straight off the North Sea, whipping icy particles of sleet into their frozen faces. Paul bounces from foot to foot, alternately tugging and hugging his raincoat around him, shivering, and grabbing at the brim of his hat.

'Shit, it's cold, shit, where's Grantham's shitty factory?'

Phil shrugs down even further into his collar, hunching his shoulders, eyebrows sparkling with drops of water below the edge of his beany, the legs of his jeans darkening with moisture below his tightly zipped leather jacket.

'Well, you talked Jonno into letting you come on the recce, I could have done this on my own.'

'The brochures needed to be written, you saw the brief, and he said that as we'd done all the work getting McBrides in; some fucking thank you.'

They're standing outside an obviously long abandoned factory. Rain drips from broken gutters and streaks the black grime coating the old brick walls. A pair of tall, wrought iron gates sag tiredly. Phil pulls at a large, rusted padlock.

'Shit, this is the address. I wondered why the cabbie asked if he should wait for us. I thought he was just after an extra quid. And I left the car back at hotel.'

Hands sunk deep into pockets, Paul nudges Phil with an elbow and raises his eyes, indicating he should look up. On the parapet of the building they can just make out some faded lettering. Grantham Industries.

They stand there, looking up and down the empty street with its cracked, uneven paving stones, stunted weeds clinging forlornly to the bottoms of walls, windows like black broken teeth grinning down at them. They both refuse to be first to acknowledge the truth.

In the end Phil relents, letting out a long breath that turns immediately to vapour. 'He's done us.'

'Like a dinner,' confirms Paul.

Trudging back to the hotel through the rain, Paul and Phil spot a phone box and cram into it, as much for temporary shelter as to make the call.

'We could do it from the hotel bar,' suggests Phil.

'No, let's get it over with.'

Paul pushes some loose change into the callbox and dials the office number.

'Grimshaw and Welby,' answers Grace.

'Grace, Paul Johnstone,' he says flatly.

'Ooh Paul,' she lowers her voice, 'it's funny here today.'

'Funny, Grace?'

'I can hear Jonno laughing. I don't know what about. Hasn't stopped for ages. I'll hold up the phone and you—'

'Grace, please, just put me through to him.'

'Perfect,' Jane answers the phone. 'Perfect,' she repeats.

'Perfect, I know it's you.'

'No, Paul,' she starts giggling, 'that's what Jonno said when he called the hotel and they said you'd gone down the docks. Perfect, Perfect.'

'C'mon, put him on.'

Phil motions to give him the phone, but Paul holds the handset up between them. There's silence at the other end, then a gale of helpless laughter. Phil, inexplicably, starts laughing, too. Paul looks at Phil, questioningly. Phil pushes the phone box door open, indicates the forlorn neighbourhood and shrugs.

Paul nods in acknowledgement. 'Alright, you bastard, Jonno, you got us. Shafted like a coalmine.'

He pulls the phone away from his ear at the shriek of helpless laughter from the other end. Phil wrestles it from him.

'Jonno you bastard, you know what's even funnier?' Phil turns to a now sanguine Paul, 'Paul spent all last week wrestling with the brochures. The fish swim in the fields; shitty line, anyway.'

Paul, anger ebbing fast, gazes through the clouded glass at the sad relic of England's industrial past. Taking the phone back from Phil, he says 'Touché, Jonno, nice one,' before putting it back onto its rest and squashing his wet trilby back on his head.

'Didn't expect you two until tomorrow.'

Phil's mum Beryl puts two steaming mugs of tea and a plate of buns studded with currants down on the table.

'Fresh from t'oven, I still do bit of baking.'

Beryl's hair is newly, crisply permed, and she wears the faded, oft laundered apron that Phil affectionately associates with trips home. It was Freddy's idea to send Phil and Paul to visit Phil's family before they came back to London.

'We can spare them for a day or two, Jonno,' he'd said.

'Absolutely. Be my guest.' Jonno turned away to hide a thin smile, 'Wakefield's not *that* far from Hull, is it?'

Paul's dad Laurie bustles in. Lean, sinuous, clear eyed, his curly hair still black, his eyebrows bristle like his son's.

'Good to meet you, lad.'

He steps back and appraises Paul quizzically. Laurie sticks out his hand and Paul grasps it, feeling a little like a soft, privileged Southerner as he feels the hard, calloused welts of the workingman's fist.

'Philip, he's nothing like what you told your mother; still, Northerners and Southerners, we like to talk stereotypes, don't we? Put each other in boxes. Ey oop.'

Laurie leans forward conspiratorially to Paul, 'Ey oop. I bet that's the only time you'll hear that oop here all weekend. I bet you hear that all the time in office in London from the lad eh, Paul, son?'

He claps Phil on the back.

'Top or Bottom club tonight, Son?'

Paul was someone who, sensitive to place, mood and moment fits in anywhere. He warms instantly to Laurie and Beryl.

'You'll be up for match tomorrow, you two?'

Paul has never been to a rugby league game. In truth, he isn't much of a football follower, whatever the code. His family supported West Ham. As it was the team nearest their home, it was only natural. Like most Londoners, Rugby League was alien to Paul, but he loves new experiences.

He knows game day follows a ritual. Down the village pub for a pint, "not too much, don't want to have to go for pee before half time, might miss something". Laurie counselled him.

Then into Wakefield for the game, a few rounds in a town pub after the game, the amount of beer dictated by a win or loss then back home for poached eggs on toast.

'I don't know how it started,' Phil shrugged, 'always has been, always will be, then it'll be down one of the village clubs.'

It's no different from going to The Boleyn to see the Hammers, muses Paul, probably the same the world over.

On the way up Paul, perhaps to reassure Phil of his sensibility, recounted an advertising story of the '60s, the days of long hair and flower power when outlandish fashions, especially as far as the opinion of the rest of England was concerned, had taken off in London.

A film director was invited back to Sheffield by his parents for the weekend. The film director's London friends talked him into a short back and sides and into ditching his trendy tight bottomed flared trousers, Regency velvet jacket and paisley shirt for the weekend.

He dug an old Harris Tweed jacket out of a second hand clothes shop and made the trip up to his home one Saturday, pausing only for a hug and chat with his mum before meeting his dad in the pub. As Paul's cautionary tale had it, the film director's dad, a steelworker, sat with three of his workmates.

Dad stood, shook his son's hand, appraised him, 'You'll do, lad,' and introduced him to his friends. 'Well, get 'em in, lad,' he instructed his son, 'and seeing as it's you, we'll have a whisky chaser each, eh boys?'

Film director son approached the bar and ordered the drinks as he would in London's adland, where a single shot of spirits was considered so meagre it was normal to order a double. Borrowing a tray, he placed the drinks in front of his father and his workmates and went to sit down. His father's eyes narrowed as he picked up a whisky and held it up for his workmates to see. He turned to his son.

'Hold up, are these large ones? Ye flash git, get thee back to London.'

Paul sits with Phil and Laurie in the Top Club under fading photos of past club presidents and village football and cricket teams. They'd strolled there up quiet, now dark streets past dour, reassuringly stolid stone houses and the 15th century Church.

Paul is relaxed, attempting to decipher the older patrons' conversations spoken in a largely impenetrable local patois, honed to companionable shorthand over many years. Tomorrow, they'd buy lunch for Laurie and Beryl in the pub before leaving for the drive South.

'I can't leave without Yorkshire pudding, liver, and onion gravy,' Paul would say.

'I'm having the roast pheasant seeing as it's in season,' affirmed Phil. 'You too, Mum, Dad, as it's my treat?'

'Ooh son, you shouldn't, are you sure you can afford it?'

'Mum. How often do I get to see you and Dad? Anyways, I'm a flash London git, now.'

'Language, Philip, language.'

Tonight, Jonno's windup forgotten, Paul is happy, comfortable as he raises his glass to a beaming Phil and his proud father.

'Afters in the pub, Laurie? As we're staying there, it shouldn't be a problem.'

Chapter 12

Working late, Paul looks up from his computer, rubs his eyes, and thinks better of it. Phil's out, shooting the new packs for Aunt Nora's Pies. There's noise in the street outside as pubs and restaurants fill.

Unlike New York's South of Houston Street and Hong Kong's South of Hollywood Road, the original word Soho doesn't refer to anything geographical; it was a hunting cry from the time of Henry the Eighth, when Soho was all fields. So-ho, was the huntsman's cry to call off the hounds when the hare went to earth. Another of the arcane bits of information Paul so loved to share.

'Not many people know this,' he'd say to Phil, 'but—'

The coming of the McBrides account has lifted the agency's workload considerably, and Freddy and Jonno are hurrying to hire new people.

'A planner first up, please Freddy,' Paul implored, 'someone to really work out the consumer's needs and focus the briefs.'

Jonno is in his element, disappearing for clandestine lunches with writers and art directors from other agencies.

Beer, thinks Paul. Beer, who will have beer in their fridge? He knows if he leaves the agency, he won't come back, so wanders down the corridor. Jonno's office door is closed, blinds down. Light slips through the slats. Paul looks at it disinterestedly as Jonno doesn't have a fridge.

Suddenly, surprisingly given the hour, Jonno's office door opens and Jenny Brownlow slowly emerges, brushing her hair back as she cautiously looks left and right. Seeing Paul she reddens, turns and pokes her head back through the open door.

'Right, Jonno, right, good thought, I'll convey that to the rest of the team.' Then a little too loudly, 'oh, hi Paul, Jonno invited me in to hear a mix of our India Light Ale jingle.'

'Hi, Jenny,' Paul replies casually, 'Yeah, great, isn't it? Good one.'

'See you, Paul.'

He smiles as she hurries off down the corridor, discernibly flustered.

'Yeah, g'night Jenny, and goodnight to you, Jonno,' he shouts, prudently declining to look around Jonno's office door.

And then sotto voce, 'By the way, Jenny, you've got your skirt on back to front.'

'It's none of our business.'

When Paul and Phil want to talk in private, they invariably go to Riley's, a dive bar in an old wine merchant's cellar down by the Thames.

'It's not that, Paul, Carol's OK.'

Carol is Jonno's wife. Sensible, with a good sense of humour, she views the ego ridden world of advertising with a healthy degree of scepticism.

Seated in a dark alcove under Riley's sooty, arched stone ceiling, a legacy of England's early involvement in the Portuguese port industry, Phil picks at the thick collar of wax on a candlestick.

'I've only met her a couple of times at agency does, and I like her. And the thing is, Jonno's not the sort of guy who normally chases around after other women.'

Paul stretches, exhales, and brushes his hair back.

'And?'

'One evening, Jonno will confess. He'll get home early in time to see his kids before they go to bed and read them a story and Carol will open a bottle of wine, cook him a nice dinner, they'll get all lovey dovey and he'll get all guilty and the idiot'll confess. He'll spill his guts, tell her.'

Paul pauses, looking up at the old, pitted ceiling.

'Not our problem, old son, nothing we can do, and Jonno knows we're not the sort of people who'll ever talk. The horrible thing is, he's going to know we suspect something. He's going to be so *nice* to us in future. You guys OK with that brief? You know.'

Phil flicks some wax across the table.

'But Paul, Perfect will get to know, too; if she doesn't already sus something, and I don't like the thought of her getting involved. On the one hand, she'll be loyal to Jonno but she'll hate it, she'll just get upset.'

'Which is all to your advantage, Knotty, a shoulder to cry on. She doesn't know that you know about Jonno, you can play the sensitive guy, the guy who sees something is wrong.'

Paul puts on a silly, wheedling voice.

'What's upsetting you, Perfect? Perfect, I can see something is getting to you, won't you share it with me? Let me offer you solace, comfort you, let Uncle Philip display his deep, sensitive, caring side, just put your head on my shoulder so I can look down your blouse.'

Paul's already ducking as Phil swings his arm.

'Arsehole.'

'No, seriously Knotty, there's nothing we can do. We're not close mates of his. We tell him it's not a great idea, it'll just makes us look like sanctimonious turds, and the more we tell him not to the deeper, he'll dig himself in and the more guilty and twisted he'll become. Knotty, stay away. Never pat a burning dog. Guilt could be a real trip for him. I reckon his big problem is Jenny. She's no angel, she's manipulative, she's—'

Paul shakes his head.

'She's a real worry, mate. Still at least we know where we stand.'

'He'll be knee deep in his own shit if Carol finds out.'

Chapter 13

'How did the trip up north go, Paul? Interesting?'

'Not really Nige, they've decided to shelve the project for the time being, eh, Jonno?'

Jonno had uncertainly joined the group in the pub.

'Er yes, correct Paul. Bit of a wild goose chase that. Hope you two didn't get too cold, that Northern weather can give you piles. Of grief.'

Jonno had kept the wind-up to himself, as it involved expenses on one of Michaels' accounts.

'It's funny, isn't it?' Nigel looks reflective, 'the fishing industry shrunk in Hull years ago. You'd have thought a Norfolk company would have gone home, then.'

Paul shrugs. 'Anyway, we had a great weekend. Learned a new expression.'

'Not many people know this,' they all chorus.

'Perfect, this isn't very nice.'

'I'll go and talk to Knotty then.'

'Come on, Lord Byron,' urges Bitsa.

Paul loves the euphony of language, rhythm and rhyme, loves song lyrics. He loves to twist, tease, bend, shock, and gleefully juxtapose words. Above all he savours new expressions, wordplay, and slang. He puts his pint down.

'Well, we're having afters in Phil's village pub Saturday and I'm talking to one of his old mates, this bloke called Demo. See, he's got a local demolition business, he's a really great down to earth guy.

'Anyway, Phil's gone to the khazi, and on the way back one of the locals grabs him for a chat. So, Demo puts his pint down, all serious, looks at me and he says, "Paul, that mate of yours, Phil, what a bloke he is".'

Cynthia, Claire, Bitsa, Roddy, Nigel and Jimmy lean in closer.

'He's being really sincere, Demo, so I put my straight face on. And Demo produces this business card out of his pocket and he says, "Phil designed this, here, look at it, I can't tell you how many jobs I reckon I've got just by giving this card to a prospective client".'

'The round one like a wrecking ball?' Interjects Bitsa, 'I got that printed for him.'

'Yeh, that one. Anyway Demo goes on, all proud and serious, "didn't cost me a penny. Wouldn't charge me, Phil paid for it himself".'

'Didn't know that,' says Bitsa, impressed.

'Anyway, Demo looks around the pub, makes sure Phil's not coming over, puts his pint down, looks me in the eye and says, "Paul, your mate Phil, he'd give you his arsehole if he could shit though his ears".'

'Paul,' Claire grimaces, 'that's not very nice.'

'No, it's not nice, it's marvellous and I'm trying to keep a straight face,' Paul's laughing, 'and look serious and—'

Cyn gives him her raised eyebrows "Men" look. 'We get it, Paul, we get it.'

Chapter 14

Freddy, cherubic face beaming, buttonholes Paul and Phil in reception.

'Paul Johnstone, Philip Arbuthnott, I'd like you to meet our newest member of staff, Brian Arnold.'

Good looking, spiky blonde bleached hair, tanned, Brian grins widely at the boys through his freckles, revealing a perfect set of white teeth.

'G'day, pleased to meet you.'

'Do you sun drenched cliches of Aussies always say g'day?' enquires Paul amiably.

'Not all the time Paul, it's just that you Poms expect it. Like us parking a tiger after we've had a drink. Phil, good to meet you, heard all about you two.'

'Complimentary, I hope.'

Freddy takes Brian by the arm.

'Mustn't linger, you'll be seeing a lot of each other later. I'm putting Brian straight onto McBrides.'

Brian Arnold is one of the many Australians in London advertising. His affectionate nickname has followed him from Sydney; Bungalow Brian, nothing up top. In fact, he's shrewd, sharp as a tack. He wanders cheerfully through life, giving off an air of diffidence. Useless at contact reports, forecasts and all the other paperwork, he never ever seems to be around the agency.

'Where's Brian?' enquire harassed secretaries.

'Handsome lessons, charisma classes,' the creative department invariably replies.

Creative departments love him, just as Freddy knows Ralph will. Bungalow has an uncanny knack. He can sell ads to clients. To Brian, it's a matter of pride. His job, the bridge between agency and client.

'And I don't like going backwards and forwards over that bridge too many times,' he once observed.

To him, any change to an ad is time and money wasted.

'Every ad you do for a second time is a new ad you're not doing for the first time.'

His most disarming selling technique is not to eulogise about the core idea but to carefully tick off where it meets the brief.

'I've no idea if it's a great idea,' he was once heard to say, 'but it certainly meets the brief. Lunch, Arthur?'

Brian had followed his brother Trevor to England. Trevor Arnold became a much loved member of his agency before returning to Australia. He ignited Brian's interest in a London job with stories of London agency life.

His stay culminated in a leaving party that fast became, as Paul recounted to Phil, an advertising legend.

After the customary speeches the staff repaired to the Feathers. As the long, boozy evening wandered on Trev's colleagues started to drift away, leaving him with a small group of diehards as landlord Jimmy called time.

Gloria, Glorious to regulars, was Jimmy's colleague behind the bar. Big, buxom, larger-than-life, she looked like a 1950s starlet. Agency members lusted after her, yet none had ever managed to get a date. There were rumours Gloria had another life, that she'd been seen out nightclubbing in Soho with politicians, actors and famous footballers.

That evening in the Feathers Gloria managed a three deep crowd at the bar with humour and aplomb, remembered everyone's names and drinks, and to Trevor's surprise, beckoned him over as closing time approached.

'Trev,' she said, looking at him over the pint glass she was polishing. She paused, holding it up to the light as she casually suggested, 'Trev if you can hang on while I cash up, I'll give you your leaving present.'

An astonished Trevor had momentarily gone weak at the knees before looking around to see if any of his workmates had heard this extraordinary proposal, but by then they'd all disappeared into the night.

The flatmates who delivered Trev to the airport the next morning reported he only just made the flight.

"When he didn't come home from the pub, we were really worried. We didn't know where Trev had got to," one explained.

"He came wandering in at about eight in the morning with this soppy grin all over his face. Like it was painted on. He was all over the place, didn't know his arse from his elbow, we almost had to pour him onto the plane."

In the days after Trevor left there was muttering from agency staff that they never even got to see his leaving present, the matching luggage to which they'd all so generously contributed. They readily accepted, however, that it had been sensible to give the money to one of the creative group heads so he could buy the luggage and take it straight around Trevor's flat so Trev had time to pack.

Trevor, arriving back in Australia with the same battered old suitcase he'd carried to England, might have wondered for a moment why the only thing he'd been given was a leaving card but he was never any the wiser.

'Or was he?' pondered Phil?

Chapter 15

'Fuck me.'

Phil is piloting his aged Ford over the Hammersmith flyover when the billboard comes into sight.

'Nice layout, Phil.'

'Nice line, Paul.'

Their first piece of work for Aunt Nora is out there, larger than life.

'Next,' they chorus.

Paul glances around Phil's car.

'I've just noticed something, Phil. There's no cans or burger wrappers under my feet. And you can see through the windscreen. Don't tell me you cleaned the car just because we were going to see a client?'

'What?'

Phil is listening to Madness at warp volume.

'You heard me. And Madness isn't from your part of the world. What's the matter with The Smiths? The Cure?'

'What?'

Phil turns the tape deck down.

'C'mon, mate. Cleaning the car; I've never seen you do that before. It's a bird, isn't it? And you even know what music she likes.'

'I like Madness. They're fun.'

'Don't change the subject.' Paul gestures theatrically, 'if the car's perfect it's got to be: Perfect.' He glances at Phil. 'Wow, Jesus, it is. Alright Phil, seriously, none of my business. It's too late to go back to the office, let's go up to Camden, drop the car off, I'll buy you a pint.'

It's not like Paul not to get a few cutting remarks in. Could it be that he actually approves of me seeing Perfect? Could Paul, just for once be acting like the gentleman he tries to pretend he isn't?

A half hour later, they're seated at the bar of the Dublin Castle.

'You and Perfect? Paul looks at Phil, searchingly and slowly shakes his head. 'Well fornicate with my ancient footwear. At last. Mind you, I can't really see what a classy bird like her sees in a scruffy herbert like you.'

'Shut up and drink your beer.'

Two weeks before.

'Have you asked her yet?'

Phil's silence says to Claire, "No."

'Phil, trust me. You ask her, she can only say yes or no. Don't you want to know? I'll bet you a haircut she says yes.'

'You'd stand me a haircut in that poncy place you go to?'

He lifts his head to look at her, eyes guarded. Claire's eyes narrow.

'You haven't asked her already, have you? Well, ask her, you big lunk, just ask her, jeez, you've no idea you blokes, have you?'

'A haircut's quite expensive in that place, isn't it?'

'Win, win, Phil.'

The week before Claire's offer, Phil had carefully stayed away from Jonno's end of the corridor for several days. He kept telling himself there wasn't a certain questioning look in Perfect's eyes when he talked to her.

'Oh, by the way,' Claire had remarked as an aside to Perfect in the pub, 'I think Phil wants to ask you out.'

'I'd worked that one out,' smiled Perfect. They both laughed and returned to their previous conversation.

Phil had taken a layout to Jonno for his approval and instead found Perfect in Jonno's office.

'Just leave it for him, Phil.' She returned to her scrutiny of Jonno's diary.

'Perfect, Jane, if you're not doing anything one night,' Phil found himself saying.

'You'd have to come round my place, Phil.'

'Your place?' Phil managed to look surprised. He tried to indicate it was highly unusual for a girl to invite you around to her place even before you'd got around to finishing asking her out.

Yet, he knew full well Jane meant her mother's house, as she was loath to leave her alone.

'I was thinking of Fiorelli's, or,' he shrugs.

'Or no, Phil, if you don't mind coming to the boondocks, we'll have dinner Friday at my place.'

'Love to, thank you. Yes, that's perfect, Perfect. Jane, I'll bring the car in Friday. Yes, on Friday.' He exited backwards like a courtier bowing out of the presence of Her Majesty.

Jane looked up from Jonno's desk as Phil's voice carried from the other end of the corridor. 'Yes!'

Chapter 16

'You been for a lunchtime swim, Phil?'

'No?'

'I dunno, your hair looks different. Blimey, you've had it cut. Properly, for once. You almost look fanciable.'

'Knock it off, Cyn.'

Cyn completes an appraising circle of Phil.

'Claire, you been working on him?'

'Note, Cyn, the fresh T-shirt, the Levis 501s and freshly sponged leather jacket. Note the eyebrows that don't meet in the middle anymore.'

'He's not?'

'He is.' Claire nods slowly, finger to lips.

Cyn puts her hand on Phil's shoulder, leaning back to appraise him. She goes to make a comment and thinks better of it.

'Good, Phil, good. She's a good lady.'

'We're only having supper.' Phil squirms under their scrutiny.

'Strange people, blokes, eh Cyn?' Claire comments, 'put them in a rugby team and tell them to knock over a 200-pound fridge with a head on it and no bother. Put a 100-pound woman in front of them and they turn to jelly.'

'At least he had the guts to ask her.'

Claire looks at Phil, raises her eyebrows and cocks her head.

'I just bought you a haircut, you cheeky.'

'Win, win, Claire.'

Phil smiles a smug smile, bowing first to one, then the other and leaves the office.

Chapter 17

'My housemate will be home, Phil,'

Phil and Jane are in heavy traffic that snakes sluggishly South of London. As they get further from town, the less Jane is the assured West End advertising agency PA.

'Phil,' Paul had counselled him, 'Phil, work out what you're going to say, your attitude, she's got to tell you about her mum sometime. Just be cool.'

'Paul, just what sort of Neanderthal Northern anus do you think I am?' he'd replied.

'Sorry Phil, apologies, you're right.'

In the car, Jane is scrunched up against the passenger door, face turned to the window.

'Knotty, Phil, I said my housemate's going to be in tonight.'

Phil pauses before breezily replying.

'Mmm? That's OK, love. Hope there's enough food for her, for him?'

'It's my mum.'

Phil quickly calibrates the level of the tone of his reply down to neutral with a patina of surprise, followed by a cool nod of acceptance, taking care to concentrate on the road ahead as he speaks.

'Oh, that's—your mum's your housemate, eh? Lovely, yes.'

'Knotty, you didn't know already did you? Scrub that, forget I said that.'

Phil smiles inwardly, keeping his face straight, eyes on the traffic.

'Are we there yet?' he asks in a high-pitched child's voice.

Jane laughs, relaxes, and laughs again.

'Take the next turnoff left. Mum's, she's cooked for us.'

'Lovely.'

The front door of the small terrace house opens as they approach. Jane's mum hesitates and then stands back, not venturing out onto the front doorstep.

'Phil, my Mum, Lily.'

'Please to meet you, Mrs Saunders.'

'Please Phil, Philip? Call me Lily.'

'You can call me what you like, Lily. Perf, Jane calls me all sorts of things, and sometimes even to my face.'

Phil lets Jane lead him into the small front room, admiring her pert bottom in the tight jeans. He tries not to moan out loud. The room is dominated by a large flat screen TV. A family of photos have been forced en masse onto a mantelpiece over a fireplace fronted by with a contemporary gas fire.

Lily indicates the TV and fire. 'Jane spoils me, I don't go out much now.' She motions Phil towards an armchair.

'Not many men have sat in that since my Reginald left. I took that wine out the fridge, love. I expect Philip would like a drink.'

She bustles out of the room.

'Don't mind mum, she's not used to male visitors. My brother Julian comes around some weekends. I can't stand him.'

Jane stood up, 'I'll help her in the kitchen.'

Paul looks up, reaches out, puts his hand on her forearm.

'Jane, I, it's great being here, really. You know, glass of wine, home cooked meal and,' he squeezes her arm, lets go as she turns to the door.

Jane's mother reappears with wine bottle and glasses.

'You sit there, Phil, I've cooked a special meal for you, roast beef and Yorkshire pudding. My Reginald said no woman South of Barnsley made Yorkshire pudding quite like mine. Though in retrospect, I'm not sure what he meant by that. And Brussel sprouts, of course. And Jane told me to leave the meat pink, not well done like Julian likes it.'

'Lily, I'm sure it'll be lovely.'

'Mum, stop fussing.'

Saturday in The Engineer, Phil and Paul lean against the bar, cradling their pints.

'OK, Knotty, c'mon, spit it out. C'mon what happened?'

'Well, when we got there—'

'You didn't get pissed, did you? First date and all that? Sat there nice and quiet, directed all the conversation at her mum? Didn't push it, left at a reasonable hour, you did, didn't you?'

'For fuck sake, Paul, for fuck sake.' Phil's grits his teeth, voice intense.

He collects himself, lets out his breath in a hiss, turns and stares at the bottles behind the bar.

'What? Didn't it go alright?' Paul's voice has genuine concern.

Phil slowly turns to him.

'Paul, please, I can't stand it. Knock it off mate, please?'

'What?'

'You're being nice. Concerned is not you. Please, be yourself.'

He puts on his estuary English voice.

'C'mon Phil,' he mimics. 'C'mon, be honest. Few milk stouts down her neck and I bet Mrs S had the false teeth out and the eyes rolling. How about a threesome, Phil, I know what you Northerners like, bit of rough, bit of mature gusset twanging, c'mon me and Jane don't get much male company.'

'Blimey,' exclaims Paul, slapping Phil on the back. 'Wow, is that what really happened? Wha hoi.'

Paul pauses to assume a hurt expression.

'Actually, I'm a bit upset you think I can't be nice to a mate. I mean,' he sits up straight and puts on his serious face, 'If you're not happy, how I am going to get any layouts out of you?'

Phil puffs his cheeks, exhales slowly, smiles and shrugs.

'You can bloody guess what happened, can't you?'

'Well at a guess, her mother fussed and was embarrassed and overdid it a bit, and then she suddenly said, "that's enough of me, I'm going to go to bed early and leave you two to it." And after she'd clattered noisily upstairs to signal she'd gone, you sat there looking at each other, looked at your watch and said, "that was perfect, Perfect but goodness me is that the time, it's a long drive back to Camden Town. I'd better be going", and she said "OK but thanks for coming down, Phil" and you stood on the doorstep and her mother's bedroom light was still on and Jane went to give you a decorous kiss on the lips,' Paul smiles evilly, 'and you stuck your tongue right down her throat and grabbed—'

'Yeah, yeah, something like that. You were right, I didn't want to push it. She's a great girl, Paul.'

'I know, you great hairy git but don't forget, office romance and all that.'

'Aye, you might shit on't doorstep but never on't carpet.'

'Yeh, something like that. Pint of Guinness this time, and a large Powers?'

'Yeh, if we must. You can always crash at mine.'

Chapter 18

'Clayton Howell's joining us,' announces Nigel to Bitsa, Paul and Phil. 'Group account director on McBrides.'

'What about Ralph?'

'Braithwaite's kicked up, said with McBrides, Ralph wouldn't be able give the brewery the attention it deserved. And anyway, Ralph's got new business to worry about, too.'

'Anyone know anything about Howell?'

'He's got a big,' Nigel looks around him.

'Head, ego, wang, schlong, todger, willy, hampton? It's alright Nigel, no girls about.'

'Hampton?'

'Hampton Wick, prick, you dick.'

'Oh, I see, yes that's it, yes,' Nigel reflects, 'It's really big. He calls his cock Doctor RedFace.'

'How do you know, Nige?'

'My mate Chris worked with him. He and Howell were juniors at Halo. Shared an office.'

'They weren't saucing the saveloy?'

'No, no, nothing like that. Howell's boss was this real overbearing arsehole. Every morning it was, "Howell, get me a cup of tea two sugars and don't forget to stir it." And his boss would wait for it to cool and slurp any spill from the saucer. Real old school.'

'One morning,' his audience waits patiently as Nigel takes a slow sip of his beer, 'one morning, his boss says, "tea, Howell, and don't forget to stir it. I know you don't bother sometimes".'

Realising he has his audience hanging on his every word, Nigel relishes another pull at his beer. 'So, Howell comes back with the tea and Chris says, "don't forget to stir it, Clayton," and Howell snaps. "I'll fucking stir it for him."

'He puts the tea down on the coffee table, unzips his fly and pulls out this enormous cock. Chris says he just stared at it, said he'd hate to see it when it got angry.'

Nigel relishes the moment.

'And?'

'Oh yes; "No, Clayton," shouts Chris but Howell just looks at him and flops his cock into the cup. "Aaah Aaah," he goes and lifts it out quick and runs out of the office. "I was only going to remind you it was hot," Chris shouts at his back.'

'Did Clayton's boss drink it?'

'Well, yes. Chris took the tea down to the boss's office then legged it down to the gents. He had to hold the door closed while Clayton stood on tippy toes, hung his cock over the basin and put his knob under the cold tap.'

Nigel stands there as the listening trio explode into cackles of laughter. He straightens his back with satisfaction. He's now one of the boys. Nigel gives it a moment before concluding, 'every morning after that Clayton waited until the tea had cooled down a bit before he stirred it.'

Chapter 19

'Jimmy, what are you two doing for lunch?'

'Roddy's arranged to call a friend in Singapore, I'll probably just get myself a sandwich, and do some stuff.'

'Come down the pub with us.'

'That's so '60s, Phil.'

'Careful. No, really, come down there, rub shoulders with some real live human beings for once.'

'Let's all join hands and contact the living.'

'Nice line, Paul.'

'Not mine, James old son, Ronnie Scott's. You know, the jazz musician, the one who said never pat a burning dog, founded the club down the street. C'mon, last chance, down to the Dog and Duck.'

'Your friend George will be down the Dog and Duck.'

'He's alright.'

'He'll only be in my ear with his old advertising stories. "Jim, before your time, this, but I remember when".'

Jimmy looks resigned.

'Not if you shut him up,' Paul tells him.

George was a copywriter who,

Possessed of a wicked grin and a fund of filthy jokes and anecdotes, he still regularly caught the tube to Soho, his old stamping ground, where he'd insinuate himself into the conversations between agency members. Out of respect, and because George also had the rare gift of knowing when he was being boring, they were happy to let him join them.

'That'll be you, one day, Paul.'

'No mate, I'll be a published novelist. I'll be down at The Groucho with my agent and the other literati. And you'll be up in the dales, having your way with a sheep or two.'

George wasn't at the bar. They got Jimmy a pint, 'Oh alright,' and a ham roll and stood there, relaxing.

'Are George's stories true?'

'Well, some of them are, but you know what they say about memory, Jimmy. With time, it gets all twisted and honed and shaped the way you want it.'

Jimmy looks reflective, 'I thought the one about his first writing job said a lot about society, and advertising then, maybe even now.'

He pauses to chew his roll.

'Come on.'

'Well, George said, though London was becoming more, enlightened, as he put it, there was still some antipathy towards Jews in business.'

'There still is. Say it like it is, Jimmy, anti-Semitism.'

'Well, George said his first agency's founder and MD was Jewish. And there was this meeting when a new client was introduced to the agency and he suddenly said, "I say, Morris, is this a Jewish agency?" And the MD answered, "Not necessarily".'

'Great, but sad,' nodded Paul, 'get 'em in, James, I need some inspiration for this afternoon.'

Chapter 20

Ralph was a career Group Account Director. He didn't want to be MD of an agency or have his own shop with his name on the door.

'You lack ambition, Ralph,' said his wife Sonia, sitting down on the sofa and running her hand over his prematurely balding head.

'Sonia, relationships are what my job is all about, particularly yours and mine. That's why I'm home at a reasonable hour, the kids still remember who I am, and we're having a G and T together for the pure pleasure of it, not because I desperately need it.'

Ralph's lucky and he knows it. He's satisfied Freddy Grimshaw is loyal to his senior staff. Ralph has a contract and the trust of his MD. Freddy relies on him and perhaps subconsciously plays on it. New business manager is the worst job at G and W.

As Ralph makes it clear to anyone who questions his ability to attract clients, 'it can take two years to get a new client in the door. And the more you get in, the more new ones you're denied by relationships, and account conflict. This isn't Japan, where a large agency might handle three different whisky brands.'

Fortunately, Ralph also looks after Braithwaite's beer. He'd be up there next week, looking at the towering brewery chimneys leaking steam into a lowering sky, smelling the sour sweet vegetal wort and listening to the kegs being trundled over the flagstone yard below.

Ralph had kept quiet in the meeting when Jonno's idea found favour. Much as he might disagree before or after a meeting, the agency had to back each other in the boardroom. Traditional beer values was Ralph's strategy, he genuinely felt that Braithwaite's was one of the few beers from older breweries that could still justify that positioning.

Perhaps when he had Jonno to himself on the train north, CDs of the new jingle in his briefcase, and an animatic of the commercial, a rough compilation of footage from other sources put to the music to give client an idea what a finished commercial might look like, perhaps then he could broach the subject of changing the packaging slightly and make India Pale Ale just a little less fustian and tired looking.

He'd first thought of it when Jonno dropped into his office to discuss work in progress but decided to bide his time before broaching it.

'You see, Ralph, it's the juxtaposition, as Jenny puts it, that works so well. The stylish modernity of the personal computer, the Mackintosh next to the brown bottle and its label with the old lettering, and the way we've introduced a little sitar and tabla into the music to make the subtle India Pale Ale connection.'

'Ravi Shankar.'

'Who?'

'Sitar player. He was back in my teenage days. You been working on Jenny?'

Jonno bristles. Colouring slightly, he aggressively pushes a brightly waist coated chest towards Ralph.

'What, Ralph, do you mean by that? Are you inferring something?'

Ralph is genuinely perplexed by Jonno's reaction.

'Well, no, I mean, you're the best person to worm their way inside her defences, catch her with her pants down, so to speak. She reacts very positively to you.'

He sees Jonno's expression. *Ah Jonno, Jonno you underestimate me.* Ralph assumes a hurt look, trying to keep his face straight.

'For goodness sake don't take me literally, Jonno, I wouldn't suggest for one moment that you had, have, that you'd try to, to get into her knickers. No, no, I meant it in a purely business sense.'

Jonno, momentarily picturing Jenny's G-string hanging off a Cannes Gold Lion award, reddens even more.

'Well, Ralph, well, from a purely business perspective, I suppose it's a good idea. Perhaps, from a purely business perspective, I mean where your budget and my expenses are concerned you wouldn't be surprised to see, in fact you might even sanction my taking her out to dinner or lunch occasionally, on expenses.'

Ralph nods his serious nod.

'Absolutely Jonno, you're the creative director, you can't expect us suits to do all the footsy, I mean legwork, and carry all the afterhours fraternising and late nights with clients, can you?'

Ralph's understated sense of humour is not fully appreciated by his colleagues. He's thought of as being very conservative, something of a fuddy duddy and uses it to his advantage. Capable of a straight face, he employs it now.

'Perhaps a few power breakfasts with her are in order?'

Jonno immediately gives himself away by going on the defensive. He could have shared the joke with Ralph, colleague to colleague, laughed off Ralph's inferences, defused the situation and allayed his suspicions. Instead, flustered, he goes onto the back foot.

'Well, well, I think, I'd hate people to think, Ralph, people aren't talking, are they?' Jonno gathers his papers together, 'things to do Ralph, good to talk with you. As always.'

'Absolutely Jonno,' Ralph smiles disarmingly, *absolutely as I suspected,* he says under his breath.

Chapter 21

'Your place or mine?'

'Get a pizza, the action.'

'This'll make you change your tuna.'

'When it comes to spaghetti, we're pasta masters; wonder how often that's been used down the years.'

'Must be getting late. When one puns, it's time for pub.'

'C'mon, one in Riley's on the way home?'

'That's the opposite direction to home.'

'The Feathers, then, Glorious Gloria might be there tonight.'

'You wouldn't have the energy.'

As McBrides brands trickle into the agency, Paul and Phil are constantly working late. As the workload builds, so have their hours and it's well into the evening when, brains frazzled, they decide to leave the office. The boys stroll towards Soho Square.

'Stupid prick.'

'Who?'

'Jonno, that's his Beemer over there.'

'I thought he'd gone up to Braithwaite's with Ralph.'

'That's just it, the meeting's not until lunchtime tomorrow.'

'I'm not with you?'

'Knotty, what's just down the street?'

'True love? Christmas? The Feathers? Ah got you, Fiorelli's.'

'Exactly. I'll bet he's in there with Jenny. Told Carol he's going up there tonight, bingo, night with Jenny and they drive up there together tomorrow.'

'Paul, sometimes your Machiavellian mind really, really—'

Phil stops and appraises his mate. A passing taxi slows and moves on.

'Jonno's not stupid. He knows someone from agency will see his car. And he's already made it clear in the office that he *is* having meetings with Jenny to get her onside, as he put it. And we might know what's going on but no one else does.'

'I reckon Ralph suspects.'

'Mebbe, but rest of the agency doesn't.'

'Got you, so he quite blatantly has dinner with her tonight.'

'Exactly, but goes home to Carol, picks Jenny up tomorrow on the way through, she lives in Highgate, maybe gets there before she gets up.'

'And he gets up.'

'Like a rat up a drainpipe.'

'The dirty bastard. And diverts all suspicion.'

'Easy to prove, bet they'll have a window seat.'

Deep in conversation, they casually wander past Fiorelli's.

'Oh, look, there's someone in the window of that restaurant waving to us. Turn around and look surprised.'

They both turn and, theatrically overdoing it, mouth 'blimey if it isn't Jonno. And good gracious it's Jenny, so it is.'

Jenny raises her glass and beckons them to come in. Paul and Phil raise their hands and semaphore exaggerated thanks but no thanks, looking at watches and putting hands over yawning mouths. Jonno, looking every bit the serious creative head, mimes an OK chaps and they all wave goodnight. Paul mimes kisses, and the boys continue towards the Feathers.

'Crafty bastard.'

'No, sensible bastard.'

Next day, Ralph and Jonno gaze out of the window of George Braithwaite's office.

'Could make a whole commercial out of this view, couldn't you Jonno? It's like a, like a Lowry come to life. The grey, the black, the shiny cobblestones slicked with drizzle, the brewery workers hunched in their raincoats arriving under brooding clouds, the smudged red of the walls, white steam drifting from the chimneys, they've even got the delivery dray with the Shire horses out today.'

'Very poetic, Ralph. Lowry? Which agency is he with?'

'L. S. Lowry, Northern painter. Famous for his local scenes.'

'Yes, and oh look Ralph, there's guy in a cap and muffler,' says Jonno sarcastically, 'and another. It isn't Phil, is it? Saw them last night, Paul and Phil, they walked past Fiorelli's.'

Raising an enquiring eyebrow, Ralph feigns interest.

'I was in there with Jenny, having an early bite, getting her primed for the meeting today.'

'Well wouldn't want it to go off half cock, would you,' smiles Ralph, maliciously. 'Ah,' he raises his voice, 'here they are now.'

George and Jenny had excused themselves to sign off some internal business before continuing their meeting with the agency. While they waited, Ralph found his gaze drifting outside to the brewery tap, the pub by the factory gates where the draught beer came straight from the brewery and where they served a legendary meat pie.

He willed George to say, 'Half an hour's break, gentlemen? Time to sample the product.'

George appears, his black suit jacket settling like a funereal shroud around him.

'Half an hour's break, gentlemen? Time to get a cheese sandwich and a glass of milk from the canteen,' he announces as he joins them.

Ralph's shoulders droop. Jonno picks up the ball.

'We'd love to join you, Mr B, bit of protein, jolly good, can't afford to sample the product, not if I'm giving Jenny a lift back to town, later.'

How far can you crawl up the client's arse, Jonno, especially when he knows very well that you're brown nosing?

Ralph thinks back to the advice he'd once sought from a famous Australian adman, who, when asked by the eager young account executive how he approached clients had answered, "Ralph, young man, I breaststroke majestically up their arses, keeping my nose one inch above the shit".'

If only George Braithwaite was like his father, an old school marketing man. Marcus Welby had always spoken warmly of him.

"Old Sid Braithwaite, you'd come all the way up here to see him, get the ads out and every time he'd put his hand on my arm, say don't bother Marcus, just leave them with me. If you say they're good, I'm sure they are. Like I always say, I make the beer, you make the ads.

"If only all our clients were like that," Marcus would say wistfully to his offsider, 'It's called trust, Ralph, trust."

While they wait for their lunch to come up from the canteen, Jenny turns on the TV, plugs in the videotape of the animatic. She and Jonno tap their feet enthusiastically to the song while George looks closely at the screen.

'Mmm, pretty good. No, pause it there. The nightclub scene, some of those girls' dresses, bit flimsy, that's not Braithwaite's, we've got impressionable young girls working here, might put ideas in their heads and I'm not racist but...'

'I believe our producer Steve pulled the footage from a Brazilian commercial, Mr Braithwaite, it's purely indicative, representative of the mood and the milieu. When we shoot it, our dancers and the other patrons will be accurately cast and dressed to represent a cross section of the demographic Jenny so carefully defined.'

Was that my mouth moving? Did I really say that? It must have been me, Braithwaite's nodding and Jonno and Jenny are also nodding in agreement. Will I, one day, say what I really think and feel to a client, especially a stitched up paternalistic racist like him?

'Ah, good, here's our lunch. I do think a bit of lettuce adds that final touch to a cheese sandwich, don't you Ralph? Seeing as you're a bit of an epicurean. I must get them to get some piccalilli in, do you have that down south?

'Ah,' he says, again, taking a bite, 'perhaps not quite what you chaps serve me in London but I'm not sure focaccia or panini really does justice to a slice of fine local English cheese, anyway. Tuck in, at this rate Ralph, I'll have you on that 3 o'clock train back to London.'

Chapter 22

Jane perches on the corner of Claire's desk. 'Claire, I've been going to a local salon for years, girl I went to school with cuts my hair. I hate to be disloyal but I think it's time I got it styled, you know.'

'Perfect, I've an appointment Friday, why don't I see if I can't get you done as well? There's a couple of good cutters at the salon.'

Claire appraises her. Jane's normal style of dress is quite prim. It suits her, the plain skirt and blouse, her hair neatly bobbed in a style that, as Paul had cannily noted, owed something the sixties. You could actually think that Jane's was a studied retro look, one that suited her chiselled turned up nose, well defined cheekbones and hazel eyes.

She wanted, however, to change her looks. Be more, contemporary, she thought. That's it, contemporary. Hip. The word had been around forever; it was still relevant. Glancing at her fleeting reflection in the window of the train home, paperback open on her lap, she was suddenly dissatisfied with herself.

She disapproved of some of the excesses of advertising, perhaps not reconciling the normality of an office job, the hours, computers, schedules and invoices, with some of the unreconstructed and uncouth personalities she worked with; the contrast of an executive's pair of brightly shined brogues with an art director's scuffed hi tops, the open derision with which the creative department greeted Friday mufti day, as executives, plainly uncomfortable, tried to dress down.

She ignored the fact that little mousy Sheila from the studio took orders for weed and marching powder every Tuesday and delivered on Fridays in the Feathers. On the other hand, she recognised that under the veneer of irresponsibility and crumpled, shabby clothing, the alcohol and the drug fuelled excesses, there were some genuinely nice and very clever people in the creative department; however much they cloaked it in sardonic asides, cruel jokes and a general disregard for PC respectability.

And perhaps, compared with her workmates, she was a little, dowdy. Yes, she felt, dowdy. Or was she thinking of Phil, again? Her first sight of him shambling through the office had frankly repelled her; maybe not so much repelled, as she explained to Claire but the wild unkempt hair, the shaggy eyebrows and beard left her cold.

However now there was the cleverly cut hair, trimmed beard, clean T-shirt, 'and underneath all the eee by gum, there's this genuinely gentle, caring guy. It's like having a big, shy kid around, until he puts his arm around you, and you realise the strength there, the quiet strength.'

Her words die away as she thinks of him.

'Lovely,' Claire's lips crinkle, 'this is Phil, the guy down the corridor, the guy who gets down the pub and shouts, "C'mon you Southern shite hawks, let's do the full gallon." That Phil?'

'The very same, Claire.'

The girls sit next to each other in the hairdressers.

'Has he been around again?'

'Yes, not such a success this time. He met brother Julian, and I got upset with him, sent him back over the river with a flea in his ear.'

Claire settles back in her chair, 'tell me?'

'Well, I suppose Julian thought he had to have a look at Knotty, so he invited himself around for lunch. Mum had cooked this roast lamb, well done, which didn't sit too well with Phil from the start. And I think he and Paul had had a few before he came down, his car was in for a service and he caught the train.

'You know, Saturday he and Paul came into the office for a couple of hours to finish something, so we had lunch late. I heard Phil do this enormous belch as he came up the front path and he had this silly grin on his face when I opened the front door. The breath mint was a bit of a giveaway, too.'

Claire relishes this, conjuring up the scenario in her mind.

'Then Julian comes in wearing this pink golf shirt and blue trousers, and I saw Phil trying not to smile. Then when he shook Julian's hand he was almost, what's the word, obsequious, fawning. "Julian," he went, "Julian, alright if I call you that love? Or darling, like we do on the moors? Eee oop, I'll get thee an ale if that's alright with you, Lily".'

'Doesn't sound like Knotty to be like that, sounds like he was, well, sort of on the defensive,' Claire comments thoughtfully, 'his, I know I'm only an uncouth Northern lout routine, like when he first joined us.'

'Claire, I told Phil the other day that Mum had described him to Julian and Julian had turned up his nose. Julian just said, "comes from north of Watford does he," and sort of tossed his head. "Chip up both nostrils, eh? Will he bring his whippet with him to lunch? You watch him Lily, he'll have the Wedgewood out of that cabinet before you can blink." I thought Phil would just think it was Julian's attempt at humour and he'd laugh it off. I thought he could take it.'

'Obviously not. He's a sensitive lout, lad. Yes, Annabel,' she turns to the enquiring studio junior, 'another espresso please. What happened next?'

'Phil just sat there at lunch, with this odd smile on his face. Just said please and thank you, made Julian do all the talking. Not that he needed much encouragement.'

Jane was very good at imitating accents. Other clients in the salon started to tune in. "Do you play golf, Phil?"

"No, not really. Had a round of crazy golf in Skegness once. That were fun, making flowers pop out of flowerpots and the sails on the windmill turn. Think I broke par that day. I was a bit pie eyed though. What's your handicap, Julian?"

"I'm currently shooting a fourteen."

"That's good, isn't it? Or is it?"

"Not too shabby Phil, we'll have to have a round sometime."

"I think I'll save my rounds for 19th hole, if that's alright with you, Julian."

'Phil was, you know, off. Wouldn't look at me, talked to mum a bit, and just sat there uncomfortable. Then Julian brought out this bottle of wine. "This is impressive, Julian," Phil said. "Cranleigh Golf Club Founders Day Reserve. Eh oop, we don't have anything like this at Top Club at home. Pint of Boddies with a cream top, mind and that's it. Oh, and a Rose, eh? Coming into fashion, Rose. This a Provencal number?" Then he looked at the label. "Spanish, eh, they do a good Rose down there right enough. Go nicely with lamb especially if it's underdone like that shirt of yours." Then he'd just shut up. It was really nasty. He was being purposely awkward, and supercilious.'

'Sounds quite mild to me.'

'Phil was drinking steadily, I could see it was upsetting mum, she was going quieter and quieter. "I hope you're not driving, Phil," Julian said. "To drink and drive, Julian, requires that you have a car. Any more of this golf club plonk and I'll be driving the big white bus".'

'Just sounds, jocular to me. You know, he's joshing a bit.'

'No, it was like he wanted to provoke Julian.'

'Well, you'd told him your mum was, you know, disappointed in your brother and it sounds like Julian's so thick skinned, he didn't get it, anyway.'

'Yes, that was it, short of Phil really insulting him, he couldn't get a rise out of him. Just made Phil nastier.'

'He was half in the bag, Perfect.'

'That's not a good look, round my house, with my mum and all, seeing how often Dad was out of it. On the turps, that is.'

'Suppose it wasn't,' Claire ponders, 'so why are you bothering to work on your looks?'

'For me, not Phil. When we'd eaten, he couldn't wait to leave. Mum had retreated to the kitchen by then. Julian just sat down behind the Sunday papers. Then Phil tried to give me this big smoochy kiss when he left. "C'mon love, give me a smacker," he said. I just pushed him off and said to talk to me when he'd sobered up.

'Walked back indoors, shut the door in his face, just left him there on the doorstep. I could see him through the glass. He stood there a minute then he stomped off. I was really upset, went up to my room. Left mum at the mercy of Julian. Thank goodness he left soon after.'

'Perfect, Phil was looking for a reaction. For goodness sake, get him outside the office and give him a real mouthful, come on girl, all this miss goody two shoes stuff, you don't look like a prissy librarian anymore. He wanted a reaction, so bloody give him one. Right. You look great, when we leave here, we're going for a drink.'

Chapter 23

Paul and Phil occupy their usual seats in the Feathers.

'You idiot Phil, you big plonker.'

'I lost it, Paul. Acted like an idiot. I felt embarrassed, I sort of went into my shell, I was, I dunno?'

Phil shrugs and toys with his glass. Paul shakes his head in disgust.

'You didn't even give that Julian guy a good going over. Put the boot in. At least give Mrs S and Perfect something to remember the lunch by. If you're going down in flames, take someone with you. Bloke comes in wearing a pink golf shirt, brings a bottle of golf club wine, what an opportunity. Pink shirt; pink plonk, fuck it, forget it. Right, send some flowers. One bunch for her mum, one for Perfect, and a note.'

'You're the writer.'

'Well, sorry is a good start. Don't need any more than that. Just sorry.'

'You're an arsehole.'

Perfect has entered the pub. She directs her remark from some distance away, loudly. Paul looks up, sees her in the mirror behind the bar, gets up, picks up his pint and wanders off without a word, leaving Phil wondering what's happening until he swings around on his stool and sees Jane.

With a new outfit, and the new haircut framing her face, Perfect looks great, even more so because she's angry. Phil looks at her and says the worst thing possible.

'Love, you look great when you're angry.'

Perfect doesn't pause in her progress through the bar. In one smooth movement, she picks up Phil's pint, pours it over his head and keeps walking out. There's a round of applause and Bitsa shakes his head in wonder. 'Blimey Knotty, she must really fancy you to do that.'

Phil just sits there, beer trickling down his back. He then stands, shaking himself to get rid of the beer that has pooled in his crotch and is now running down his leg. Glorious appears behind the bar. 'Fresh pint, Philip? I'll pull you one while you go and mop up. On the house. Haven't seen that done in years. Must have done something pretty spectacular to impress the lady.'

When Phil reappears from the gents, Paul wanders back to the bar.

'What was all that about, she didn't like the flowers? Not into roses?'

'Dunno, Grace chose them.'

'You didn't get Grace to send the flowers, did you? You idiot. You didn't think she'd say something to Perfect? You know what Grace's mouth is like. Our clients don't need media, all you need to do to get something broadcast is to tell Grace. I bet half the female staff knew in five minutes. And now they know you're seeing Perfect, which she'll really like, the staff talking behind her back and now they'll all be wondering what you did to have to send her, and her mum flowers. It's really funny.'

Bitsa appears and butts in. 'You've got to tell us what you did, Knotty, Grace got me to help out with the notes on the flowers.'

Phil spins round, suspicious.

'Oh no, tell me you didn't rewrite them, you Irish Jamaican git.'

'What did they say, bog rastaman?'

'Well, I thought that just putting sorry, was a bit, well, short. Sort of thing you'd write, Paul.'

Paul merely shrugged. 'And what words of wisdom did Jamaica's answer to J. P. Donleavy come up with?'

Phil now leans back against the bar, his eyes fixed on the nicotine amber glow of the ceiling, awaiting the worst.

'Well,' continues Bitsa, 'seeing as Paul's cards were grovelling and highly uncreative, I merely adjusted them to suggest that Phil was truly sorry, Perfect, as he'd really like to get into your panties pronto and have hordes of curly haired bearded children with you; and to Mrs Saunders, how much you'd like to present her with a tribe of Knotty replica grandchildren, so she could look after them while you were down the pub, as long as she didn't mind moving to Yorkshire and sharing her daughter's future with a flock of sheep.'

As he explains, Bitsa prudently edges towards the door.

'No, you didn't, Bitsa,' says Phil tiredly.

'No,' says Bitsa, 'I had a better idea.' His voice echoes as he quickly exits the Feathers, 'we swapped the cards.'

'Shit, fuckin' dreadlocked Irish git,' says Phil, half rising from his chair.

Hand on arm, Paul restrains him.

'Shit, clever bastard, why didn't I think of that?' Paul's voice rises in admiration, 'then I could have really made the apologies work. But thinking about it, they probably did. I mean, the one to Perfect said you were sorry for upsetting her mum,' Phil's eyes widen as he realises. 'And the one to Lily said how much I liked and respected her daughter, and how my anti-social behaviour had let myself, and them down.'

'You know, I bet Bitsa saw the implications.'

They track Bitsa down in Riley's. Phil walks straight up to Bitsa who turns and flinches, expecting the worst, as Phil clamps his hands on his ears: and gives him a big kiss on the forehead.

'What am I doing with you?' enquires Jane, 'look at you, you caveman,' she says, leaning sideways as she hangs off his arm. 'Look at you,' she says affectionately.

Phil is still surprised that, two days before, as he'd slunk down the corridor past Jane's desk, eyes downcast, she'd said quietly without looking up, 'am I seeing you Saturday?'

'If you like,' he'd mumbled, completely nonplussed.

'Give me a ring as you leave Camden Town.'

Pleasantly surprised, Phil had relaxed, but as instructed by Paul, kept his face straight later when he approached Jonno's desk with a layout.

'Remember, Phil,' Paul had suggested, 'knowing what we know, Jonno's in no position to say anything to you. Just don't react.'

As Phil sat down, Jonno made a great show of looking around him at Jane and waggling his eyebrows. Phil merely looked puzzled.

'OK, then,' said Jonno, suddenly understanding, 'what are we here for, frozen peas?'

Phil waggled his eyebrows suggestively and grinned evilly.

'Just do me a favour and sign it off, Jonno.'

'I actually quite like the idea,' replied Jonno, stiffly.

Chapter 24

'Mmm?' Phil turns to look at Jane as they continue their Saturday stroll around her local park.

'P, you were miles away. I was just about to tell you something.'

'Mmm?'

'They delivered your flowers all wrong. They were lovely, by the way. I wouldn't have thought you knew a flower from a patch of moorland gorse.'

Phil shrugs noncommittally.

'They mixed up the cards.'

'No, really?' Phil is learning not to overreact. 'Oh, I hope Lily wasn't offended, upset in any way.'

'That's the strange thing, all she said to me was she didn't realise you were shy, and you had reacted much as Dad did when they went to parties where Dad didn't know people. He got all defensive and self-conscious and proceeded to drink until she took him home. She even noticed you'd trimmed your beard and that your eyebrows didn't meet in the middle anymore.' Jane starts to giggle.

'What did Julian say?'

'That you were exactly how he expected you to be, that's all,' she concludes diplomatically. She looks at him, head on one side. 'At least the card to me didn't say you wanted to get into my—'

'Been talking to Bitsa, have you?'

'I was a bit worried until mum showed me her card. And Bitsa told me you'd written them, not Paul.'

Jane stops, looks around, and seeing the park is empty, pulls Phil towards her in an embrace. She shivers, tentatively pushing her lips against his, her mouth exploring his gently, until after some moments they break apart.

'I've never kissed a man with half a beard before,' she smiles, colouring a little.

'I love it when you blush,' he looks at her, inclining his head.

At the park gates, Jane again turns to him and this time kisses him passionately, sucking at Phil's top lip, touching her tongue to his. After a moment he reacts, his hand sliding down her back to cup a buttock and pull her to him.

'Oof, we'll never get to the pub at this rate,' he murmurs when they finally pull apart.

'Oh c'mon, you big lummox, beer's not that important.'

'Lummox?'

'Northern word, isn't it?'

'Never heard of it.'

At the pub, they find a corner table and continue talking. Jane puts her hand on Phil's.

'Shame mum won't, I mean, can't leave us alone at home.'

Phil shrugs. He's spent some time reading up about agoraphobia. It wasn't hard to understand how Lily had totally lost confidence in herself after her husband had abruptly left. He could see how her world had drawn in on itself, to the point where the safety, the sanctity of her home had become everything to her: If she didn't go outside, she didn't have to face the world and justify herself to it.

'Mum gets upset if things get misplaced in the house, aren't where she put them. Even the smallest thing upsets her equilibrium.'

'But she hasn't let herself go,' observed Phil. 'Her hair, clothes, makeup.'

'That's because I jolly her along. And when you come around, she makes a special effort. Though she was frightened as all get out that you'd whisk me away, leave her alone, trapped in that house: I had to reassure her.'

Phil knows when to keep his counsel. He smiles, gently, reaches over and strokes her cheek with his thumb. It hadn't struck Phil, until that morning that if he wanted to continue with Jane, how important was to foster his relationship with Lily. He mustn't be seen as a threat to her: and he knows Jane's first loyalty is to her mother, however attracted she is to him.

Paradoxically, ironically, his behaviour the other Saturday would have made him seem less of a threat.

'If that's the way he behaves, he couldn't be that keen, Mum. He's a lout,' was Julian's summation. He'd snapped his newspaper shut dismissively. 'No couth, those Northerners.'

Phil knew he had to work, gently, on Lily's phobia. Persuasively but not obviously. Making his interest too apparent or cajoling her would not work. The more she thought he was encouraging independence on her part, the less she'd respond. In fact, any suspicion he was could be deleterious to her health. She might regress even further. He had to be subtle.

Lily opens the door to the couple, smiling happily. Phil steps forward tentatively.

'Lily, Mrs Saunders.'

'Oh, hello Philip, thank you for the flowers, you shouldn't have.'

Phil's taken aback, instantly changing tack.

'It's getting parky out here, don't leave the door open, don't need to be outside on a day like this, looks nice and warm in there.'

Jane looks puzzled as it's a lovely, mellow afternoon. Phil pushes in, rubbing his hands. *Don't overdo it, you lummock, he says to himself, steady on.*

They settle into afternoon tea in the sitting room. It reminds him of trips home, of his mum.

'Have another scone, Philip, I know how much you like them. My Reginald, he was partial to them.'

Jane had already explained her mum always referred to her dad as Reginald, not Reg. "Call me Reg," he'd say to everyone he met, "don't stand on ceremony that's not our way, is it Lilian?"

"Lily," she'd say with a disarming smile, "so pleased to meet you."

These days, Lily had an aversion to shortening names, even though she perversely preferred to be called Lily.

'No Philip,' she continues the teatime conversation, 'we never really had a garden, just a yard.'

Phil relaxes. His voice softens.

'You obviously enjoy gardening though, Lily, that flowerbed.'

'Jane keeps the weeds down at present.'

'I could use a bit of help though, Mum,' Jane looks up reproachfully.

'Only happy to oblige,' Phil says brightly.

Phil's steadily working on Lily. He's noticed the art books on the bookshelf, and a couple of watercolours on the sitting room wall.

'Mum's, but she's rather given it up since Dad left.'

Phil carefully stores these little nuggets of information.

'I walk across Hampstead Heath up to Kenwood House sometimes, Lily, to have look at the amazing Rembrandt self-portrait, one of his best. Vermeer's guitar player. There's only 37 of his canvases in the world. The Franz Hals. And the Constables. There's even one of Hampstead Ponds, doesn't look that different now.'

'I thought advertising art directors were all philistines,' says Lily archly, tongue in cheek.

'Absolutely. Especially rough Northerners. Don't tell anyone I'm not, Lily, or you Jane, it'll ruin my image.'

'What about Henry Moore, and the Hepworth Gallery and Wakefield Sculpture Park?'

'Just up the road from my home. Been doing your homework you two, have you?'

'I'd love to see them, one day,' comments Jane quietly.

'Maybe you will, one day love, maybe you will.'

Lily smiles encouragingly at Phil. *Breakthrough, he thinks to himself controlling his smile, breakthrough.*

Chapter 25

It was Saturday morning. The cleaners were in the office, Paul didn't have to remember the alarm code to let himself in. Just as well after a night at the Feathers that ended up on Phil's couch. He'd got up in the night and tripped over the bucket thoughtfully left there for him.

His shin was sore, and he cursed as he made his way to his office to retrieve his car keys and bag; he'd bumped into some production company people in Soho after a longish lunch, had gone back to their office for a glass of wine, justifying it as work as he looked at their latest reel of commercials and gone straight to the Feathers.

This morning, Jonno's office door is open, unusual; then Paul remembers the cleaners are in. Paul retrieves his keys and is going past the toilet when the door opens and Jonno emerges, carrying a towel and British Airways toiletries bag.

'I've just been for a—' Jonno's voice trails away. He looks crestfallen, forlorn, like a chubby schoolboy who's been caught doing something naughty behind the bike sheds.

He raises his head and looks up. 'I stayed in the office last night. Had a bit of an evening so I slept on the couch. Paul, Paul, you won't say anything, will you?'

Paul shrugs it off, exaggeratedly.

'So? Nothing to do with me, me old china, happens; buy you a coffee?'

'No, no, no Paul, I'd better get home, you know, Carol and the kids.'

His voice breaks as he turns away to hide his emotions. Paul claps him sympathetically on the shoulder.

'See you Monday.'

'Yeh, see you.'

Paul turns away.

Poor silly bastard, something must have happened at home, Jonno came into the pub late and was there late, almost willing himself to be there. Not that I remember much. Ooof, my head hurts.

Paul turns back to his office; there are aspirin in Phil's top drawer.

Phil and Jane settle down in the corner of Jane's local. She suddenly breaks the silence.

'I've been talking to Jonno. But I know you and Paul. If I tell you, you'll use it somehow. Do something.'

She looks at him, reproachfully.

'Love, no, anything we say is just for you and me. And anyway this is different, Jonno's a silly bastard, but this is out of the office stuff. If we're going to wind him up, it's about work, not personal. Anyways you know we both like Carol.'

'Jonno confided in me.'

'No, he didn't, Jane love, you asked, he told you. Heart on the sleeve stuff. And it won't go further than me and Paul, if there is anything he needs to know. And this we do know. Is this Jenny's doing?'

'Carol didn't need her help. She just suspected something was up. You know that weekend she went away and took the kids to her Gran's and Jonno stayed in town that day?'

Phil nods.

'Perfectly legit, he had to work the weekend. He had the Braithwaite's post production. They'd pulled the media forward, and he had all that to sign off.'

'Maybe, but he took Jenny down to his house, after.'

'C'mon, not even he's as stupid as to do something like that. Mind you, if there was nothing in it, there's no reason she couldn't have been with him.'

'P, she lives in Highgate.'

'Anyway, stupid git if he did.'

'So, the other Tuesday night he gets in early, puts the kids to bed, reads them a story, Carol cooks dinner, candles and wine, and they retire to the sofa with a liqueur.'

'Jonno's telling you all this?'

'Yes. They snuggle down on the sofa, Carol suddenly pulls away, reaches down behind the cushion and pulls out a G-string, holds it up, waves it about.

'What? Who?' She shouts, 'who Jonno?'

'And he spills his guts?'

'Absolutely.'

Jane looks around the pub to check no one's listening in, but the other patrons are into their Saturday lunchtime drinks ritual, picking up the threads of Home Counties conversations where they'd left them last week; house prices, four wheel drives, double glazing, school fees, golf tomorrow, George? Oh, you're going ahead with the conservatory, Angus, are you?

She turns back to Phil. 'Jonno gave her the whole, contrite, what a fool he'd been, wouldn't happen again, please forgive me, I love you really, you and the kids are everything to me.'

'Not very inventive for a creative director. What did she say?'

'Out.'

Jane leans back and sips her drink. She tries to look serious, but her eyes say something else.

'You're looking—'

'P, there's something else. The thing is Jonno didn't really have to admit anything.'

'Jane, this isn't like you. What do you mean he didn't have to tell her?' Phil is bemused.

'The G-string, the thong thingy wasn't Jenny's. Carol had put it there, planted it under the cushion.'

'You're kidding.'

'No. Carol did it to provoke a reaction, must have suspected something. Jonno *did* take Jenny home, and according to him, she was very, you know, keen, hot, I think that was how he described it. The moment they got in the door. And according to him they, they got down to it, but he just couldn't do it.'

'Couldn't get it up?'

'P, really, he wouldn't say as much to me but he felt guilty. Jonno's no lover boy, so he dragged Jenny out of the place and back to London, hardly a word on the way back and she just got out of the car in Highgate and left him with the parting words, "If you didn't want me, couldn't even do it with wifey away, why drag me all the way down to the country"?'

'So, he could have legitimately, well almost, denied it, called it off with Jenny and got things back on an even keel.'

'I wonder if anything had ever actually happened, before.' Jane mused.

Phil chooses not to be forthcoming about the evening Paul found Jenny in Jonno's office. He ponders for a moment.

'Beer's not bad here.' He marshals his thoughts, momentarily distracted by a braying laugh from a tweedy local at the bar. 'Mind you, her reaction wouldn't make Jonno's job any easier, hell hath no fury, etc. Could turn the Braithwaite's account into a nightmare.'

Phil frowns. 'She's trouble. I still remember how Ms Brownlow talked down to me in that presentation.'

'Talked up to you, P, up. Paul said you were looking down her blouse.'

'That were the old Phil, before I met you. I mean, you three.'

Phil wards off Jane's casual slap.

'Reckon Lily's got the spuds on yet?'

Chapter 26

'Jonno sends his apologies, couldn't make it. He's given Paul a full brief.' Ralph looks up, the portraits of Braithwaite's ancestors glower down at him suspiciously. He turns to his copywriter.

'Paul?'

Paul looks around him before starting to speak. He likes to project an aura of quiet authority when he presents creative work. He wears a dark suit, white shirt and subdued tie. In an off-handed manner, he described it to Phil as his sucker-the-client outfit, when privately he believes in showing a certain respect and deference to those who contribute to his salary. Paul clears his throat, looks up and smiles disarmingly at Jenny and George.

'As Jonno's deputy, I like to get on top of most things of his.'

Paul directs the remark straight at Jenny, who looks back at him, stone faced, then looks down at her notes and, for a moment, smiles. As usual, her flame red lipstick is absolutely precise, as is her makeup, mascara, and hair. She wears a beautifully cut black business suit that clings to her thin, spare frame and high heels that flatter her trim calves.

Like the black widow in that Italian movie, Paul reminded himself as he saw her approaching that morning at King's Cross Station. And Daddy's obviously got money.

'Here's Jenny. Odd, she normally sits with us,' remarked Ralph as she strode past their carriage. 'Must have some work to do.'

Now they sit in the dusty, fustian gloom of the brewery boardroom. Ralph gazes out of the window as Paul speaks. The sun is casting the long shadow of a chimney across the yard below and up the opposite wall. The patriarchs of the Braithwaite family continue to gaze sternly and disapprovingly down. Jenny appears to have borrowed her expression collectively from the founders.

Paul continues, 'I have the finished commercial here, Mr Braithwaite, Jenny. In Jonno's absence, I went through all the amendments in your contact report of the 18th scene by scene and made sure the editing house accommodated them. I've also taken it upon myself to use the material, plus some outtakes, to complete the video of the whole D'Ciples track for selected cinemas. With a different target audience from the TVC, I'll make it a little more, youthful. But let's look at the commercial on the run as it works best as a cohesive whole.'

As usual, the scene framed in the window rather than the TV screen captures Ralph's attention. He lets Paul get on with it. Paul slips the video tape into the player and the large screen brought in especially for the meeting lights up. The Braithwaite's beer song bursts into the room. The portraits look, if anything, even more disapproving. Ralph absently taps along, George and Jenny stare fixedly at the screen.

'Too loud,' comments George suddenly.

Paul picks up the remote and turns the volume down.

'Not the music, Paul, the girl's dress in the bar scene.'

'It's the way this monitor's been adjusted,' says Paul, 'the magenta's far brighter than when I last saw the film at the editing house on their equipment.'

He's making that up, thinks Ralph. Probably used that excuse a hundred times.

Mr Braithwaite nods his head in acknowledgement; he tends to defer to those with superior technical knowledge such as his head brewer.

'Hrmmph, I'm still worried by that dancer's cleavage.'

Ralph has been listening with one ear.

'I think you'll find she's wearing a body stocking, Mr Braithwaite, I had Paul go through the bar scenes to check that an undue amount of flesh wasn't being exposed, it wasn't until then we realised all the dancers were wearing body stockings,' says Ralph, reluctantly tearing his attention away from the brewery yard.

'Hrmmph. It's not my kind of music, anyway.'

'I don't think we're really the demographic for this one,' Ralph confirms, 'We're more draught bitter, Mr B, than bottled Pale Ale. Sorry Mr Braithwaite, for the familiarity. Music must have got to me.'

'Jenny? You're unusually quiet.' Mr Braithwaite waits for her opinion.

Jenny looks at Paul with a calculating expression. 'I think it's very good, Mr Braithwaite. I think Paul has added a little something of his own. Made it stand up a lot more than Jonno did, so to speak.'

Paul nods very slightly, indicating to Jenny he understands the tenor of the innuendo. 'Well when you're the creator of something, as Jonno is,' Paul says disingenuously, 'you can sometimes get,' he turns to Jenny, 'a bit too close. I suppose I see things from a different perspective.'

They smile falsely at each other, two generals who've grudgingly agreed a ceasefire.

'Mr Braithwaite, Jenny, I've arranged for a tape of the song to go out to every one of your reps, and Jonno's looking to get the D'Ciples for this year's sales conference.'

Ralph stirs in his seat. Before he can speak, Paul continues. 'Mr Braithwaite, I haven't been up here for some months, and if you might indulge me, I'd really like to see if your best bitter is as good as it always is.' Braithwaite's eyebrows narrow. 'Unfortunately, the agency pub doesn't have it on tap, and anyway it never tastes quite as fresh down there as it does up here.'

'No need to make a speech, lad, I can see Ralph's been breaking his neck for a bevvy for the last half an hour. And you boys can find out what a real meat pie with lardy pastry tastes like, not those mamby pamby fi-lo thingies you get in London. Thai green chicken curry pie indeed. I've some reports and suchlike to go through anyway. Take Jenny with you, you can talk about promotions to boost sales. And Paul lad, just for the record, no more Light Brigade, flat 'ats, mufflers, eee by gum, trouble at mill.'

He waves his forefinger back and forth, ticking off the items in a dismissive arc. Ten minutes later Jenny looks on, bemused, as Ralph and Paul share a long, loving look with each other. It could be misinterpreted, but the object of their mutual affection is the pints of Braithwaite's Bitter clasped in their hands.

'Get it down you, Paul, we've time for another.' Ralph turns a warm, appreciative gaze on Jenny. 'Jenny told the cab company not to hurry the taxi.'

Chapter 27

'I almost feel sorry for Jonno, you know, blokes together, so to speak. Shall we invite him down Boardroom Five lunchtime? Jane says he's not been eating properly.'

'Never pat a burning dog, Phil. Mind you, I don't think lunch at Locanda and eating properly are mutually compatible phrases. And I bet his hotel has never had such a run on room service. There'll be scorch marks in the carpet outside his room.'

'Suppose you're right. I'd hate to be the maid who cleans it. Mind you, it could be a good career move to listen to his moaning for an hour or two.'

'Alright, alright, you soft Northern pussy. I know you're only doing it to impress Perfect.'

'She's had his self-pity for a week. I said we'd take over.'

'Blimey, Jonno, you'd better give me those jeans to take round the dry cleaners, the weight's falling off you,' remarks Phil.

Jonno looks around at Locanda's faded décor.

'It's an ill wind,' Paul contributes sardonically.

'Parmigiana for you, Paulo, you Filippo and the boss,' announces Maria, slapping three plates down on the table.

The crumbed veal escalopes had been pummelled to within an inch of their lives and hang in limp supplication over the sides of the plates. Maria leans across the table and pinches Jonno's cheek affectionately.

'Look at you, sad man. I take you home introduce you to my daughter.'

She bustles off to the kitchen.

'Last thing I need,' mumbles Jonno disconsolately.

'She's never said that to us, boss man.'

They chew away, silent for a moment.

'You OK in that hotel, Jonno, you're not looking too flash, those bags under your eyes.'

Jonno waves his fork in a say-it-and-get-it-over-with gesture.

'You're not still bonking Jenny, are you?'

Jonno looks up, takes a long, slow breath.

'She finds the whole hotel thing exciting. What's the word?'

'Illicit? Frisson?' Suggests Paul.

'I swear,' Jonno sighs, 'she hasn't got an off button. If she has, I can't find it.'

'I bet you have fun looking for it. And at least you're getting some,' Paul says brightly.

'Paul, I know you look at me like I'm a pompous prick.'

'You're telling us you're not going to put lunch on expenses?'

'That's not the point.'

'Jonno, this isn't about you, or work, or anything.' Phil pauses for a moment to sip on the house red, grimacing. 'Well, it is work in a sense. Listen, you're in London, we needed to eat, we asked you to join us, and you bedded down Braithwaite's—'

'Literally,' interjects Paul.

'Ha ha,' Jonno stabs at his veal, which flaps back at him.

'Jonno,' Phil looks at him levelly, 'Jonno, Paul can handle Braithwaite's. Braithwaite thinks Paul's some sort of aristo arsehole with a country estate, and Jenny won't do anything to upset the business now. We'll be straight with you, we like Carol, though frankly we're not that keen on Jenny as a person, but she pays the agency bills. It's your business, absolutely.'

Paul pitches in.

'Jonno, for fuck sake, it's no fun having you moping around the place. Takes the edge off the atmosphere. By all means, keep apologising to Carol, but don't be hang dog. Just say you made a terrible mistake, moment of madness.'

Jonno looks up. His eyebrows furrow. Guilt? Anguish?

'Carol phoned up the other night, and I picked up the phone.'

'And Jenny was there and thought this is fun, and got hold of your todger and—'

'And I put the phone down, well, dropped it actually.'

'Great move, Jonno.'

'Then I got really annoyed with Jenny and she went off in a huff. And all I could think of was her walking through the hotel foyer naked with just her raincoat buttoned around her. If only they knew. Had quite an effect on me.'

Jonno smiles wistfully at the memory.

'Jonno.'

'I phoned Carol back. Got the answering machine. Funny, talking to your own voice. Just said sorry, I was sleepy and dropped the phone.'

Paul pushes his plate away from him.

'Jonno, it's OK to tell Carol you love her, but there is a time and a place. Well, is this on expenses?'

Jonno nods resignedly. Paul leans over and gives his shoulder a friendly pat. 'Get the bill or get another bottle,' he looks at his watch, 'scrub that, The Colonial Club is open. C'mon Jonno, you haven't got a home to go to.'

Chapter 28

'Shit, shit, shit,' Ralph bangs his head on his office wall, 'got to interview all these girls for the new secretary's job tomorrow, and I've got a long report to do on new business, and some leads I must follow.'

'Why don't you get Brian to do it? It's his birthday tomorrow, he'll love having a procession of eager, young, attractive totty in his office.'

'Good idea, Paul. I'll do just that.'

'How's it going, birthday boy?'

Paul, Phil and Brian stand in reception, balancing paper plates of the traditional G and W birthday carrot cake. Brian leans forward.

'Cripes, I've never had a birthday quite like this.'

He looks around and leans closer, his voice dropping to a conspiratorial whisper.

'You know I've been doing these job interviews all morning for Ralph?'

'Yes,' Paul and Phil answer in unison.

'Well, this beautiful girl comes in. Stunning looker. Very self-assured, business suit, Gucci briefcase.'

'I saw her in reception, *when I paid her*,' Paul mutters under his breath, 'I agree. Beautiful. Those lips. And I must say she looked very, capable, handy.'

'You got that one right, Paul, phew. She swanned into my office, sat there in front of me and smiled this amazing smile. I asked her if she had her CV with her and she said, "No, I'm the hands on type, but I do take dictation." Then you wouldn't believe it, calm as all get out she gets out of the chair, pushes it aside, slips under the desk, pulls my old feller out and gives me this amazing blow job.'

Brian pauses for a moment, savouring the memory.

'I'm sitting there going cross-eyed and I'm thinking what happens if Freddy or Ralph waltzes in? Sort of added to it, in a way. Then she gets up and I'm just lost for words. I say something stupid like, "you must really want the job."

"Blow the job," she says, "happy birthday, lover boy," picks up her handbag and sashays out of the office. Wonder how she knew it was my birthday.'

'Grace would have told her,' Paul answers quickly.

'Yeh, happy birthday, you Aussie plonker,' adds Phil affectionately.

'She obviously got the position, so to speak.'

'Mate, I was speechless after that, just sat there.'

'Happy birthday, indeed, lover boy.'

'Hmm,' says Brian, eyes narrowing as he studies a grinning Paul and Phil. 'Hmmm.'

Back in their office, Phil pulls out some money.

'Great idea, d'you want a contribution sunshine, we could do that again on someone else's birthday.'

'I don't know if it'd work twice, but I've kept her number. Put your dosh away, you can buy me a pint after work.'

Chapter 29

It's Friday lunchtime in Riley's. Claire and Cynthia are fidgeting, Claire checks the time. Cyn absently drinks half her glass of Macon Blanc in one go.

'Cynth, Cynth, I've been looking forward to seeing you all the way from New York, and all you can do is crack your neck to get back to the office. Girl, the work's not going to go away.'

'I know Becs, but we've got to get it done this afternoon; deadline?' Cyn's voice trails away, unconvincingly.

Her best friend Rebecca Young is over from New York. Becs went there to further her career in film, signing up for a course at New York University. She's unconventionally beautiful, slim, angular framed, nose crooked, with a large mouth and full lips, high forehead and hazel eyes framed by loose corkscrew curls of natural red hair.

'Cynth, you won't come up with anything if you don't stay loose. You've got to stay cool. All that angst and adrenalin won't help.'

Paul and Phil, alerted by Grace, stroll in. Paul walks straight up to Becs, hand outstretched.

'You must be Becs, Cyn hasn't told us all about you.'

Claire does the introductions.

'Becs, Paul Johnstone, copywriter, bon vivant, deputy CD and resident arsehole. Philip Arbuthnott, art director, Northern Neanderthal, and nice guy though he doesn't look it.'

Paul orders drinks.

'Right. Bottle of indifferent Macon Blanc for you et moi Cyn, Stella for you Phil, bourbon and coke for you Claire, Becs that bottle label reads Dos Equis. May I call you Becs?'

'Everyone else takes the liberty.'

'Paul, please, not a bottle, we can't be here long.'

'I'm thirsty Cyn, I'll finish it if you have to rudely rush off and leave us to entertain your friend. What's the problem, anyway, it'll keep to Monday, won't it, Jonno's not about.'

'Cyn doesn't want to work the weekend, Paul, not with Becs here,' explains Claire.

Becs turns to the boys.

'I've been sat in cattle class half the night next to some fat git with B.O. and this is how you welcome me to London. Paul, you're the boss here, have a word with them. Pull rank.'

Becs looks at him. Her oval eyes seem to widen further. *Any wider, thinks Paul, and I'll dive in.*

'What's the problem, Claire? You going to tell us?'

'It's not your worry, Paul, we've got to crack it.'

'OK but sharing probs sometimes helps. You know that. The job's always easier when it's on someone else's desk.'

'One of your lines, Paul; Johnstone's ninth law of advertising?' Asks Cyn sarcastically. Paul ignores her.

There's silence for a moment. Glorious strolls by, picking up empties and tops up Cyn's glass before she can demur. Paul helps himself. Claire looks around the group and exhales, resignedly.

'It's Greenway. They've got this corporate strapline, "Its Possible." Don't even know if the grammar's right. The idea being, if one of their front office guys dreams something up, the nerds in the back room can make it happen. You've heard their IT bullshit.'

Greenway Software Solutions is a new client, recommended to G and W by one of their old international affiliates. They have growth potential and the agency has seen the need to respond, quickly, to their first campaign brief. Becs picks up her bottle and necks it, puts it down on the bar and looks around at the furrowed brows of the agency creative teams. In the silence, Paul shrugs and sips his wine. Becs looks at them, amused.

'Do elephants dream of being small?' she scratches her nose as she thinks, 'do babies dream of Chateau Margaux? Did Einstein dream of a better haircut? It's possible. I dunno, is it possible? I'm not an ad guy.'

Phil looks at her in wonder.

'A mouse and an elephant the same size; a lovely shot of a baby blissfully breastfeeding, or even bottle feeding, wine does come in a bottle. Einstein with a short back and sides,' he extemporises, quickly.

'D'you reckon?' asks Cyn.

'I reckon,' says Claire, 'I reckon you're in the wrong game, Becs. They'll be expecting all this moody visual impressionistic stuff, and you come out with something with a bit of wit and flair.'

She leans forward, pulls Becs towards her, kisses her on both cheeks and then her forehead for good measure.

'Bisous. We'll give you a credit. Better still, one day we'll give you a script to direct.'

'Is this all you guys do for a living?' asks Becs in wonder, waving her beer bottle, 'stand around in bars all day, talking crap?'

'Let's get back and put it down,' says Cyn decisively.

'No, guys it's my idea, I make the rules,' poses Becs with a superior smile. 'First, you buy me another beer, then a half decent bottle of wine, we have lunch, I come back to the agency with you; no, scrub that, I'll stay with the boys.'

'And we'll see you in the Feathers later,' says Cyn, relaxing.

'She's your sort of bird, Paul,' says Phil later when Becs goes to the ladies. 'Here today, gone tomorrow. No ties, no hang-ups.'

'Mmmm,' says Paul.

Paul can still taste the dark peat of the last malt whisky as they burst through his front door, giggling and theatrically shushing each other. They stumble over the doormat, grasping at each other for support.

'Why are we shushing, I live here, by myself.'

Paul removes Becs' finger from his lips, holding her hand while attempting to undo the buttons of her shirt with his other hand and kiss her, all at the same time. They relax a little and kiss deeply, Becs' hands cradling the back of his head as Paul finally opens her shirt and awkwardly slips a hand into the top of her bra.

Becs takes her hands from his head and moves them down and under the edge of his T-shirt. He flinches as her fingertips stroke his stomach. She moves to deftly undo the top, then the other buttons of his jeans, slides her hands inside his jeans, down his hips and around to his backside, squeezes for a moment then pushes his jeans and boxers down his thighs.

'Ooo, mmm,' She looks at him appraisingly for a moment, as he struggles to stand up then breaks from his embrace, spinning around.

'First,' she says, 'where's the bathroom?' Giggling, Paul shuffles around grabbing at his jeans, gesturing vaguely towards a door.

'That way, next to the bedroom.'

'See ya,' she says, waving teasingly.

Paul weaves after her.

'This is one night when,' he thinks to himself, first in rueful admonition and then with a grin, 'I won't be making my apologies and leaving early.'

Saturday morning. Cyn and Becs sit outside a Soho café. Becs downs her espresso in one gulp and shudders.

'First time in weeks I haven't heard someone ask for a skinny hot soy decaf latte.'

'You can't,' says Cyn, 'there's a sign on the cash register. No skim, no soy, no decaf.' They sit for a moment in silence, watching the passing parade, staring blankly at those men who give them a lingering glance as they stroll past. Becs draws in a breath and flexes her shoulders, which draws even more looks, then relaxes.

'Why,' she says, 'why can't men understand that sometimes you just want to fuck them, not fall in love with them?'

Cyn puts her toasted sandwich down and looks at her in astonishment.

'I don't believe it, not Paul.'

'Yes, dear Cynth, I went home with Paul.'

'No, I gathered that, you were all over each other on the pavement outside the Feathers, pawing each other like demented teenagers. No, I mean Paul, well normally, he can't wait to get away the moment he's done the deed.'

'He couldn't last night, could he, playing at home. Hey,' Becs looks at Cyn, mouth opening in astonishment before a grin crowds her face. 'Cynth, you haven't, with Paul?'

'No, of course I haven't. He confessed one night when we were sharing a bottle and lovelorn woes at Riley's. He said he got frightened whenever he fancied anyone and ran a mile. He's one of those guys who'd love a relationship, but he's far too far into himself and analyses the shit out of everything. He couldn't handle a proper relationship. Mind you.'

'Well, he wasn't like that with me. I expected him to be jokey and offhand in the morning but he treated me like fragile porcelain. Hopped out of bed, just when I was all warm and toasty and—'

'Becs, too much info.'

'OK. So it was all tea in bed and "are you OK, you sure you're OK, Becs, would you like some toast," said with his silly little boy voice and smile.'

'Becs, I don't believe it, not Paul, that isn't the offhand ironic git we all know and don't love. No snide comments on the side, no jokes: tea and toast, I don't believe it. And, and, he didn't offer to run you a bath?'

'How did you guess?'

'No, no, it's too much.' Cyn laughs gleefully, clapping her hands and raising her eyes to the heavens. 'And you know what the worst thing is, I can't use it, can't tell. Claire would side with him anyway. "Becs saw the real Paul, I think it's lovely," she'd say.'

'Well, after I've gone back, you might use it. But I'd rather you didn't. You know, he's going to know I talked to you. Anyway, so I saw another other side of Paul and he was trying to be sweet. But gee, he doesn't know me.'

Cyn looks at her friend quizzically and circles her finger at an approaching waiter for two more coffees.

'Becs, you'll be gone in a few days. And the thought of Paul being nice and doing a cow eyes thing, I can't even envisage it. You've made my day.'

'What time does the French open, I need a hair of the dog.'

'Not sure on Saturdays. Anyway, which dog?'

'Probably the burning one.'

'Jeez, Paul was using all his favourite lines last night, was he? Must have been pissed.'

'And he chose me? And I fucked him? Thanks, Cynth, I'm flattered.'

Chapter 30

Phil turns from his layout pad. 'Shit, you and Ralph should compare notes.'

'What?'

'You've been staring out of the window for the last hour.'

Paul shrugs.

'An idea might be something else you could think about, we've got to get this in by Friday.'

'Ah, hell.' Paul caps his fountain pen, drops it onto his layout pad and puts his feet on the desk. The office is in its normal state. Paul's side almost anally clean to the point where Phil's discarded layout pages, piles of magazines, old coffee cup holders and three pizza boxes constitute a clearly defined border.

Paul no longer comments or complains, knowing Phil thrives on disorder, and Perfect will, once a week, dutifully pile up the magazines and throw any detritus into a garbage bag.

'Paul, Paul, Becs goes back to NY tomorrow. You won't see her for yonks. You said yourself that all she wanted was a bit of holiday fun, and you happened to be the one standing in the way at the bar, buying the Scotch and Tequilas. Now, you're moping and we've got work to do. What you're worried about is that Mr Casual couldn't care less who doesn't like relationships, scared of a bit of emotional,' he catches his breath and appraises Paul, 'scarring, has let someone get right under his skin.'

Phil pauses for breath, waving his Pentel in the air.

'And she's wriggling about, isn't she? You know why? Because she treated you exactly like you do most of the birds you go out with. And you're not used to that, and it knocked you sideways, and I find it oddly amusing. OK, so you're actually human, I might even let you join me in shagging a few sheep sometime but we've got work to do.'

Paul looks at Phil glumly. 'So?' he shrugs again.

'There's nothing you can do. Hold on tightly, let go lightly. Your words.'

'That's ideas, not a beautiful woman with a tiny bluebird tattooed on a beautiful lovely, lively, lissom bum.'

'Paul, I doubt Becs would like me to know that.' Phil thinks about it for a moment, 'really? Any more tatts anywhere else?'

Paul looks up, purses his lips. Phil gazes at him seriously.

'Paul, all you can do is be honest with her, because she's the one with the get out clause. Tell her the other night meant more to you than just a pissed porking, ask if it would be OK to keep in touch, you know, call occasionally. Take it easy now, two steps forward, one step back. You know, you soppy git, cool it.'

Bitsa sticks his head around the door.

'Love,' he warbles, 'is a many splendored thing.' He withdraws his head and disappears up the corridor, voice fading, 'it's the April rose that only grows in the Feathers, on a Friday night, in the early spring.'

Paul doesn't respond.

'Paul,' Phil says, quietly. 'Paul, I owe you lunch. Dinner even. We sit down quietly at Fiorelli's. A Tuscan T-bone and a glass of that red, you know, the real Chianti not in the flask.'

He shakes his shaggy locks.

'It's a fiasco.'

'No, no, it's not, the situation's saveable. And funny, too, sorry mate.'

Paul jumps to his feet.

'Fiasco, fiasco is Italian for flask, you smug, sheep diddling dolt.'

Chapter 31

Roddy and Jimmy sidle into the Claire and Cyn 's office.

'Good weekend, Roddy?'

'Terrific. Brighton's a great place, even if you are down there with your Mum. Anyway, she spent all her time with her sister, Aunt Vera. Hardly saw her. Claire, who does our editing?'

'Film, video?'

'Yes.'

'Well, we don't do any ourselves, though I suppose you could. Production houses tend to have deals with those editing houses where a director has a relationship with an editor. We have been to post production houses where they have an editor on staff, you know, when we're doing a sales conference presentation, or something. Even commercials. Some of them are very good, why?'

'I had an idea for an ad for my Uncle Jim's car yard.'

'Roddy, he asked you to do an ad?'

'No, I went to him with the idea.'

Cyn looks over the top of her PC.

'Roddy: taking an idea to someone when they haven't asked for one is a scam ad. A quick way to get yourself a bad name around town if it's ever entered in awards.'

'It's not really, Mum had already suggested to Aunt Vera that I do ads for Uncle Jim.'

Claire pulls at her spiky, gelled hair.

'Roddy, but Uncle Jim didn't actually commission you to do the work. Give you the account, or even a brief?'

'No, but I'm sure Aunt Vera spoke to him.'

'So when your ad does well at an awards and the organisers ask where are the brief and paperwork, you'll say, I'm sure Aunt Vera spoke to my Uncle Jim.'

'I'm sort of committed now, Uncle's bought some spots on Southern tele and he's got these Fiats to sell, I saw them there when he showed me around the showroom.'

'OK. You're committed. Do the ad, don't enter it for awards, tell people, be honest when you show your book. It'll sound good that way. Proactive, but ethical.'

Cyn speaks up again.

'Your Uncle's well off, is he? He can afford to shoot car ads?'

'He's got all this promo footage of a Fiat driving around Rome.'

'And you're going to cut it into an ad? Boring.'

Roddy and Jimmy look hurt.

'Cyn,' Claire turns on her, 'you're a right bitch, sometimes.'

Roddy looks crestfallen.

'You don't want to hear the idea then?' He quietly asks.

'There is one?' Cyn spits back sarcastically.

'Leave it out Cyn, don't dishearten them, we've done enough retail shit in our time.'

'Only because we had to.'

'Go, Roddy.'

'Well, we've got all this footage of the car driving around Rome, and we pick these shots with Roma on the signs, and there's some freeway footage as the car leaves Rome, with road signs.'

He pauses for breath, looking around for support.

'Promising so far,' sneers Cyn.

Claire nods encouragement. Roddy ignores Cyn.

'Well what we do is we cut the film, and flip it left to right—'

'So the car's driving on the wrong side of the road. Well, the left side, which is the right side of the road over here,' interjects Jimmy excitedly. 'So the driver's on the right side.'

He flicks his hand back and forth in explanation.

'Yes, we've got it.'

'So you've got the car driving around Rome on our side of the road but all the signs are all back to front. Roma says Amor; hey that spells love, almost, anyway,' Roddy continues enthusiastically, 'It'll look real odd on the freeway and at that point, the voice over says, "The new Fiat blah blah. Now available in right hand drive".'

'At Uncle Jim's car yard,' Cyn finishes for them. 'Actually that's pretty good. Very neat, I take it all back. I'll vouch for the fact that you got a brief, if you want to enter it?'

Chapter 32

Paul is swimming underwater. Above him is the hull of a boat, anchor chain disappearing into the blue. He grasps it and pulls himself towards the surface, towards the light, chest tightening. Paul bursts into the air, gasping to the shrill of his flat's intercom. He groans and rolls out of bed. He'd been deep in the first wave of sleep.

The alarm clock says 12.30. Picking up a pair of boxers, he struggles to the front door and fumbles to lift the handset on the doorjamb.

'Yes?'

'Becs.'

He makes his way to the front door and opens it. Becs pulls her hand across her forehead, moving an errant curl of hair.

'Bec. I thought you were—'

'I put my flight back to the afternoon.'

Paul nods wanders back up the hall.

'Bathroom, me,' he mumbles, points and turns into it.

He pisses, leaning his head on the wall, rinses his hands, takes a mouthful of water and as an afterthought, scrapes a toothbrush across his teeth.

His brain's whirring, analysing; what's happening, what's her motive, what are the ramifications? His below-the-belt-brain prevails; "man, she's beautiful, she wants you, and she's on a plane in twelve hours' time."

Paul gets back into bed, turning his back as he surreptitiously digs around in his bedside cupboard for a condom. She slides into the bed after him, her hand creeping around his body, gently pulling him back towards her.

They make love again in the morning, slowly, gently discovering each other, almost reluctantly admitting a mutual attraction. They hardly speak at breakfast, sharing the odd smile. Paul prudently leaves things unsaid.

'Paul, I'd better go and pack.'

'Yeah, I've got a meeting at 9.30. Mmm, er, thanks for coming around.'

'Our pleasure. Mutual.'

On the doorstep, she pecks him on the cheek. *Paul, I only came around because you're good in bed. No. Crass. Trite. Flippant. Not true. Don't say it.*

'Be in touch Paul, please?'

'I'd like to. I really would. I will, Bec. Bec, promise. Safe flight.'

He watches her as she walks off down the street. *She'll turn and wave just there.* And Becs does. Paul waves once, smiles to himself. Hey, she said please. And then quietly, uncharacteristically, to his reflection in the hall mirror, 'don't go out of my life yet, please Bec.'

Chapter 33

It's been two months since Jonno separated from Carol. He's taken a small flat near Phil in Camden and now appears regularly in the Feathers on a Friday night. Some of his pomposity has ebbed away. 'Like the beans from a split beanbag,' Bitsa had suggested.

'After Jonno sat on it,' concluded Paul sardonically.

'A general has to keep a certain distance from his troops,' Jonno once explained to Phil.

'Saves buying them a drink, *with your own money,*' Phil quietly observed, swallowing the second half of the sentence.

Jonno's self-importance, and waistline, has diminished along with his self-confidence and he's now svelte, rather than chubby.

'Deflated,' as Ralph put it. Jonno's once regularly barbered hair is now unkempt.

'Jonno, you're almost human now,' Perfect had said it encouragingly as she served him his morning coffee. He'd looked up, a little boy hurt by his nanny. 'I mean that as a compliment.'

Jonno wanders into the pub and Glorious puts a glass under the gin optic before he's halfway to the bar. Jonno catches her eye, shakes his head, points to the bottle of Plymouth on the shelf and raises two fingers. Glorious flips him a V sign back and pours a double. Jonno perches himself on a stool at the periphery of the group and indicates with a tired sweep of his hand to serve a round. The group shuffles around to include him.

'Newlands,' Jonno mutters to himself.

'You going somewhere, Jonno?'

'Mark Newlands, Phil.'

Phil shrugs, still none the wiser. Paul and Claire react with surprise.

'He's not looking to?' asks Paul, so surprised he pauses his pint on the way to his lips. Mark Newlands is London's most notorious, and many consider most talented art director.

Jonno nods. 'He could be.'

Paul looks at Jonno searchingly, 'He's been at HLT about three years now, and management patience might be wearing a bit thin.'

'I admire him,' says Cyn. 'He might go over budget occasionally and be a bit of a handful but as Mr. Johnstone here would say, "if it's good, they forget how long it took and how much it cost".'

'Thank you, Cynthia,' Paul raises his glass.

Like G and W's experience with Crash Cranshaw, agencies looking to lift their quality and profile suffered Newlands' excesses, but when this didn't translate into new clients and increased budgets, it wasn't long before the CFO pointed out the impact on the agency's image, internal equilibrium and bottom line.

"Mark Newlands is not so much a loose cannon," a creative director once observed, "as one directed at the rest of the agency and any client who happens to be within range."

But Newlands was also a multi award winner, capable of ground breaking advertising that actually surprised and entertained.

'He's a big brand guy, builds them,' says Nigel admiringly, 'but are any of the stories true?'

'Exaggerated beyond belief, and the stuff of legend and urban myth; yes, they are,' confirms Paul. 'We'll soon find out if he joins us, won't we?'

He turns to Claire, raising his eyebrows theatrically.

'Claire is acquainted with Mark. Is he hard to handle, Claire?'

'Fuck off dick features, as Cyn would say. I just have a drink with him occasionally.'

Paul turns to Jonno.

'Do you really reckon he'd come?'

Jonno shrugs, now noncommittal.

'Well, we need someone to work on the brewery,' says Phil. 'I mean Jonno, you don't want to anymore.'

He turns away, raising a mollifying hand. Jonno nods his head, accepting Phil wasn't being personal. The creative department has made a point of showing they're sympathetic towards Jonno, irrespective of their personal views on his behaviour.

Admittedly there is a certain amount of self interest in their sympathy.

'Glorious, could you, please,' Phil raises his empty pint glass and indicates Jonno and the rest of the group.

Chapter 34

Michael Michaels makes a rare appearance in Paul and Phil's office. He clears his throat. The couple ignore him for a moment before turning from their computers.

'Excuse me, chaps.'

'Certainly, Michael. It's perfectly OK to rudely interrupt us when we're trying to have an idea, isn't it, Phil?'

'It is that, Paul, how can't we help you, Michael?'

'The girls are tied up on that software campaign and I'm looking for a team to work on Friendship. It's a global effort with our affiliates, short notice, they're thinking of launching a new range of household cleaners. Sort of an international brainstorm.'

He looks at them both seriously.

'Fuck, it's not as if we haven't got enough on our plates. You've cleared it with Jonno?'

'It's in San Francisco. For a week.'

Phil drops his marker on his pad.

'You serious, Michael?'

'Have you ever known him to be frivolous?' asks Paul. 'Bloody hell, when?'

'Week after next. You've both got passports and all that, haven't you? No convictions for drug offences?'

Paul pointedly ignores this.

'And Jonno said yes?'

'Freddy said yes.'

Paul is magnanimous, for once.

'Good on you, Freddy. And you, of course, Michael.'

'He said you're not to come back unless we get the project.'

'Who else is involved?'

'The Australian affiliate, and the American.'

'There's some top talent in that Australian office. Should be good for a laugh.'

'It's not a jolly, Paul.' Seeing Paul's expression, 'OK, OK I know you two take work seriously. I'll take that as a yes, then.'

He withdrew from the office. Paul leans back in his chair. 'Fantastic, never been to San Francisco. Must find SF Chronicle's top 100 restaurants. And bars. Should be able to do a few in a week.'

Cyn and Claire appear.

'You lucky, jammy bastards, I hope they open fucking Alcatraz again just for you pricks.'

'I left my heart,' warbles Phil. 'Macarthur Park is, seriously, girls, if you'd like to do it, it is your account.'

'Oh yeah. I can see you two giving up a week away. Holiday the Johnstone way. Just remember you owe us, big time. Anyway, Freddy already explained it to us. They wanted the senior team, dum de dum, la la la.'

'You can buy us a drink for that, a few drinks,' stipulates Cyn.

The girls wander disconsolately off.

'I feel a bit rotten,' says Phil.

'It's the way it goes, Phil. You know the game. It is a bit nasty, but they'll get their chance. You know why they aren't going, the software thing. They just sold Bec's idea and client wants it finished.'

'You can just hear Michaels. "We'll send you our top boys. I think we can spare them for something as important as this." Though interesting to see if any female creatives will be there. I'd be willing to bet it's down to a female planner, female account service. Anyway, we're on the big bird.'

'Pointy end? Business class?'

'Maybe if we're very lucky. Agency policy, hours in the air determines class.'

'So you only get in Business if you're going all the way to Australia?'

'Something like that'.

Michaels reappeared at their door, with Nigel.

'We're sending Nigel with you to keep tabs on the work.'

'Actually, Michael,' says Nigel, 'Freddy termed it babysitting.'

'Welcome to the party, Nige.'

Phil and Nigel appear at the door of Paul's hotel room.

'Can you see the Golden Gate Bridge from your room, Phil?'

'No, nice view into an office building though.'

'How about you, Nige?'

'I can see the top of the bridge if I stand on my bed.'

'Well done, young man, then you get the first round in.'

'Are we meeting the trolly dollies you chatted up on the flight?'

'Nige, that's offensively sexist; flight attendants. You didn't have to tell them we were in advertising, I'd already convinced them I was a neuro surgeon.'

'What about Phil?'

'Bass guitarist with an up and coming Sheffield band.'

'The younger one liked that. Actually, nah, they didn't buy any of it, they get it all the time from passengers. Still, they were liberal with the drinks.'

'I thought we were pretty circumspect?'

'You both slept most of the way,' observes Nigel.

'Let's get out of here. I've done my research and there's a great bar down the street. Can't stand hotel bars, anyway.'

Michael quickly checks Freddy's office door is open, swears loudly as he walks past, repeats it several times just in case Freddy didn't hear, and goes back into his office. Freddy resignedly gets up from his desk, follows Michael into his office and closes the door.

With the agency growing, hiring new people, attracting increasing media coverage and perhaps interest from larger agency groups who were constantly looking at mergers and takeovers, G and W couldn't afford any adverse publicity. Certainly nothing that could impact on the client base and bottom line.

'Everything OK, Michael?'

'Those irresponsible, idiotic, I know I shouldn't have, we shouldn't have sent them.'

Freddy tries to stay relaxed.

'Problem, old boy?'

'I just had Nigel on the phone from San Francisco. Well, in fact I called him to see how it was all going and he said he wasn't sure, as Phil and Paul were out in the limo and he hadn't seen them for some time.'

'Limo? As in limousine?'

'Well, I had to wheedle it out of Nigel, threaten him actually, and he told me Phil and Paul had hired this car and this very large driver and the driver had brought two of his cousins along as companionship for the lonely Brits.'

'I take it these cousins are?'

'Well-endowed was Nigel's phrase. Evidently, Paul and Phil bribed Nigel by taking him on a bar crawl last night to gain his silence. Nigel said he thought he had to do the right thing by the agency and keep us in the loop. He said he didn't even realise bars like they took him to even existed, that they were only in the Hammer books he'd read under the covers at boarding school. Hammer books?'

'Mickey Hammer, Michael. He's a character in Raymond Chandler novels. More likely Dashiell Hammett, he's more San Francisco. But go on.'

'Well, they went to this disgusting bar where the woman next to them was holding a leash. It was round the neck of a man down on his knees next to her. And Nigel said he went to the toilet and there was a half dressed man chained to the wall outside and you were supposed to slap him around the face as you went in, disgusting. M and S, they called it.'

'That's Marks and Spencer, Michael, you mean S&M. That sounds more like Bukowski than Hammett though. As you said,' Freddy hurriedly adds, 'as you said, Michael, disgusting.'

'And then they went somewhere else and Johnstone and Arbuthnott asked for someone called Don Peri-something. I was getting a bit angry by then.'

'Probably Dom Perignon.'

'You know him, Freddy?' Michael enquires. Freddy sits back and looks at him questioningly. It dawns on Michael.

'Oh, I see, Freddy. Oh no, not Dom Perignon the champers, that's near a hundred quid a bottle, isn't it? Just wait till they try and get their expenses past me.'

'Maybe even more in a San Fran titty bar,' says Freddy quietly, his thoughts going back to when he was a young executive on overseas jaunts with per diems and an expense account. His thoughts return reluctantly to the moment.

'As long as they haven't compromised the project in any way?'

'Or you and me. Or G and W. I'm not sure, shall I call Nigel back?'

'Best not. Bloody creatives, at a time like this.'

'A time like what?'

'Oh, nothing Michael, just thinking generally, bad publicity and all that. Join me in my office at close of play for a drink, eh?'

The project was going well. Phil and Paul had no illusions; a raft of product concepts and advertising ideas would be presented to the local client, there'd be a major follow up presentation in New York and all this evidence of industry would, in the end, probably come to nought.

Still, you never knew. Given a couple of hours break, they were taking a look at the city. They stand at a tram stop, stamping their feet and wrapping their arms around themselves.

'Blimey, I didn't think I'd be wearing a T-shirt over a T-shirt this time of the year. I'm bloody glad I bought my leather jacket.'

'Mark Twain said the coldest winter he ever spent was a summer in San Francisco.'

'He wasn't far wrong. Still, great town. Yeh I love these trams, like travelling in an old deco diner, all curves and chrome. Terrific idea, going round the country buying them up and putting them to work again. And I love the mix of architecture. Those Victorian houses on Fillmore.'

'I still can't get over all the old hippies around the place.'

'And there's some stylish chicks. What about those two with their tongues down each other's throats in Zuni Café?'

'Local colour. Lovely to see, Phil. But I don't think anyone's going to believe how well behaved we've been. Least of all us. And Perfect.'

'Good meal last night though, few glasses of wine. Didn't overdo it.'

'But we can't come here without having an Old Fashioned or three. And must get across the bridge to Sausalito.'

'Still, we can tear the arse out of it on the last night.'

'We could always get some practise in tonight. And tomorrow. Better get back to the office, seen Nige today?'

'Yeah, he's been around. Michaels has been demanding regular reports off Nige, he's making his life a misery, phoning him at all hours, woke him up last night, got right up Nigel's nose.'

'As long as Nige hasn't told him we've been behaving, could ruin our reputations.'

'Nah, you said it, no one would believe it anyway.'

'The irresponsible stupid bastards, just the sort of stroke I'd expect those two to pull.' Jonno storms down the corridor.

'Oh yes, that's the sort of bloke you're going out with, Perfect, let him off the hook and—'

'And what, Jonno?'

Jonno softens his voice as he talks to her.

'That was for Michael and Freddy's benefit. I've just been talking to Michaels and he's been talking to Nige and evidently, Paul and Phil have been leading Nige astray. They were on the tear last night. Actually, I envy the guys a bit.'

Jane looks puzzled.

'On the tear? Out on the town? Jonno, I talked to Phil, earlier. He sounded perfectly alright. Surprisingly, he and Paul have been having a pretty quiet time. When I phoned, they'd been out with the account team and a few of the overseas guys having a meal. They'd worked late, evidently and—'

'I phoned Nigel again.' Michael Michaels, bristling, red of face, interrupts their conversation.

'What now?' enquires Jonno mildly.

'Nigel said Paul and Phil hadn't been sighted all morning and everyone was getting a bit narked when this gold, stretch limousine pulls up outside the agency with soul music blaring and Paul and Phil stumble out, and these two hookers pop up through the sun roof and start waving goodbye to them and blowing kisses to the staff watching from the agency windows.

'Paul and Phil staggered out of the limo, and, excuse me Perfect, Paul pulled a pair of panties out of his pocket and threw them to one of the girls then bowed to the agency personnel at the windows, goodness knows what they thought, they can be pretty straight laced, the Yanks,' Michaels pauses for breath.

'They went into the agency, laughing and they looked appalling and didn't smell too good either evidently.' He takes another deep breath, then splutters on, indignantly. 'Yes, the police had held them in the drunk tank, or something, overnight and let them off with a caution; drunk and disorderly, criminal damage, lewd behaviour, they were swinging off poles in a nightclub with these girls.

'The police doctor had to have a look at them they were in such a state. They even thought of calling the British consulate. They lent Paul a pair of overalls, his clothes were unwearable. And Nigel said they dropped an indecency charge as well, can you believe it?'

He then answered his own question.

'Well, you can when it's those two, can't you? Nigel said it cost us a large contribution to the Police Balls fund to get them out. Then Paul had the temerity to tell Nigel they'd had rather a good idea in the cell. Phil said Paul looked rather good in fluorescent orange and Nigel seemed to think it was funny, actually started giggling down the phone. I shall have to have a word with that young man.'

'Excuse me Michael,' says Jane, puzzled, 'Nige said they were in at the agency? We're, what, we're nine hours ahead of San Francisco. Not behind. That means it's well after two in the morning there. It's night time there, Michael.'

Michael Michaels stands there for a moment, processing the information, eyebrows knotting and unknotting, pursing his lips, eyes darting from a grinning Jonno to Perfect.

Jonno nods to him affably a couple of times, slaps him on the back, shakes his head, raises his eyebrows before disappearing, chuckling, into his office. His head appears back around the door.

'Michael, I think young Nigel's been winding you up.'

Chapter 35

It was one of those London evenings when the streets, warmed all day by an early summer sun, draw people out to share the pavement. They spill from the pubs, sprawl at café tables. The G and W crowd are contemplating going outside when the double doors of the Feathers burst open and Jonno stumbles in, waistcoat unbuttoned, hair tousled, tie awry.

'Got 'im,' he slurs loudly. 'Got 'im, oh yes sirree bob.'

The agency group steps back to appraise the swaying Jonno.

'Long lunch, Jonno? Got who? Or whom?' enquires Paul.

'Newlands.'

'No,' squawks Claire. 'I'd kiss you if you weren't spoken for. Well, sort of spoken for.'

'What?' enquires Nigel.

'I think Jonno's trying to tell us he's signed Mark Newlands to make your life even more of a misery, young Nige.'

'Hrrrm,' Michael Michaels clears his throat. 'His reputation precedes him. I doubt he'll be working on my business.'

'I doubt he'd want to Michael, you pompous git,' says Phil amiably.

'Fantastic news, Jonno. What a coup. When? Who'll he be working with?' ask various voices.

'Himself,' says Jonno. 'And me when he wants a wordsmith.' He pulls his tie back from over his shoulder and looks serious. 'I've a cab waiting, gotta go.' He spins on his heels, almost falls over and projects himself out of the pub.

'I'm going outside for a ciggy,' announces Claire, catching the door before it crashes shut.

The others follow her outside. Paul leans against the old red brickwork, stretching his shoulders against the warmth captured in the wall.

'Well done, Jonno,' he says, quietly.

'Alright, missy?' enquires Phil, putting his arm protectively around Jane.

'Yeah', she says, 'I'd better find Newlands an office, Monday, he won't want to share with Jonno?'

Paul shakes his head, squinting as the reflected sunlight catches a window across the street.

'No, he's a loner, and if they share an office, it would make him look like a creative director. Newlands is brilliant on the page, and on film, but the rest of it is a calculated act. A great one, though he can be terrific company. I was with him at Kinsale for the Irish Awards a couple of years ago. He was reeling about pissed, only ever drinks G and T, that's when he's not drinking champagne, when an Irish trade journo came over with a camera.

'Newlands sobered up in about two seconds flat. Put on his serious, only slightly amused face, then the moment the guy moved away, he let it all hang out again.'

'Jonno obviously forgets he isn't a writer,' says Phil, with a wry smile.

'He once told me he's a generalist,' supplies Jane.

'Generally mediocre?' asks Phil, drolly.

'Leave it, Phil,' says Paul. 'Takes the heat off us. Though it's going to make creative budgets a bit tight if he's going to pay Newlands the sort of money he's reputed to earn.'

'Yeah, Paul, might be an idea to ask Jonno about account alignments and responsibilities, Monday.'

'No, let's keep our powder dry. And speaking of dry,' Paul holds up his pint glass. 'One for the gutter?'

'Mad if you do, mad if you don't,' says Phil, looking quickly at Jane who purses her lips and shrugs what-sort-of-a-say-do-I-have?

'Same again then,' says Paul, taking their glasses.

Chapter 36

Angela Ainsworth, the Friendship client, settles back in her seat, her two assistants following her lead. Claire thinks she might one day write a paper on clients and their collective, imitative body language.

I suppose agency people are the same. React to each other, take boss' lead.

She scratches her tattoo and notices one of the Friendship team looking at her warily. She smiles at him enquiringly for a moment and he quickly looks away.

'Claire?'

Michael Michaels attracts her attention.

'Sorry Michael, Angela. Cynthia will present the work this morning. Cynthia, you got the layout there?'

Cyn indicates the rough idea for an advertisement, face down on the table in front of her. To start the presentation, she picks up the brief.

'Angela, Tom, Brian, Claire and I—'

Michael interrupts her. 'Cynthia, if I might pre-empt you and set the scene?'

Cyn shuts her mouth and looks down at the table. Claire looks pointedly at Michael. There's nothing quite as annoying as when someone else jumps in as you're about to start a presentation.

Especially when you've your opening remarks all worked out with absolutely no idea what the other person is about to say. Michael purses his small lips, takes off his round reading glasses and strokes his cheek seriously for a moment before focussing his attention on the clients.

Claire thinks for a moment of the pig in a suit she'd seen on the cover of a children's picture book in a bookshop window.

'Angela,' he continues smoothly, ignoring Claire's malevolent expression. 'Angela, when I approached Jonno to put Cynthia and Claire on your business, it was of course to get a more female approach into the area of household cleaners, and disinfectants.'

Angela shifts her attention to Michael. In her early forties and wearing her usual conservative peach suit and cream silk shirt, she's wary of agency people and their motives. She often appears uncomfortable in meetings. Now she looks guarded, brow furrowed. She inclines her head, twisting her pearl necklace in her fingers.

Michael suspects she'll show antipathy towards Claire, her confronting looks, spiky hair and tattoo. In fact, Claire has dressed down for the meeting, and Michael's snap judgement is totally speculative and unfounded.

In her university days, Angela was something of a radical herself and is even now liberal in her views; far too intelligent to judge someone by looks and looks alone. Michael smiles benevolently at the girls.

'Though of course, unlike you and I, Angela, Cynthia and Claire are yet to be blessed with children.'

Michael warms to his subject.

'Their creative work, with which you're unfamiliar, normally tends to be provocative and edgy, aimed at grabbing attention. Whereas, in this market segment most ads are warmer, softer, gentler, sympathetic to the young mother and the task, the hard work, so often underestimated, of bringing up a baby. So this work might come as a bit of a shock, I know it put me back on my heels.'

He pauses for breath, continuing to ignore the girls' acid looks.

'So we might review it now then pull back a bit, I know the girls have a lot of other approaches we could consider. And we will, of course, diligently research any material we decide upon, anyway.'

Having put the Friendship team totally on their guard and the agency on the back foot, he finishes his preamble and turns to Cynthia.

'Cynthia?'

Cyn stands, pulls her Danish tub plywood chair out from the table and climbing onto it sits precariously on the seatback, feet on the cushion.

'What are you doing, Cynthia?'

'Well, you just pulled the rug out from under my feet, Michael.'

Angela puts her hand to her mouth to hide her amusement.

'Actually,' Cyn puts the brief down. 'We're all familiar with the brief, and Michael is right. Normally advertising in this area is all soft and nice.'

Cyn comes down dismissively on the last word as she gets down from the chair.

'Nice, but here we're in a serious area. Germs are not nice. And it's easy to forget that there are millions around on every surface in the house and if all my experience with my nieces, minding them for my two sisters, house sitting, babysitting, has taught me something,' she smiles at Michael, 'It's taught me that babies get into everything. They touch, they crawl, put their fingers in things, put things in their mouths. Mums know this, they're wary, constantly on guard, they don't want their children getting sick.'

She pauses and turns to Angela for confirmation.

'This is all there in your brief of course, Angela.'

Turning, she includes Tom and Brian, 'And the brief also states the disinfectant is powerful; yet gentle so it won't harm children. The product might be gentle; the advertising doesn't have to be. It should be as powerful as the product, the descriptor you use on the label. Powerful yet gentle. Mothers can take it. They're not soft like their children, they're strongly protective, like our product.'

Cyn turns to address Angela directly.

'That's why we shouldn't be scared to talk to them in a straightforward, powerful way, one that, yes, attracts attention. Because, Angela, that is what you pay G and W to do. Make respondents look at our ads. And that's why Jonno gave the brief to us.'

Cyn picks up the layout from the table and holds it up for everyone to see. They see a charming, close up photograph of a baby crawling across the floor of a highly contemporary open plan kitchen, all clean gleaming surfaces, the mother in soft focus at a counter in the background.

The headline asks:

Is your baby crawling with germs?

Angela nods approvingly.

'Love it. Tom? Brian?'

Her assistants both nod assent.

'Well done, you two. Will we see any germs, if we do TV?'

Claire takes over.

'We wondered, Angela, whether it would be overdoing it to have animated germs wiggling about, or just see the baby exploring the kitchen, and then pose the question. Leave respondents to imagine the germs. We rather wanted to bounce the concept off you, first.'

'When we research—' interjects Michael.

His voice trails as Angela starts gathering up the papers in front of her, signalling conclusion of the day's business.

'I think the girls have just saved us that expense, Michael. We might put the money towards experimental animation or commission a really beautiful photo by a top photographer for the magazine ad.'

'Maybe a Friendship portfolio of baby photos, a promotion on the net, have your baby shot by a famous photographer?' suggests Claire.

'Or at least have its photograph taken, Claire?' Angela smiles.

Her assistants smile in unison.

'Perhaps,' suggests Cyn sweetly, 'we might discuss it over lunch, Michael?'

Michael's constipated expression indicates a tight, forced acceptance.

'Well, seeing as we don't get into the West End that often Michael, and Tom and Brian always appear to be hungry—' Angela concurs.

'I'll get Perfect to book us a table,' says Claire. 'is Fiorellis OK with you, Michael? Or the new place on Frith Street?'

'Client decision,' says Angela, 'the new place. What's life without adventure?'

As she gets up, Angela smiles to herself. *In advertising, it's left unspoken that it doesn't matter who picks up the lunch bill, the client always ends up paying for it.*

Chapter 37

'The way to a girl's heart,' comments Paul sagely, 'is through her mum, is it?'

He'd wandered around Phil's side of the desk and was looking over his shoulder, as Phil read a medical magazine article about agoraphobia.

'I like Lily, Paul, and I want to help her. If I don't know how her condition is treated, I might make a terrible balls up and put her back months, even make it worse and yes, you're right, there's that as well.'

'Interesting,' says Paul, reading, 'so it isn't literally the fear of open spaces, it's more the fear of being in one and having a panic attack?'

'Yeah,' says Phil, 'Something like that. Look here, Lily's insecure, her old man's pissed her off and pissed off, she's alone, can't handle social situations, crowds, travelling so it brings on panic attacks. Home is sanctuary.'

'So it comes down to sympathy from you, plus some real professional help?'

'Yep, which costs money.'

'So you've got to persuade Jane to get help for her mum, but that entails getting her there; unless a social worker, psychologist, doctor comes round to her first.'

'No idea how it works, Paul, but her first panic attack was a classic. Jane told me about it last week. Husband's been gone a week, Lily's alone at home, suddenly starts hating it, calls a friend who says "come around here," Lily leaves the house, runs for a bus, misses it, heart rate goes up, short of breath, gets panicky, sits down on the pavement, almost passes out and has to be helped home by a neighbour.'

'But you said she talks of going out?'

'Don't understand that either. Wishful thinking? Torturing herself? Anyway, Jane's agreed professional help is the way forward, she'll talk to Lily's GP, it's a start.'

Paul shakes his head.

'Anxiety, panic.'

'Like when we've got the McBride's client coming in Friday and we've got some ads to get out?'

'Knotty, that's nothing. It's frozen pies, not real life. And you've also got a severe case of lover's nuts to worry about.'

Chapter 38

'Halo's gone all open plan. The guys are hating it. Can't hear yourself think. Spend all their time in the café downstairs or have their ideas out of the office. We're lucky.'

'You can thank Paul for that, Nige, there was a move for us to go open plan once. Paul talked Freddy out of it.'

Cyn puts her wine down and ferrets for a crisp in the open bag on the table.

'These are good crisps these.'

'Go well with the Loire Cabernet Franc,' says Bitsa.

'Ooh Bitsa, the wine buff,' says Claire archly.

'I can bloody read, you moll,' growls Bitsa. 'It's this week's pub blackboard special.'

'Nige, any repercussions from Michaels after the SF windup?'

'No, but he's not speaking to me much. I snuck into the office on the way back from the airport and put a full written report on his desk, with copies of all the creative work except the Australians'.'

'Why not the Aussies?' enquires Bitsa.

'It was better than Paul and Knotty's, even they admitted that. And I apologised to Michael and pulled my head in for a few days. I reckon Michaels is too embarrassed to hark on it, not even realising we were ahead in time, not behind.'

'He he he he he,' Claire starts giggling, throwing in a few of her characteristic snorts.

'Tell us again about when he asked you to describe the hookers?'

'Well, it was a bit embarrassing. He was trying to be indignant, but he kept saying, and with this real sort of excited voice, you know, did they have big, you know, and I'm going, cor did they, Michael, I reckon they'd have to be enhanced to be that big. Nipples that would give a baby lockjaw. By the time I got to the lack of a panty line on their tight satin dresses and the way the light caught—'

'You said silk last time,' corrects Cyn.

'Doesn't matter now, does it?'

'You must be the big man in Paul and Knotty's book.'

Nigel grins, 'they still don't know. Well, they know they're supposed not to know.'

'What?'

'Jonno grabbed me the moment I came in and said, don't tell Paul and Knotty about your calls, it's delicious, their not knowing. Jonno's loving it. Went and got Michaels to keep quiet, reckons it turns the wind-up around on Paul and Phil, they're like the unwitting victims, the pawns Jonno calls them.'

'But Perfect will have told Knotty.'

'Of course.'

'I still don't understand why you did it, Nigel?'

'Michael hadn't got the time difference right so he's phoning me at all hours, and the third time he phoned and asked me if Paul and Phil were behaving, I just said, they're out in the limo. I was half asleep. It just sort of just came out. He shouted "what?" down the phone so I just went on with it. Sort of had to.'

Nigel starts giggling himself, 'especially as Phil and Paul were working so hard and told me not to tell Michael or you lot they were behaving for once, so I didn't, did I?'

He thinks for a moment, his voice reflective, 'Knotty pole dancing with the girl sitting on his head was the highlight, Michael really went to town on that.'

Chapter 39

Saturday afternoon. Phil holds his mug of tea in both hands, looking out of the window.

'Eee oop,' says Jane.

'Mmm?' says Phil, pretending not to hear. He turns, 'I were just thinking, lass, how good a couple of sheep, bloke with whippet, a few flat hats and a couple of factory chimneys in't background would complete the picture like.'

Jane nods, inclines her head and looks at him.

'You're a soft bugger underneath it all, aren't you?'

Lily enters the room.

'I was wondering what those yellow flowers were out there. Did you plant them, Lily?'

'Some time ago, Phil, some time ago,' Lily says quietly, defensively, 'Jane keeps the weeds down now.'

'I could do with a bit of a hand.' Jane's tone is slightly reproachful.

'Only happy to oblige.'

Phil jumps in quickly then changes the subject.

'I were admiring the paintings, always work in watercolour, Lily?'

'And gouache. I did them ages ago, Phil.'

Phil's been quietly yet assiduously working on Mrs S, as he calls her. He knew that she was already on medication, and due to see a cognitive therapist when they can get her out of the house. Her GP had been rather brusque in his assessment when called around by Jane.

He'd visited on the flimsy, hardly believable premise that he kept tabs on his old patients and had heard about Lily's split with her husband. 'As I was in the neighbourhood wondered if you were OK.' He'd written a prescription, 'Calm you down a bit, Mrs Saunders, nothing strong, your reaction is a common one in this sort of situation.'

On the way out, the doctor had taken Jane aside, confirmed Lily hadn't admitted to any recent panic attacks, or episodes of anxiety and that Jane hadn't seen any unusual behaviour.

'He seemed a bit offhand to me,' Jane reported to Phil.

Phil turns again to the painting.

'The Tate Britain have a lot of their Turners on show at the moment.' Phil kept his tone light and conversational, directing his comment to Jane, 'sketches and unfinished canvases. We'll have to go and have a shufty.'

Lily abruptly leaves the sitting room.

'Jane, let's do it, go tomorrow, get your mum a catalogue at least, or a book, get her interested again. Get her to do some views out of the window.'

'I'll get her to include an outside lavvy in the painting, just for you. And a pile of coke.'

'Oh no love, nutty slag, we kept coal in the bath in the kitchen.'

Jane ignores him. 'Let's get you a pint in before lunch.'

Chapter 40

'Good weekend?'

'Yeah, saw Jane Saturday and Sunday.'

'Two days eh, before we know it you'll be getting your end away.'

'No need to be nasty Paul, I know you get Mondayitis.'

'Well, I hope you copped a feel, at least.'

'What's got into you?' Phil sniffs, 'I've got it, it's Becs, isn't it, it's because you bottled it in San Fran. I told you to take a couple of extra days, get over to New York, and turn up on her doorstep.'

'I can't do that, Knotty, she's got a life, I can't just turn up, say hello Bec, get your gear off; ooo sorry, who's the big tattooed bloke in the kitchen?'

'Yeh, suppose so. You could have got in touch with her, asked.'

'I did.'

'You did?'

'She said, no. If you must know, she said if I came over it would be like, you know, when you're just relaxing after dinner in one of those restaurants where they have sittings and they say, excuse me sir, you have to go, we need the table. You know, come in number 23, your time is up.

'And anyway, I don't know who she's been talking to here but she reckoned it would be perfect for me, as it would give me a reason to get up and leave after a few days, you know.'

'It seems the Johnstone patented romantic modus operandi has preceded you?'

'Cyn might have said something?'

'You can't blame her, Paul, girls together and all that. Cyn is Becs' best mate.'

'Bec has this real dark side, negative, almost self-destructive.'

'Well, look at yourself, that's pot calling kettle black or at least dark grey. One thing though, she obviously still fancies you.'

Paul swings his legs off his desk and looks out of the cracked office window onto the back alley.

'We haven't spoken since, not phoned or anything, I reckon we'd just sit and look at each other and then say something we regretted.'

'Jeez, Paul, you are a fucking lost case. You're your own worst fucking enemy. Jeez.'

Paul slings down his pen and exits the office.

'You negative prick,' Phil shouts at a disappearing back, 'when you're feeling human again, I'll be sitting outside Bar Italia getting some Vitamin D. Shit, you Southerners are fucking arseholes sometimes.'

Dear Bec, dear when I'd like to say darling, but if I do, you wouldn't read any further, you'd just screw this up and throw it out of the window. I spent a lot of time in SF thinking of you, in your very different city, wondering what your little apartment on the fifth floor with its kitchen in a cupboard almost and the fold down bed is like.

And if the neighbours really are as noisy as you say and Coltrane's Chasing the Trane really does last twenty minutes and you watch the roaches dance to it, or whether you really live in an enormous loft with big windows and a bed on a platform on the mezzanine floor and there are miles of old, wide, wooden floorboards, some grey and some polished brown and studded with big copper nail heads and your apartment's caged by cast iron fire escapes.

And I think of sitting in Fanelli's with you nursing a hangover and a Bloody Mary watching you complain and eat a cheeseburger or like you said eating Massachusetts Belons in Balthazar and you will screw this up in a minute and say just because he's a writer and thinks he can write, he's trying to write me a love letter that doesn't look like one, because he's obviously shit scared to let his feelings out because he knows I don't let mine out too often except that time I actually said please keep in touch.

So he's keeping in touch and when I said, don't come to NYC he should have come anyway, but then he didn't have the guts to get on a plane and just turn up and that's what's really shitting him and what he wants me to say is if you're doing nothing the next long weekend, Paul, come over, because I get lonely on long weekends when my friends all leave town and I need someone to eat eggs Benedict with and drink mimosas with, etc.

'Got an envelope, Perfect? And if I give you the dosh you couldn't put this in the post for me, could you? No, I'll need a bigger envelope than that, thanks, it's on layout paper and I don't want to fold it too much.'

Jane looks up smiling, inquisitive.

'Paul, give me the address and I'll find an envelope and post it. And if you ask nicely, I won't read it or tell Knotty.'

Jane glances at the letter and looks at Paul coquettishly. 'As long as you share Becs' reply.'

Chapter 41

Roddy and Jimmy trail Paul and Phil down Frith Street. The old buildings look imperturbable, leaning against each other familiarly, scruffy old friends out on a binge. They've been weathering change for centuries, and with a bit of luck will do so for a long time to come.

'Up there, that's where John Logie Baird made the first TV broadcast.'

Jimmy shows some passing interest. Roddy speaks casually over his shoulder to Phil.

'Mozart lived in Soho, and Canaletto. And Marx wrote Das Kapital in a Dean Street garret over what is ironically now an up market restaurant. George told us.'

Paul and Phil make to go into the Dog and Duck, Roddy and Jimmy keep walking.

'Please, Knotty, no George and his stories today, let's go down the French, I like the bar food there. And Jimmy and I prefer a glass of wine anyway. You two can always dog and duck in there on the way back to the office.'

At the French, they decide to stand out on the pavement. They sip their drinks quietly, watching the passing lunchtime parade.

'Are any of George's stories true?'

'Hard to tell, some are, I don't think he makes them all up, most are in the "you should have been there" genre. You know marvellous at the time if it happens to you.'

'Like his Doctor Who story.'

'What one's that, Paul?'

'It was well before your time.'

'I used to watch the re runs, Mum was a bit of a fan, collected the VHS tapes. And now its been on again.'

'Well, the way George tells it, he's going back to the office one lunchtime and suddenly it starts pissing down, so he ducks in here and it looks like the rain's set in so he orders a drink. There's only a couple of people left in here and suddenly Tom Baker—'

'He was the tall Doctor Who, the one with the big hair and the scarf a few years back.'

'Correct, Jimmy. Well, he comes rushing in, shaking the water out of his hair, and he's wearing the scarf and starts to unwind it to get the rain out of it, big smile, everyone looks round and there's this old bloke at the bar with a flat cap on.

'George has never seen him in the French before. So the old bloke looks at Tom Baker and says, "Are you Doctor Who?" And Tom Baker says "Yes, I am."

'And the old bloke says, "well stop it fucking raining".'

Jimmy and Roddy afford Paul wan smiles.

'Well you asked, and I think it's funny, and I bet you use it.'

Jimmy looks reflective. 'Yeah, but George also said he sometimes can't remember if it happened to him or a mate or it's just one of those apocryphal Soho stories. Myth, legend, The French? The Coach and Horses?' He shrugs. 'My mum will like it.'

'Tell them his other lunch one and get it over with so next time we go into the Dog, they can tell George he's told them before. He won't remember.'

'Bloody will, his mind's a steel crap trap.'

'Alright. Get 'em in for me, could you Phil. Another cider, Jimmy? Glass of Rose for you and me Roddy and whatever you're having, Phil. And see if you can get us a table.'

Paul pulls out some money and Phil waves it away.

'Right, Morecambe and Wise. Ring any bells?'

'My dad loves them,' says Roddy. 'Like Doctor Who, we watch all the reruns. He'd tell me their jokes when I was little, used to make me laugh.'

'Well, not that long ago, the ad and film industry used to use this trattoria on the corner of Romilly Street and you'd get celebs in there but you know, you ignored them. Morecambe and Wise came in one lunchtime, nobody took much notice but Eric, Morecambe, did his wiggly-glasses thing, and attracted everyone's attention.'

'My Uncle Bernie does that, drives Auntie mad,' interjects Roddy.

'Anyway, Eric and Ernie Wise sit down, the waiter approaches and Eric does his silly glasses waggle thing so everyone's looking and he goes, "waiter, do you have frog's legs?" The waiter looks at him puzzled, and Eric says, "Then hop off and get me a steak".'

'And?' asks Roddy.

'Probably made up,' adds Jimmy.

Phil returns with the drinks.

'What do we have to do to make you laugh?' He says to Roddy.

'I heard that one when I worked in Manchester,' remembers Phil, 'and the other one about the trat.'

'Enlighten us?' says Paul.

'I've been told it's been done about a hundred times.'

'What?' asks Jimmy.

'You give a waiter a message on a piece of paper, point him at a diner at another table and ask him to take t'over and wait for a reply.'

'What does the note say?'

'I'm a lonely Italian waiter and I'd like to sleep with you.'

This amuses Jimmy and Roddy, who both start laughing. Phil and Paul shake their heads at each other.

'You two have been watching too many of those crass American comedies.'

'About as subtle as a turd in a washbasin.'

This provokes a fresh bout of giggles from Roddy and Jimmy.

'We're being signalled at, our table's ready.'

Chapter 42

Freddy walks down Dean Street from Oxford Street, occasionally pausing to look around, somewhat furtively He doesn't want to bump into any other G and W staff. On the other hand. Should he, he has every right to do so. He's the boss, he doesn't have to justify himself. But there are production companies and recording studios in Soho the creative department uses.

So Freddy didn't cut along Bateman Street, as there was a café there the agency frequents. His feelings fluctuate, wildly. After all, he has regular breakfast meetings in the Groucho Club in Dean Street, anyway, so why should he feel guilty?

Perhaps it's because he's going behind the backs of his board, without talking to them first. And, after all, the agency is, as he'd once said expansively at Christmas drinks, "my other family." And as he's head of "the family", he feels he can initiate and guide agency policy. And he rationalises, he's the largest shareholder and has the deciding vote anyway.

Freddy pauses, looks up and down the street and straightens his shoulders and strides purposefully into the club, one of the first advertising people to be allowed in, Freddy has lots of friends among authors and publishers, is often seen in The Groucho and, again he rationalises, after all he's only here this morning to listen.

He goes into the bar. There's only one person in there, who rises creakily to his feet, ruddy, lined, weather beaten face registering the effort. Christian Lafond is a huge man, shoulders straining at the seams of an aged tweed jacket, prematurely white hair standing in an untamed clump above a wide forehead.

He looks like he once played number eight in a tough, South Western France rugby club forward pack, which he had, and where he'd obviously suffered several broken noses. He's now President of the club.

'Fred, Freddy Grimshaw? Christian Lafond, I'm pleased to make your acquaintance.' Christian's English is curiously formal.

He extends a huge, gnarled paw of a hand. 'I now understand the expression; a bear of a man,' Freddy reports later to his wife, Polly. 'But he has a sort of slow, gentle handshake, as if he wants you to know he could crush you, literally and metaphorically, should he so decide.'

'Christian,' says Freddy, pleased he doesn't have to speak French, 'my pleasure.'

Christian gestures towards his teapot. Freddy nods yes. The Frenchman drops back into his armchair, speaking as he goes.

'My knees, Freddy, may I call you Freddy?' he doesn't wait for assent, 'too many rucks, mauls, scrums, not enough good surgery, back then.'

He looks steadily at Freddy as he settles back in his seat.

'I will be direct. The Argent Group, I, we would like to buy your Agency.'

Freddy doesn't react, merely lets himself down into the cushions with a slight exhalation of breath.

'Freddy,' Christian continues, 'Freddy, you have been thinking of it ever since I asked you to meet me. You were thinking of it all the way from your office. Am I betraying my colleagues, you are thinking? No, you also think, I'm in my sixties, I run the place, it's time for me to relax a little, maybe do something else.

'It's not worth giving those Frenchies only fifty one percent, as I would have to work more years, again you are thinking, yes? I'll accept a takeover, a buyout, a pay-out, retire to the country; you like racehorses, remember we were first met at the Prix de L'Arc de Triomphe, you could have your own horses. I am correct? What's your answer, seeing as you already know it?'

Biding his time, Freddy pours a cup of tea and looks around him at the slightly old fashioned English design of the room. Reassuring. At the contemporary art and cartoons on the wall. I'm happy here, he thinks, I'm in the heart of Soho, my stomping ground, my turf, my manor since I was a messenger boy all those years ago. But I'll have to let go one day.

'Christian,' he hears himself saying, as if he was in the third armchair listening to Freddy Grimshaw thinking aloud, 'you too have to go sometime. You too once had a small but growing agency and were bought by the Argent Group, but you had the clout, the influence to stay on and become chairman.'

Freddy pauses for a sip of tea. Christian gazes at him, intently.

'So, your bean counters have looked at London, we're one of the few independents left, we're growing, attracting attention, you could say it's inevitable we'll fall into the hands of one of the big groups soon. If we do not sell to Argent, someone like you will then come along and offer our clients better deals, things we can't possibly match.'

He pauses to top up his cup of tea.

'So your people said to you, talk to him, Christian, approach Freddy, be direct. Christian, you should know that I'm fiercely loyal and protective of my people, you should also know they're all talented, some will stay with Argent, some will move on, some won't do either, your bean counters will give them the Spanish archers.'

Christian wrinkles his brow questioningly.

'El bow, the elbow, the sack.'

Christian nods in understanding.

'There'll be people surplus to requirements, so I must look after them.'

Freddy thinks of Ralph for a moment, Ralph who'd probably seen this coming for a couple of years but hadn't thought to look after himself. His voice trails away, he's silent for a moment.

'Freddy, you were saying?'

'Christian, sorry, I lost the thread for a moment there. I have to say I don't resent your approach to us, and I, I admire your bluntness. You're the chairman, your executive committee will have said, ask them, make an offer, and I know the Cordier Drinks Group are eyeing Braithwaite's.'

Christian raises his eyebrows in mute surprise.

'Our brewery client,' explains Freddy. Christian nods, lets him go on. 'My answer is yes. I think you expected that. Yes. But we'll have to work out the details, and I want to be able to reveal everything to my people before this gets out at your end.'

'Thank you, Freddy, I was told you would not, prevaricate. I, in my turn, will only tell my people you are thinking about it, and you will talk only to me, until our lawyers and, what you called them, the bean counters, get together. We will keep this—'

'Amicable, gentlemanly, sociable.'

'Gracieuse,' concludes Christian. He extends his hand and they shake, once, formally. Freddy notices the Frenchman's grip is much firmer now. 'It is too early for?' Christian gestures at the bar.

'No, I think I might need one. I mean we deserve one. Both of us.'

Back at the agency, Ralph asks, 'anyone seen Freddy?'

'I believe he said he had to go home,' says Grace.

'I thought I saw him in Dean Street earlier,' says Nancy, the traffic lady.

Ralph shrugs. 'It's nothing that won't keep,' he says, disappearing into his office.

Chapter 43

'This is yours, isn't it, Lily?'

'Thanks Phil, I must have dropped it.'

Phil hands Lily an embroidered handkerchief, one he'd often seen her take from her apron pocket and absently clutch and wring it around her fingers like a child's comforter. He didn't reveal where he'd picked it up; at the end of the garden by the shed.

Phil could have let the moment go. However, he looks at Lily levelly, the question in his expression. Lily looks around. Jane's shopping, they're alone in the kitchen.

'I've been reading that book on cognitive therapy you gave me, makes a lot of sense. I went into the kitchen to make a cup of tea and opened the back door, you know, let a bit of fresh air in. Then one moment I'm on the back step holding onto the door jamb, I looked up into the sun, was blinded for a moment, then the next thing I know I'm walking down the garden, it was lovely.'

Lily smiles in memory.

'I could smell next door's freshly mown grass, I was looking at those yellow flowers, going to pick some before they got too blown, then I saw the shed and thought of Reginald and I got all, anxious, and the next thing, I'm back in the kitchen again, sitting in the chair, my heart going.'

'Lily, the garden's like an extension of the house, you're comfortable there, it's understandable you got a bit, panicky, when you saw the shed. Blokes and their sheds.'

Phil is out of his depth. Lily is looking at him as if she's done something wrong, not right. Phil draws in a breath and speaks decisively.

'Lily, it was very brave, brave of you. Not many people have the strength to face up to their demons and you just did. You did, didn't you?'

Lily still looks uncertain, wringing her handkerchief in her hands.

Phil keeps going. 'I can see where Jane gets it, gets her certainty from. Well, come to the Tate Gallery with us. We won't go for long. Reginald's not in the Tate Gallery, is he? And all you have to do to go there is walk to the front gate to my car, and I can drive you there and drop you and Jane at the door and then join you. And you'll have the both of us there with you.'

Jane appears with two shopping bags.

'Mum, I got neck of pork, your slow cooked recipe is Mungo of the Moors here's favourite. You look guilty, both of you, Mum have you been talking about me?'

'Why would we talk about you?'

'What else do you have to talk about while I'm braving the Saturday shoppers and you're here having cups of tea?'

'And cake,' Phil adds. 'We were talking about going t'Tate tomorrow if that doesn't interfere too much with your agenda.'

Lily suddenly looks fearful.

'I'm not, ready.'

Phil looks at her, eyes questioning, encouraging. Lily looks back.

'Yes, I am.'

Jane's eyes betray her emotions as she struggles to keep her face straight. Turning to Phil and Lily, she manages to keep her voice level, her manner casual, almost offhand.

'I don't see why not, Mum, saves cooking, is the restaurant open Sundays?'

Left alone together, Jane moves into Phil's arms, burrowing her head into his shoulder, digging her fingers into his back.

'Thanks, P.'

'It was nothing to do with me, she went for a walk in the garden of her own accord. I found her hanky on't lawn.'

Chapter 44

'Paul Johnstone, Philip Arbuthnott, Christine Parmentier.'

Christine is tall, slim, maybe early forties, with a mass of tangled blonde hair and faint freckles, blue eyes and a Roman nose that lends authority to an otherwise very soft, English face.

'Back in the workforce,' she says with some chagrin, forcing a hand through her hair and eyeing the fading cream paintwork of the boys' office with the window, sash cord broken, propped open by an old Perspex radio award. They stand and shake hands with her.

'You're the reason I'm here,' she says, looking at the boys.

'And of course, you, Freddy,' she turns to Freddy, 'he can be very persuasive.'

She points to the small Aunt Nora's point of sale sticker on the wall.

'Single-minded, a product truth, and made me smile.'

She addresses Paul and Phil directly. 'One of the McBrides clients told me at an ad gathering how Freddy supported the idea at the pitch. She said all the other agencies skirted around their campaign recommendations. Wouldn't plump for the one. But you did, Freddy. That's the other reason I'm here.'

Freddy nods his thanks, lowering his eyes and reddening slightly at the compliment.

Christine is a top planner. Her job is to see things from the consumers' point of view, work out exactly how and what ads should be communicating. She's tenacious, she supports the creative work that stems from her briefs.

She's been described as fierce, dogmatic and had attracted less complimentary epithets. To the point where her last agency was relieved when she'd taken maternity leave, and secretly pleased when Christine told them she wouldn't be back.

'Pie,' said Paul, 'we're looking forward to working with you.'

'Pie?' said Phil, puzzled, when Christine had been whisked away to meet the rest of the agency.

'It's been her nickname forever. Someone said it was because Parmentier is a sort of French cottage pie. Not that I've ever heard that. Blimey, she's going to scare the shit out of Michaels.'

'What's today's word to be, then?'

Christine halts Cyn and Claire as they join her at the boardroom door.

'Word?'

'It's a game I play in meetings, we take it in turns to work a word into what we say.'

'Any word?'

'The more irrelevant to the subject in hand the better. That's what makes it fun.'

'I wouldn't want to upset Angela,' says Cyn. 'Are they in there, yet?'

'No, no, Michael will bring them in. I just wanted to make sure the AV is working. Never does when you want it to. So, I'll choose today's word and you, Cyn have to work it into the meeting.'

Cyn looks suspicious.

'What's the worst word you've ever had to use?'

Christine looks around. 'Cunnilingus.'

'You're kidding.'

Christine grimaces.

'No, and it was a very uptight client, and my only out was I knew he'd requested that I didn't work on his business anymore as they preferred to formulate their own approaches and strategies, thank you very much.'

'So how did you do it?'

'I just couldn't, there was nowhere I could use it, no way, but as the meeting was running down, the bloody art director who'd suggested it kept catching my eye and making this little come on hand movements. Then the client stood up, picked up his briefcase and said, "let's get down to it, then".'

Christine takes a breath.

'It was like a cue so I said it, out loud, "what, cunnilingus"?'

'Blimey, what happened?'

'There was silence for a moment and then everyone looked appalled and tried to act as if they hadn't really heard it. Chairs were scraped, throats were cleared, the little idiot of an art director and goofy writer were looking at me and grinning, so I just looked at the client, contrived to look contrite, took my hand away from my mouth. I'd sort of clamped it there when I said it and said, "I don't know why I said that," and as the only female in the room, they sort of ushered me out first. It got me off the business, though, thank goodness. Ungrateful bastards.'

Christine reflects for a moment.

'And out of the agency, and in here, come to that.'

Cyn interrupts her.

'Christine, here's Michael and the clients, you'd better check the AV. What's the word then?'

'A gentle one to start, Cyn, sausages. And it must be used relevantly, if laterally. Not like the irrelevant example I just gave you.'

'I think cunnilingus is always relevant, Christine.' Claire smiles a Cheshire cat smile.

Chapter 45

'Yes, Nigel?'

Nigel walks into Freddy's office, and halts in the middle of the fine, faded Persian carpet in front of Freddy's ornate, Italian antique desk. If asked, Freddy would always cite Burt Lancaster in "The Leopard" as his example of style. It had been shown recently as part of a Visconti retrospective so at least some of the agency now knew what Freddy was talking about. Freddy gestures Nigel to an armchair.

'Freddy, I just wanted to say about San Francisco—'

'No', Freddy puts down his bone china teacup and raises his hand in a warning gesture. 'It has been, gone, done. This is an advertising agency we have fun and what you did didn't jeopardise our contribution to the project. Though it's not sensible making senior members of staff appear figures of fun, Nigel, especially those who might influence your career. Though off the record, it did show some imagination on your part. Anyway?'

'It wasn't really about that, Freddy, it's just that Paul and Phil take time mentoring me, but they come from a creative point of view and they said I should ask you about any business insights.'

Freddy leans forward, looking thoughtful. 'I did have something confirmed to me the other day, mmm.'

'Yes?' Nigel too leans forward eagerly, the young acolyte at the feet of the old guru.

'Have you not noticed Nigel that client's use the terminology of their products when describing things to you?'

Nigel looks puzzled.

'The first time it was pointed out to me was as a junior after a meeting with the Warner's Jelly people. Having bid farewell to the clients, the MD I was working with started chuckling. I asked him what was so funny and he said, "Freddy m'boy", Freddy affects an upmarket accent, "Freddy, did you not hear the client's answer when I asked about his current sales position? He said, wobbly. They're wobbly." See what I mean Nigel?' Freddy looks searchingly at Nigel.

'I see. So, if he had been,' Nigel searches for a simile, 'a fixatives client, making glue, he would have said his sales position was sticky.'

'Exactly, you've got it. Happens time and time again. It's enlivened many a meeting for me. And here, Nigel, endeth this morning's lesson.'

Chapter 46

Ralph leans against the bar in the Brewery Tap, the pub on the corner of Braithwaite's Brewery. It might well have been an extension of the brewery, as it shared the same heft of stonework and the dark mahogany woodwork carved by the same hands as that of the brewery offices, except the pub was decorated with sad mementoes of the first World War supplied, it was said, by those of the brewery workers lucky enough to return and supplemented by some faithful regulars.

Ralph takes a sip of his bitter and stretches his back. How many times had he caught the train up to this northern town with its stern chimneys forever wheezing white smoke; how many meetings had he ducked and dove and wheedled and wormed his way through swallowing his pride, as Paul put it, to sell a few advertisements to George Braithwaite?

'Well at least we get to swallow a good pint afterwards,' was Ralph's feeble rejoinder.

Paul is still upstairs, going over a promotional idea with Jenny.

'Bonjour, mon brave.'

It's directed at Ralph, in a somewhat ironic tone in a thick local accent. Ralph turns to find a smiling Tommy Jenkinson, head of the Braithwaite's sales team.

'Tommy—'

'Jenkinson' says Ralph, shaking his hand. 'We met at the sales conference. Ralph Bertram.'

'Ralph, aye, or is it allez oop?'

Ralph's look is genuinely puzzled. Tommy signals for two pints, 'another one, Ralph?' and turns to him, looking at him searchingly.

'You've either got a poker player's face or you haven't heard rumours?'

Ralph's expression doesn't change.

'Cordier, you've not heard?'

Ralph's expression tightens. 'Europe's biggest liquor group. They're not looking at?'

'Acquiring us? Me? This? Aye, so t'is said.'

Freddy's mind starts racing. Paul enters in the pub. He smiles at Ralph.

'Has something large and nasty just escaped your arse and attached itself your shirt tail, Ralph? Paul Johnstone,' he says, turning to Tommy.

'Tommy Jenkinson. Pleased to meet you, though not so pleased if you're responsible for that commercial my sales force have to get behind.'

'No, Tommy, singing and dancing's not Paul, Paul did that Charge of the Light Brigade idea.'

Tommy guffaws into his pint, spraying droplets down his suit. He slams the glass onto the counter and grips Paul's hand with both of his.

'Pleased to meet you, Paul, pleased. I'm sorry you couldn't sell it, son, in a work sense, but you'd have felt a bit better if you could have been there when Mr Braithwaite told me about it. Well, I'm not sure whether he was directing remarks to me, or to all those portraits on't boardroom wall. His eyes were stood out like prize bull's bollocks and the veins on his neck, you could have tied The Queen Mary oop with them. Ap-o-plec-tic he was aye, apoplectic when he was telling it to me.'

Tommy shakes his head and takes a long pull at his pint, relishing the memory.

'Well get one down you lad, might not taste quite the same when French take us over.'

'Sorry?' Paul enquires.

'Tommy says the Cordier group are looking at British acquisitions,' says Ralph, tiredly.

Paul takes it in.

'Well, you'll be OK, Ralph, if the account stays with us; you're the font of all knowledge on Braithwaite's and beer.'

'Aye well, I confronted Braithwaite with it,' says Tommy sombrely, 'and he denied it, but you know it's hard to tell what he's really thinking; he's friendly, right, smiles at me because I do the job but he's got a smile on him like the wave on a slops bucket.'

'Thank you, Tommy, you've just made the whole trip up worthwhile. Sante.' Paul raises his glass and sucks the froth off, appreciatively. 'And this is the bonus, lovely.'

'Eh?'

'Great expression, great beer.'

'Oh.'

'You still with us, Ralph?'

'Just mulling over all the implications.'

'Well, don't mull away too much, we've got a train to catch, and we've got to get one in for Tommy first.'

Paul gestures to the barman, smiling. 'Smile like the wave on a slops bucket, wait until Phil hears that one.'

'What was that all about, Ralph?'

Cyn and Claire had seen Ralph in reception, shaking hands vigorously with Alan Sergeant, before ushering him out and standing there, looking very pleased. Claire's enquiry is prompted by Ralph then performing a short soft shoe shuffle.

'That, Claire is new business, and if I could ask you two to keep quiet until Freddy has made the all staff announcement.'

'What, more of Reader Inc?'

'Much, much more.'

Cyn extends, opens and closes her arms. Large or small, she pantomimes.

'Oh I see, which part? The pet food division. A project to start with, on their new, dry dogfood, followed by one for an upmarket gourmet wet dogfood. The first will be mainly magazines and posters.'

'The whole dog's breakfast?''

'Yes, with TV for the Poochie Pouchie product.'

'Poochie Pouchie?'

'They haven't settled on a name yet. The research is about a foot thick already. You know, pouched dog food; small dogs for single women. Surrogate children. The ones that are fed fillet steak and allowed on sofas and in bed.'

'The women or the dog?' Enquires Cyn.

'Eeeuch yuck,' exclaims Claire, face twisted in revulsion, 'I hate it when people bring their dogs around my place and then invite them onto the sofa. Our dog lived in a kennel in the garden. It was lucky to get as far as the kitchen door.'

'Careful, Claire, I was just going to put our hand up for the TV brand.'

Cyn notices Ralph's looking a little uncomfortable.

'Ralph, sorry, that's marvellous, terrific, you've pulled a client.'

'No, Cyn,' Ralph deadpans, 'that's Jonno's prerogative.'

Claire gives Ralph a hug. She's taller than he.

'You're going a bit thin on top Ralph, must be all the worry of new business.'

Ralph shrugs her off, 'they're an existing client, after all, though it is a big bit of extra business. And for all the criticism Sergeant gets, he is a supporter of ours.'

'Just as long as Grace's school uniform fits, or doesn't,' Cyn suggests.

'Are you sure your names not short for cynical, Cyn. Cynical Cyn; you can both buy me a drink after work, especially for the uncalled for bald remark, Claire. Sonia and I are going to the theatre later.'

'She's meeting you in the Feathers then?'

'And I will put in a word for you with Jonno, though what attracted the Reader guys was the Aunt Nora's stuff, so it might go to Paul. I told Sergeant the freezer line stemmed directly from a field research insight, a consumer quote.'

'As long as he doesn't ask to hear the tape of the vox pop.'

Chapter 47

'I'm hearing things, Freddy.'

The meeting is over, Friendship Industries has gone, the boardroom table is a litter of cups, glasses and plates of fast curling sandwiches. Freddy Grimshaw slumps in his chair, idly twiddling a piece of lettuce leaf.

'Ralph, I'm tired. I've been in this game a long time. Someone once told me that everyone should have four careers. I've had just this one, for bloody over forty years. I started the day I left school, early. Office boy, trainee, messenger, tea maker, dogsbody: I worked my way up, of course there was a lot of luck on the way, right people right time, joined Marcus, ended up with my name on the tile.

'Ralph, I may have been a little under the weather in Feathers the other night, and what you heard was a rhetorical question, i.e. isn't it time you did something else, Freddy, and I said, probably, yes. And of course by the time it gets to you, it's "Freddy is selling the agency."

'Well, old friend, maybe it is time to do something else. While I've got time. I owe it to myself. And I don't mean sit on a boat, garden, or play golf. I can't stop working. And even if I, we, do accept a takeover bid, or merger, whatever, they'd still make me come in for a year or two.'

'Maybe,' says Ralph, quietly. *And where would that leave me?*

'Arts administrator, charity,' Freddy ponders. He moves slightly, inclines his head, ensures he's looking at Ralph directly. 'Fact of life, Ralph, everyone knows how advertising works. I sometimes think our creative teams are the only honest ones. They work towards personal advancement, get their faces in magazines, pay court to award juries. But people like you, loyal, happy to be where they are; at least you're irreplaceable on your business.'

'Am I?' asks Ralph. A touch of bitterness creeps into his voice. 'If industry tittle tattle is right and the French have us in their sights,' Ralph raises his hand, 'Freddy, you don't have to confirm it' *I guessed right, it is Cordier's agency,*

Freddy, your body language is giving you away. 'Freddy, those French mobs are run by bean counters, they suck their foreign affiliates dry.'

I should start looking around, putting out feelers right now. Beat the French to the punch. Take an account or two with me. Freddy's counting on me not doing that, good old loyal Ralph.

Freddy looks at Ralph, quizzically. 'You were saying, old boy?'

'Freddy, you have my support, you know that.'

Even as his voice trails away, Ralph feels pathetic.

A stupid thing to say; it's time to look after myself while I still have the time. And the energy. Before my career's put into the hands of a group of people who'll have me in the soup like a stale baguette.

'I'll see you're alright, Ralph. Trust me.'

Always have. But you can't, Freddy, even if you want to. It'll be out of your hands.

Chapter 48

Paul is in a Reader meeting. He excuses himself for a moment when the discussion side-tracks into media. Alan Sergeant, the Reader client is an extremely serious man whose whole approach to advertising is dictated by exhaustive research and a conservative strategy.

He'd been described to Paul as resembling the dean of a university, which, thought Paul, was an unfair reflection on university deans. Maybe an ecclesiastical one. To Paul, Alan looks like a Victorian cleric or temperance advocate in his cheap, shiny suit, tie tightly knotted, unsmiling demeanour and gaze penetrating from under bushy eyebrows more luxurious than his rapidly thinning hairline, his brow constantly pulled into suspicious furrows, nose wrinkled as if you had farted close by or were about to put one over him; as if his experiences of dealing with agency people, especially those from the creative department was inevitably unsavoury, at the very least.

Female staff had noted Sergeant's wandering eye early on and so Phil had suggested to Grace that she might help the agency's cause by giving him some sort of visual relief the moment he came into the agency.

'I don't mind, might help him take his mind off the other girls, Phil,' Grace had observed.

In a way, it was a bit of play acting, a game, signalling to Alan Sergeant that that agency noticed and didn't mind playing up to it. There was an element, even, of dismissive contempt in it, too. A bit of give and take as Sergeant wasn't fooled in any way.

However, as he was someone who'd be disconcerted by the opinionated and assertive Cynthia and Claire, Paul had been delegated to cover client meetings.

Paul slips into the toilet, catching a glimpse of himself in his blue Yamamoto suit in the mirror. He pauses for a moment, does a double take, looking good, son, smooths his tie.

Bitsa bursts in. 'Looking smooth Paul, client in?' he says, disappearing into a cubicle.

'Reader,' says Paul to the fast closing door.

There was a pause then, 'aaah, dog food, aaah.' Bitsa's voice strains from the cubicle. 'Aaaah,' followed by a prolonged mock fart and, 'you'd have to be proud of that.'

'You all right in there, Bitsa?'

'Aaaah,' comes the strained reply, 'Guinness and vindaloo down the loo.'

Paul rinses and dries his hands and, opening the toilet door to leave, pauses to let a volley of Bitsa's mock farts out and Alan Sergeant in. Their eyes meet for a moment. Paul obligingly holds the door open for him, keeping his expression inscrutable.

'Aaahhh, nnnn, mmm, begorrah,' the sound effects continue from the cubicle, now in a pronounced Irish accent. Paul lets the door close gently behind the client.

'Hotline to the Thames Turd Treatment Works,' Paul hears faintly as he moves away down the corridor. 'Warn the guys at Barking outfall. Tell them to get their thigh boots on. Aaaargh.'

Paul takes his seat in the boardroom followed a few minutes later by Alan Sergeant. Alan takes great care not to catch Paul's eye. Paul bites his tongue and assumes his no-expression-client-meeting-expression.

Bruce Wood, Alan's moon faced assistant, shuffles some papers self-importantly into a pile, opens a notebook at a blank page, uncaps a ball point pen, carefully writes "Creative suggestion" at the top of the page and underlines it.

On cue, Alan says, 'perhaps we could look at the creative work now, Paul?'

Paul has done his homework on Sergeant. This is one, canny client. Don't soft soap him. Don't reiterate the strategy or the brief, don't try and be clever. Just play back what he'd asked for in the brief and get to the point.

'Alan, you asked us for a line that would grab the attention and had an absolute product truth, which we've closely followed. We also stuck closely to the controlling dictums of all dogfood advertising, as per your iteration in the brief: healthy, lively, animal enjoyment, the dog enjoying its dinner. Phil, as art director asked a photographer to do us a favour and shoot a test shot with a particularly lean and muscular dog, one with short, shining healthy hair.'

He didn't say it was the photographer's dog, coat carefully retouched, as he knew Alan was stickler for the truth and actually believed his products made dogs look discernibly healthier.

'Alan the shot, or one of the others from the shoot, we feel is good enough to be used for the actual poster.'

Paul looks at Bruce who is scribbling away, waiting for him to finish. He'd underlined absolute product truth.

'OK,' Paul's bored with all this foreplay, 'OK, I suspect Alan that our line will take you a bit by surprise, but if it were more obvious, I doubt it would catch dog owners' attention. Especially as we're aware this is the more pragmatic sort of owner. We also hope the ad will be the first of series.'

Paul walks around the table and picks up an A3 Layout leaning with its face against the wall.

'You asked us to use the word tasty in relation to the product and make it a superlative. You also asked for originality, a thought, a unique aspect of doggie satisfaction with the product, as Bruce put it, never featured or pointed out before.'

Paul waits for Bruce to stop scribbling unique aspect of doggie satisfaction, MINE and underline it twice. Paul then quickly turns the layout around. It consists entirely of a photo of a dog with its face deep in a bowl of Reader Dry Dogfood, with a pack shot morticed into the corner of the layout.

The headline reads:

So tasty they'll eat it off the floor.

'Is that it?' blurts Bruce.

Paul prudently keeps quiet.

Ralph says, quite reasonably, 'We're already slightly over the six words to a poster rule Bruce, but we think the line is sufficiently engaging to carry the day.'

'And dogs do have a short attention span, Bruce,' Nigel's bites his tongue. 'Sorry Bruce, I don't want to sound facetious, but as the line's slightly tongue in cheek, research indicates the approach would be acceptable to this target audience, who as we agreed approach dog ownership and dog food purchase with a certain, pragmatism. Your words, Alan?'

True to form, Sergeant stifles a yawn as he totally ignores his assistant and Nigel's impudence. It was nothing more than he expected from an advertising agency and does no more than to confirm this long held belief.

'Mmmm,' he says, 'Ah, yes. I know I asked for something different, but this might be too different.'

He glances at Paul, inviting a reply.

'G and W rule, Alan, if we can't surprise you or set you back on your heels, we certainly won't excite the dog owner faced with a plethora of choices.'

I bet Bruce writes that down, thinks Paul, glancing surreptitiously over to see Bruce write faced with a plethora of choices.

'True, very true. We'll have to mull this one over, do a bit of tea lady research.' Alan stands. 'But I must say, and this is not a tick on the spot, thinking about it in relation to your Aunt Nora's line, Paul, I'm already beginning to prefer it, and you have promised us a few more like it.'

Bruce nods, self-importantly, stands and sticks out his hand.

'Well done, Philip.'

Paul catches Alan looking at his assistant. Alan grimaces with a "what-have-I-done-to-deserve-him" expression, casting his eyes heavenward as he turns to Paul.

'Yes, thank you. Good work, Paul.'

'What's tea lady research, Paul?' Asks Nigel on their way back to their offices.

'Alan comes from an era before they had water coolers when lovely old dears brought morning tea round the office. It means asking anyone who happens to be standing around in the office what they think of an ad. Normally forces people to double guess you and give you the answer they think you want to hear. Whereas tea ladies told you exactly what they thought of everything including your clothes and whether you looked sexually proficient.'

Claire and Cyn appear.

'Well, then?'

The work was Claire and Cyn's. As Paul was the creator of the Aunt Nora's campaign, Ralph had suggested he present it as his own.

'Nice top, Claire,' says Paul, 'I'm not joking. Well, maybe I am a bit.'

The girls don't react, merely stand there blocking the corridor. Paul holds up his hands in supplication.

'OK, OK, I think they love it.'

'If you really push him, Claire,' Nigel butts in, 'he'll admit that Sergeant likes it more than the Aunt Nora's line.' Nigel smiles maliciously and bows slightly to Paul, 'and Paul promised him a whole lot more like it.'

'Then Paul can fucking write them,' says Cyn. 'Thanks for selling it in, though.'

'You can't just be nice, for once, can you Paul?' Claire looks at him coldly. 'Standing there dressed like my dad has an expression for it, like a pox doctor's clerk. This top is a Vivienne Westwood. I wore it in case I had to meet the client. You really disappoint me sometimes.'

She snatches the layout from Paul's hand and stalks off.

Chapter 49

'Christine Parmentier.'

'Angela Ainsworth.'

The two women shake hands, openly appraising each other.

'I'm really only in the meeting to introduce myself, Angela,' says Christine, 'though I can honestly say I wish that the creative work stemmed from one of my briefs.'

'OK', says Claire, picking up the cue. Rapport. Same age, same backgrounds, Freddy was a crafty bastard sometimes.

'No surprises Angela, exactly as presented, child in foreground on the floor, kitchen styled to the tastes of the bullseye of the target audience, headline prominent, is your child crawling with germs? One line of copy with the germ killing claim.'

'I think the logo could be a bit bigger?' suggests Tom.

Cyn notes Angela's young male assistants are a lot more casually and stylishly dressed than at the initial meetings. Claire has already anticipated there would be the client response to the size of the logo. If it's in proportion and you can see it, then you can see it, is always Claire's way of including it in the layout. And inevitable, it's one of the subordinate clients who asks, "that our logo be made more important."

'The toy boys,' as Claire had dismissed Tom and Brian after the first presentation. However, they'd relaxed a lot at that introductory lunch, and she'd noticed how Brian had coolly taken Michael's suggestion that the Friendship team choose the wine.

'You bought the ad, we'll buy the lunch,' Michael had said awkwardly.

This prompted Brian to let his finger drift down near the bottom of a list that had the cheapest wines at the top. Claire pulls her thoughts back to the meeting and glances at Cynthia.

'Cocktail, chipolata or banger?' Asks Claire, brightly.

'Sorry?' Everyone looks puzzled.

'It's a silly G and W thing, within the agency,' Cyn explains.

'Our term of measurement. We measure things in sausages, for some reason.' Claire continues, smiling, Cyn nods sagely in agreement. 'It's stupid, but it's a G and W tradition from before our time. We'll increase the logo to chipolata size. We usually only use banger on retail ads.'

'How about one of those enormous Italian boiling things?' asks Tom.

'Cotechino? Certainly, on the poster, Tom,' agreed Claire, 'but here chipolata with tomato sauce, I'll push the red a bit.'

'English Mustard,' murmurs Christine, 'it's hot, this campaign,' she offers in explanation.

Tom looks at Brian and winces.

'I saw that, Tom,' says Claire. Tom grins at Claire.

Taken aback by his direct gaze, Claire raises her hand defensively to her tattoo.

Cyn catches up with Claire in the corridor after the meeting.

'Fancy a bit of toy boy action eh, Claire? Bit of a spunk that Tom.'

'More your type I'd have thought Cyn, I saw you eyeing his bum, bit young for me.'

'You never know, he might have a thing about older women. Maybe we'll see at the Christmas Party. That's if accounts department can find enough in the petty cash tin to have one this year.'

Chapter 50

Freddy is the last to enter the G and W boardroom. It's a lovely evening, shadows of the late, low sun softening and mellowing the brickwork of the surrounding offices. On an adjacent rooftop, a man in his shirtsleeves is carefully watering a row of pot plants.

Ralph is predictably staring at him, wistfully, out of the window.

Why is it, he thinks, *that wherever I am, I wish I were somewhere else?*

Freddy clears his throat to get everyone's attention.

'Right,' he says briskly, Perfect, Jane, you'll take the minutes, everyone's got a drink, nibbles there; you all have the agenda.' Freddy clears his throat again. 'Right.' He pauses, obviously uncomfortable, and his demeanour quickly focusses everyone's attention. 'Right. First, I'd like to welcome Clayton and Christine to the management group.' Paul, Ralph, Jonno and Michael nod their welcomes.

'And, and, I'd like to reverse the order of business, as any other business should take precedence tonight. This is strictly not on the agenda, nor is it, like most of tonight's business, for the ears of the rest of the agency.'

He now has everyone's full attention, especially as he remains standing.

'I'm not going to give you any platitudes, you know how I feel about you all, and your contribution to Grimshaw and Welby; you Christine and you, Clayton, have already made a mark but there are certain things that you cannot control, or times.'

'Like takeover bids, Freddy?'

Ralph says it slightly sourly, 'sorry, Freddy I shouldn't double guess but you hear things.'

Paul yawns and looks bored. He doodles Bec on his pad, absently.

'No, much as I hate interruptions when I have the floor,' his voice softens, 'Ralph, you of all people have the right to say it, but in a situation like this, I couldn't give you all a personal heads up before the meeting, much as I'd have liked to, as this only happened two days ago and it affects me, you, all of us, anyway.'

Freddy looks around him. The paintwork is looking tired, there are faint patches where pictures once hung, the blonde plywood on the Danish chairs is darkening and chipped in places, the granite table could use a good polish; windows carry the usual patina of London dust and grime.

'Yes, my friends, a takeover bid as you, Ralph, have obviously guessed.' He gestures resignedly to Ralph, giving him the floor.

'Argent,' pronounces Ralph, decisively. 'Paul and I were up at the brewery,' he explains to the rest of the group, 'and heard Cordier were eyeing Braithwaite's over. Argent have the Cordier business, Argent suggests to Cordier they look at the brewery, force our hand.'

He defers to Freddy.

'Yes, correct, neatly deduced. Thank you, Ralph.' Freddy draws in his breath.

Cut Ralph some slack, his inner voice says, *he deserves a little leeway.*

'Yes Ralph, everyone, Argent. And I'm very inclined to propose we accept their offer. It would mean I'm out of here, but all of you in this room, I'm assured as of yesterday, would have an important role with them.'

Freddy sees Ralph's eyes roll towards the ceiling.

'Yes, Ralph, and that includes you. Cordier will need someone with your local alcohol experience. In fact all of you could, would be much better off. International agency, wide range of accounts from the institutional to the creative, they admire our work, etc. and this would give us a certain degree of autonomy. You, Clayton and you, Christine, you joined a small agency with certain prospects, now your horizons widen.'

Looking around the table, he pauses for breath. Quizzical, apprehensive, interested, smiling, resigned; everyone has a different expression.

'In the light of this revelation, Freddy,' Michael says stiffly, I wonder if I might propose that we close the meeting and re-convene later in the week, when I'm sure we'll all be able to assess the situation better in relation to our own accounts, and their and our needs.'

'Seconded, Michael,' says Christine, 'and Freddy perhaps you'd be so kind as to afford us all some personal time with you to discuss the implications before we reconvene. Especially as Clayton and I have only just come on board, as it were. All in favour?'

'Aye,' is repeated several times before they all get up to leave the room. Freddy puts his hand on Ralph's shoulder and feels his body stiffen.

'Tomorrow, Freddy,' says Ralph, without looking around.

Chapter 51

Lily steps nervously outside the front door. She doesn't really have a choice, as her arms are tightly linked under Jane's and Phil's. Jane and Phil know they have to stay totally relaxed and smile at every opportunity. Mustn't give Lily a moment to feel uncertain, or anxious.

Lily says nothing. At the garden gate, Phil leans forward awkwardly to open it, pulling it towards him. The previous evening he and Jane sat together in the Feathers, choreographing every move of the following afternoon, from home to Tate Britain and back.

Jane is now completely relaxed with Phil, putting her hand unselfconsciously on his knee as they sat at the bar.

'Stop looking down my top and concentrate,' she'd chided him.

'OK, when we get to the Tate, we know we can go straight in, but sit Lily down until I've got rid of the car, and give her a guide or something to read.'

The next day, following the script, Paul glances over his shoulder as he draws away from the gallery, seeing Jane carefully help Lily up the imposing marble steps. Luckily finding a parking spot, he hurries back, slowing down and smiling casually as he approaches the couple in the foyer.

'The Turners first?'

'Oh yes,' replies Lily.

Walking around the gallery, through the centuries of art, Lily visibly relaxes. Finally, recognising an unmistakable Turner, she pauses in front of it for a long time, holding tightly to Jane's arm.

'Is that a tear, Mum?'

'His work always has that effect on me dear, and I'd forgotten quite how beautiful his canvases are. Look at that sky, so soft, the way it drifts, merges into the sea. And I'm hanging on tight, not because I'm, afraid, or anxious, but because I love you and realise just how much time you waste looking after me and—'

'Mum, no, no. Stop it. That's my choice. Phil and I don't need an excuse to come here, and I want you to enjoy the day,' Jane says firmly.

'Art makes me 'ungry,' pronounces Phil, 'let's go and get some lunch.'

Settled in the restaurant, Lily looks around.

'Years ago, when we first went out together, I used to bring Reginald here. Under sufferance, when I think about it. They had, might still have this amazing wine list. We'd pick a bottle of great French wine, and have it with the shepherds' pie.'

Lily is becoming more relaxed, but still has her "moments", as she admits later after Phil has gone, when she thinks she might quite inexplicably suffer an anxiety attack.

'One glass, Mum, if you've taken any pills today.'

'I haven't, thought I might try and go through the day without them.'

'You're doing great, Lily.'

Phil gives her an encouraging smile.

'I remember once at the end of a meal, the waiter came up and asked if we wanted a glass of anything else. "I've opened a Port and a Madeira, today," he said. Reginald said he'd have the Madeira. "It's the '37," said the waiter. "Gosh, I've never had a 1937 wine," said Reginald. "The 1837, Sir," said the waiter. Happy days.'

Jane and Phil exchange glances. There was no rancour or spite in Lily's makeup. She prefers to remember the good times she had with "her Reginald". There was nothing more to be said, they pay their bill and leave.

'I'm arted out,' says Phil. 'Can't take more than an hour or two. Leaves us more for next time, eh?'

He strides purposefully out to get the car. Lily links her arm through her daughter's.

'You're fond of Phil, aren't you love? And though I said I see aspects of Reginald in him, the shyness, I think he's a bit stronger than your dad.'

'Bloody hope so, Mum. He'll do for the time being. When we get home, let's get outside, have tea in the garden. It's a lovely afternoon still.'

Chapter 52

'Jonno,' enquires Phil, 'pint or a G and T?'

He'd seen Jonno tentatively push his way into the crowded pub. Phil could have looked down at his Times and let Jonno find him, but instead waves him over.

'Might have a pint Phil, thought you'd be in here seeing as it's Sunday.'

'Yeh, well, thought I'd have a couple and then go for a walk on the Heath. How's your weekend been?'

'Quiet. It's not my weekend for the kids so.'

'So no, er, romance this weekend?'

'No, I was going to see Jenny but she had to see her mum or something. We're only, you know—'

Jonno purses his lips.

'Get this down you.'

Phil hands him his pint. Whatever Paul thinks about "his fatness", Phil feels a certain gratitude towards Jonno. It was Jonno who'd plucked Phil out of the small Manchester agency and given him his chance in London. Jonno had his faults, but he was also very perceptive about creative talent. He had a knack for spotting it and putting together teams with a real, productive chemistry.

'I don't want to talk shop, Phil, not on a weekend but I'm out in meetings all Monday and wondered how you and Paul were getting on with the new dogfood.'

'Project Poochie Pouchie? We've done a campaign. Never been done before, can't think why it hasn't, Paul's just making sure the scripts work to length. You know, shoehorn in the things they want to say, but make sure there's still some air around them. Show you first thing Tuesday?'

Chapter 53

Ralph stands stiffly in front of Freddy's desk.

'I haven't said a word to Sonia yet,' he pronounces, 'not until you tell me exactly where I stand.'

Freddy carefully pours two cups of tea.

'Ralph, I'd prefer you to sit. Comfortably. Do take a seat on the sofa,' he says, without looking up.

Freddy picks up the tray of teas.

'Ralph, I'm not going to give you any preamble or platitudes, we've been colleagues and friends for too long a time. So please do me a favour and don't say anything until I've finished. Please.'

Ralph opens his mouth to protest.

'Ralph, please hear me through. Saying please three times is enough.'

He motions towards the sofa again and Ralph consents, moving to the sofa and leaning back into the cushions, his face strained. Freddy joins him. Ralph tends to believe, or wants to believe what others tell him, but the world of marketing has toughened, coarsened him as he puts it, his beliefs, his attitude. There are far too many self-serving people in the business.

'Ralph,' Freddy hands him a cup of tea, 'Ralph, you've never wanted to run an agency. Even this one.'

Ralph goes to protest, then thinks better of it.

'Ralph, you've never asked me if you could be MD with me taking the Chair, never looked to leave, have you, never looked to run another place, and yes, I've played on that. I might, you feel, have wilfully taken advantage of your loyalty, but never misused or abused it, or your trust.'

Ralph doesn't move. Freddy waits a moment, takes a sip of tea. After a pause, Ralph does likewise.

'So, Ralph you can ascribe whatever motives you like to what I'm about to say.'

Ralph's taut face muscles relax a little.

'These, my old friend, are the facts. If Cordier buys a controlling share, or all of Braithwaite's, and we both know this will probably be the case, then Argent, and I have this direct from Christian Lafond; he made it very clear to me that Argent want you to step up and help them into our market.

'And you'll also be heavily involved in the rest of the Cordier business, especially any international expansion. Simple as that and I, old friend,' Ralph tenses for a moment and Freddy notices his sudden antipathy. 'Old friend, and I mean that sincerely, I will get it in writing that you will go straight onto Argent's international board, though you may have to move to Paris for a while, not a hardship I'd have thought, as you and Sonia are, what's the term, empty nesters. In writing, Ralph, and in your hands before I make any formal announcement.'

Ralph succumbs, deflated. I should feel some elation, he thinks, feel that this is a late career opportunity, I should grab it, when all I want to do is run back to my office and wish nothing had changed.

'What say you, Ralph? Say yes. Trust me, not as someone you work with but as a friend. Say yes. Please.'

'Yes, Freddy. I've got used to saying yes to you down the years.'

Freddy prudently remains silent. Ralph glances towards the window, then decisively turns his head back to look directly at Freddy.

'Yes, I've just about had enough of Braithwaite, and his condescension. But that's what you pay me for. Because no other account director would suffer him for long. And in advertising, I discovered a long time ago, it's your integrity that's first to be compromised.

'Michaels couldn't handle him, and Braithwaite would abhor Clayton and his bespoke silk suits and yachtsman's tan.'

Ralph allows himself a wry smile.

'We know each other too well, Freddy, and you've earned this. Not worked towards it, I'll accept this has come out of the blue, but yes, and yes, I will take the posting and yes, I will join you in a Scotch later. I'll take it.'

'Yes, you're the first person I've talked to, Ralph.'

Ralph keeps his gaze straight, and level, as he nods agreement to Freddy. *That goes without saying. You've already sold me to Argent, Freddy, and you wouldn't look good if I said no. But you know I can't afford to say no.* Ralph stands to shake hands with Freddy, then turns to leave. 'Don't get up, thank you, Freddy. I'll see you later. Au revoir, as it were, or is, now.'

Chapter 54

Clayton Howell pauses by the boardroom door, smooths his hair, straightens his tie, realigns his pocket handkerchief, straightens his back, bends his knees, adjusts his crotch and strides in. Paul and Phil stand by the sideboard helping themselves to cups of tea, introducing Christine to Alan Sergeant and Bruce Wood of Reader.

'Good afternoon, Alan, Bruce, you've met Christine, Alan, good.'

Clayton was appointed Group Account Director on Reader when it became obvious that it had become an even bigger and more complex account than even Freddy had anticipated.

'Going to need a lot of handholding chaps, so I think Clayton and Brian should get involved.'

'Cup of tea, Clayton?' asks Paul.

'Thanks, Paul, white with one please.'

Handsome, immaculately suited, with a chiselled patrician nose, square jaw, prominent brow, a mane of prematurely grey hair kissing his collar and permanent tan, Clayton is the archetypical ad exec of the public's imagination.

'Shall I stir it for you, Clayton?' asks Paul innocently, flicking a glance at Phil, who gently rotates his hips.

'No, I'm perfectly capable of stirring my own tea thanks, Paul,' Clayton has already revealed he has something of a pompous manner, 'let's get started.'

Phil hides his amusement and leads them to the table.

'Right,' says Alan Sergeant. 'Right. You've had one success with us, Paul, am I to expect another?'

'I hope so, Alan, because this is great, really fresh thinking. And I can say that without pushing my own barrow, because it isn't mine. A lot of it is Christine's, but our female team put the real gloss on it. You asked for a female dog owner in the commercials, so we thought our female team would give it the right perspective and we think it was a clever idea to actually cast our dog owner before we, that's the girls,' he hastily corrects himself, 'before Claire and Cynthia started writing any scripts, so they could really get the mood and tone right. But you've had enough of me presenting recently, we put Christine onto the account the moment she walked in the door, and she immediately brought some fresh thinking to the whole up-market, pouched wet dog food category.' Paul notes Alan Sergeant's expression.

Stop bullshitting.

'Christine.'

Christine stands up, with Paul's rationale in her hand. Paul and Phil wrote the strategy and scripts a week before she joined. Now she has to carefully speak as if the thinking is her's, and the scripts Claire's and Cynthia's.

Paul has written at the top of the page; today's word is perineum.

Christine glances at him. It was the look of an experienced, mature woman who'd seen and done everything before the eternally childish, callow male. Paul responds with his inscrutable, "a samurai only displays emotion once every three years" look.

Christine stands to speak.

'Alan, Bruce, as you know my job is to look at things from the point of view of the consumer. And what does the consumer see when they watch commercials in this category? They see commercials that are all the same.'

She pauses and takes a sip of tea to allow Bruce, as usual furiously taking notes, to catch up with her. Alan Sergeant's body language indicates he knows exactly why she has paused. Christine quickly continues.

'Consumers see commercials that are all the same because they have to be. The hero of the commercial can't talk. Dogs can act, Rin Tin Tin, Lassie, proved that what, sixty years ago? They can run, jump, show anger or affection, they can show their approval by wagging their tails, they can hoe into their food, woof it down, so to speak.' She pauses, looking around the table for emphasis.

'Did I say, so to speak? Actually, they can't speak. Someone always has to speak on the dog's behalf. The owner, trainer, breeder, veterinarian. So, all pet food commercials tend to follow a pattern. Expert speaks, dog eats food, runs around dementedly. And as dogs are smaller than humans, the camera invariably looks down on them, diminishes, denigrates them, they're rarely the star of their own commercial. Phil?'

Christine passes the meeting to Phil, who stays seated.

'I was talking with Claire one day, Alan, Bruce, about when we were kids and Claire's mum had shown her Tom and Jerry cartoons.'

Phil pauses as Bruce looks around, uncomprehending.

'They were about cat and mouse, Bruce, black and white, hand drawn, 2D. Animators had to be careful with perspective so camera was always down at their level, on't floor with Tom and Jerry. You only saw humans, the maid it was, from knees down. So Claire says to me, why don't we do that? Live action, though.

'Of course, we'll have to show the owner, do shots of her, do shots of her talking to dog, but let's get down at ground level for some dog shots, make the dog the hero, especially when it's eating our product. Let's see things from the hero's point of view. Give them a proper close-up. See the animal's expression, but not from an odd angle.

'And as she were explaining this to Christine, I'll give her credit here, Claire says pity dogs can't talk, you never know what they really think. And Christine says,' Phil and Christine rehearsed this before the meeting. She takes up the presentation.

'I just said it out of the blue, speech balloons, thought bubbles, and Claire says yes, yes, you've got it, we can show exactly how the dog really feels but we make the captions contemporary, let the words animate on screen around the dog, do them for today's audience.'

Phil continues, maintaining the momentum.

'Alan, we realise this is a concept session, preliminary ideas, but this one seemed such a breakthrough that Cyn started writing—'

'Where are the girls?' enquires Alan, 'seeing as you're stealing all their thunder?'

'At a funeral.'

'At a shoot.'

'At shoot of a funeral.'

Clayton and Paul answer simultaneously. Phil then rescues the situation.

'For our cut-price funeral client, Alan. We should have said at outset Alan, sorry.'

Alan waves away their explanations and Phil continues. 'Cynthia's written draft scenarios so you can see how it works.'

Phil opens a layout pad. On it is a hand written script with lines crossed out and rewritten. He's copied it from a finished script on Paul's Apple.

'Alan, Bruce, we open on a shot in our dog owner's kitchen. We cast an actress called Annette, so let's call her that. We open in Annette's kitchen to give the viewer some idea of lifestyle, what she's like, the single career woman around 30, which makes her sympathetic to younger and older audiences.

'Sitting on't kitchen floor is her dog, Scout, which is a Parson Jack Russell. The girls chose the breed.'

'I'm not sure Jack Russells are a pure breed Phil because—' Bruce jumps in. Alan shifts and clears his throat. Bruce quickly apologises 'Sorry, Phil.'

'Perfectly alright Bruce,' mollifies Phil, 'whippets are more my territory, anyway. OK, we establish Scout and look up from his point of view at Annette who's on the phone. From her tone and what's she's saying, we get the idea she's been stood up, had her evening ruined. She could say something like, "John don't apologise, really, work comes first, some other time, maybe. Goodbye," and put the phone down.

'Then she turns to Scout and says, "That's the last we'll see of him, Scout. Looks like it's you and me tonight," and we look for the dog's reaction and the words appear over Scout's head. "Didn't like him, too hairy," something like that, like the dog's actually thought them and Annette says, "let's feed you anyway," and in close up, we see her get out a single serve tub of Woof, as you know that's our working name, out of cupboard.

'She pauses for a moment so we can see several packs in't cupboard and we watch her pull the tab and spoon it into Scout's bowl so we get a good look at texture and Annette says, "Woof Beef Casserole, Scout, looks better than what I'll be having."

'And Scout's speech bubble says, "Well, you're not having any of mine." And he starts to woof it up and, well, that's the last line, Woof, they woof it up.'

Alan Reader reacts immediately.

'I get it Phil, and I like it. It's a very clever and easily adjustable concept. We'll have to time the serving, food close-ups and eating shots so they're the correct proportion of the running time, it's a tried and trusted formula of ours and of course, the moment the woman names the featured dinner, she must have it in her hand and of course tonally, its relation to the background and her hand are crucial.

'We shall have to have a close look at, er, Annette's nails of course, nail colour neutral and she can practise tearing the lid off the pack. We, and our

American cousins, take the appetite revelation shot very seriously, it's pivotal, but all in all—'

'Alan, aren't speech bubbles a bit comic book? A bit down market?'

Phil and Paul turn slowly and look at Bruce, faces non-committal though Christine comments later, their expressions bordered on bored contempt. Paul looks pointedly away, as if dismissing Bruce's comment out of hand.

'Alan, if I may,' Clayton interjects smoothly, 'Bruce, the style of the animated words, the design, typography will be entirely contemporary, as Christine stated. Up to the minute is the way the words will appear, yes, we'll experiment, and of course the way the words—'

'Exactly, Clayton.' Christine jumps in, 'the words provide us with the, the, perineum, the link, bridge, between the two subjects, dog owner and dog.'

'Yes, Christine.' It's Paul's turn, as everyone is looking curiously at the agency's new planner, 'that was what Cynthia said. Anyway, you can see the way the girls are going. For my own part, I find it easy to have script ideas when your strategy and creative idea is clear cut and I know the girls have a range of scenarios including a lovely one.'

Careful Paul, thinks Phil, don't lay it on too thick.

'Where the dog's thoughts come up before—'

'Sorry, Paul?' says Alan, clearly puzzled.

'Apologies, Alan. Don't have the script in front of me, but say Annette gets out a pack of Woof and Scout's thoughts bubble words read, "No, I had lamb last night."

'Scout's thoughts are ahead of Annette so she'd say, "no, you had that one last night," and Scout's thoughts words would read, "how about Chicken Fricassee," and so Annette would then say, "how about Chicken Fricassee?" and at the end when Scout's eating, Annette says, "Scout, I swear you can read my thoughts".'

'No,' says Bruce firmly, 'not Chicken Fricassee, it's an Americanism Paul and we still have a list of product names in research. We would of course probably feature three of our most popular products but when Annette opens her kitchen cupboard, you'll see our full range lined up.'

'Full range lined oop, Bruce, hardly natural is it, it's set in't kitchen, not supermarket,' says Phil, bluntly.

'Nor are talking dogs natural, Phil,' replies Alan with a certain finality, 'and this is a commercial, not an arthouse film.'

Phil is learning fast when it's best to accede to client. He nods to Alan, conceding the point.

'Good, good,' smooths Clayton, 'good, good, you'll tell the girls, Phil and they can start working on the scripts. And Bruce, you'll get the projected timings breakdown to us won't you, wouldn't want to sell you short, and we'll make sure Steve our producer adheres to them, imperative, particularly at launch.'

'Phew,' says Clayton after the clients have gone. 'Nearly got us into trouble there, sorry chaps, we'll get our story right next time. Could have been our funeral. Glad you managed to link the shoot and funeral, Phil.'

'Provided the perineum, so to speak,' says Christine.

'What on earth does that word mean?' puzzles Clayton.

'It's the strip of flesh between the—'

'The Bruce and the Alan,' quickly finishes Paul.

Chapter 55

'See the Braithwaite's spot got a mention in Adverts Mag,' Paul casually remarks as they wait for work-in-progress to start.

'Those pricks,' says Jonno.

'Thought you were a mate of Graham Kershaw?'

'Got to be, haven't you, him and his bloody ad mag? Actually, he's a good bloke, it's those anonymous arseholes on his Campaign Comments page who get up my nose. Shit all over everything you do, snide bastards, haven't even got the guts to put their name to anything.'

Jonno shifts uncertainly, he still wasn't quite used to his ubiquitous new creative uniform of jeans and T-shirt. Or that his baseball boots, carefully selected for him by Claire, 'don't you let on, Claire,' had quite the correct balance of style and gravitas.

Meaning he actually did them up.

'Yeh, well that's the way it is, Jonno. There was a time when we were all in it together, you didn't criticise other people's work because you know just how hard it is sometimes to get anything half decent past a client.

'It's still like that to some extent but there'll always be small minded done nothings who've got anonymity to hide behind. And if Graham didn't run their half arsed opinions anonymously, he'd have nothing to run.'

Paul pauses for breath.

'Thanks, Paul,' says Jonno with genuine appreciation.

In fact Paul hadn't read any reviews of Jonno's epic, as Phil called it. Nor could he be bothered, he had his own opinion. Jonno's reaction is enough to signal to Paul the reviews have been less than flattering. Paul and Phil have a little dance, a soft shoe shuffle that they do to the Braithwaite's jingle, with substitute words.

'This is the Braithwaite's jingle, it'll make your bollocks tingle, with the in crowd you can mingle, as they sing-le the Braithwaite's jangle jingle.'

They sing it at odd times in the office and pub, repeating it until it became too monotonous even for them.

'Mr Braithwaite, what are your feelings about Cordier attempting to buy their way into British liquor interests. A wine and spirits house getting into beer, seems odd.'

The late afternoon sun crawled, insubstantial, down the old, worn walls of the brewery, its shadow tiptoeing its way across the cobbles. The weekly meeting was over and agency and clients sat there amicably, waiting for the taxi to take Ralph to the station.

With India Pale Ale sales up, Ralph had been quick to acknowledge George and Jenny's contribution to the success of the new advertising campaign. He'd prudently omitted to mention the contribution of Tommy Jenkinson, and his relentless encouragement of his sales force. 'Explosive, Tommy is, like a curry after six pints of Braithwaite's Brown,' as a rep from a rival brewery put it.

'Business, Bertram, business. Diversifying their interests. Got to expect occasional incursions from across the channel. 1066 and all that.'

George Braithwaite leans back in his chair and looks up at the implacable portraits staring him down, as they had from the first moment he'd stepped into his family's shoes.

Ralph smiles to himself. Ironic, the first time after so many years that Braithwaite has called him by his surname. It indicates Ralph has moved up the social acceptance scale, not into the intimate inner circle, but certainly to the level of business confidante.

'Were you aware historians put English victories in battle with the French in medieval times down to the sturdy English yeoman drinking beer? More nutritious than froggy's wine.'

The longbow helped a bit, thinks Ralph. But there's some antipathy there, keep prodding at it.

'Mmm,' Ralph nods, pondering, 'I'm not sure I can envisage the Braithwaite's brand in a diversified foreign portfolio, a British head on a French lance, so to speak.'

Careful, Ralph, don't overdo it.

'Bertram, you're right, absolutely right.' Mr B becomes animated, his brow darkens, 'not in my lifetime.' He warms further to his topic. 'You're probably unaware the Braithwaite family lost many faithful retainers, fine workers, salesmen, locals, to French muskets in Napoleonic times. Sacrificed to the shortarse from Ajaccio and his imperialistic ambitions. 'Scuse my French, so to speak.'

Leave it there, Ralph, you have your answer. Or do you?

'Ah, your taxi's down there, Bertram, good to see you, best to Freddy, eh?'

Chapter 56

Michael Michaels wanders into reception to look at the morning papers. Grace is neatly fanning them out on the coffee table. She looks up.

'Morning, Mr Michael Michaels, Freddy just called, he wants you in his office with Nigel as soon as he comes in.'

Michael looks puzzled, shrugs and picks up The Daily Mail. 'Thanks Grace, and well done, you almost got the form of address correct. One Michael is sufficient. Grab Nigel as soon as he appears and send him to my office, please.'

Grace smiles, sweetly.

Freddy had identified Grace's dumb receptionist act hid a sharp mind and offered to move her into the body of the agency. No, she'd said, just give me extra tasks, and a raise.

'She said it so sweetly,' Freddy reported to the board, 'that of course I said yes. Grace enjoys being "the face of the agency," as she put it, the first person a client sees.'

Ten minutes later, Michael and Nigel appear in Freddy's office doorway.

'Come in, boys, shut the door please, Nigel.'

Freddy indicates the sofa and takes his place behind his desk.

'Nice way to start a Monday. Albreachtson from Humble Funerals rang and said he no longer wanted us working on his business and was taking it elsewhere. Hmmm?'

He raises his eyebrows theatrically and looks from Peter to Nigel.

'Any ideas?'

Michael frowns and looks defensive, smoothing his tie. Nigel goes red and clears his throat.

'That, Freddy, Michael, would be my fault. I thought about it all day yesterday and my resig—'

'Hold on Nigel, hold on.' Freddy raises his hand as Michael instinctively shrinks away along the sofa, distancing himself from his young assistant. 'Why don't you tell us what's happened?'

'Well, I had a call Thursday from Mr Alphabet, sorry that's what the creative department calls him, and he said he wanted a progress meeting and to go over the accounts.'

'And?' prompts Michael.

'And I know the account's not worth a cracker, your words Michael.'

Freddy glares at Michael, then at his assistant. 'We all know that Nigel but it gives, strike that, gave us a chance to build our creative profile. And I'll come to that.'

'Not that they were allowing us to, Freddy,' interjects Michael.

'Alright, let's all calm down, I know nothing of this, Nigel, continue.'

'OK, well Mr A said he couldn't see the agency until the weekend because they were very busy with funerals and could we please come down to Godalming on Saturday to his house for a meeting?'

'Saturday.' Freddy raises an appraising eyebrow.

'I didn't want to trouble Michael so I said I'd do it and as Michael was away for the weekend, I didn't want to call him. Anyway,' Nigel pauses for breath. 'I got the train down on Saturday morning and bussed down from the station. They've got this big detached house. Did you know he drives an Aston Martin?'

'Get on with it, Nigel.'

'I rang the doorbell and a woman answered it after about five minutes. I could hear her shouting, "alright, alright, bloody tradesmen," as she came down the hall and she opened the door and looked at me and then over my shoulder and said, somewhat aggressively, "you're not the washing machine man. Who are you?"'

'I was a bit taken aback so I said, "Mrs Albreachtson? I'm Nigel from Grimshaw and Welby. Your advertising agency. Your husband's expecting me." And she says, "I know very well what Grimshaw and Welby is. But Alfred said you'd be overweight and middle-aged with a cloying, obsequious, ingratiating manner about you".'

'I don't think he could have been thinking of you, was he, Michael?' asks Freddy with the hint of a smile. 'Surely not. Carry on, Nigel.'

'Well, I said my boss was unavoidably detained on family matters but I have all the relevant material your husband wants to discuss.'

'Mrs A said, "It's a great pity it doesn't include servicing washing machines."

'I smiled and she sort of sniffed and looked at me like I was, I was, anyway, she says, "I suppose you'd better come in, then. I'll get my husband. You can wait in there," and threw the sitting room door open. I turned to thank her and she says, "You're not the copywriting fellow, are you? No, obviously not, you don't look dissolute enough. You can tell him I've already wasted half the morning re-writing that rubbish he put in our brochure."

'It's a she, Mrs Albreachtson, I said, her name's—"

"Well that would explain it, a junior secretary, with body piercings and tattoos, no doubt. I can just see them. Another modern illiterate. Save your senior people for the frozen foods business while we pay their bills. In there, then, what's your name."'

'No tea and biscuits on offer then, Nigel? I commend your fortitude.' Freddy was starting to relax. 'And?'

'So I went in and it's all chintz and heavy curtains and big cushions and thick Persian carpets.'

'We don't need a treatise on interior decoration,' says Michael huffily.

'No, Michael but that's the whole point. I went over and plonked myself down among the cushions on this enormous, overstuffed sofa and just sat there. It was really hot and stuffy in the room and there wasn't a sound from the rest of the house. I thought Mr A must be in the house somewhere as the car was outside so I just sat there and read a magazine from the coffee table and twenty minutes had gone by when I started feeling really uncomfortable and I thought surely they wouldn't mind if I opened a window.'

Nigel catches his breath. Peter and Freddy are now looking fixedly at him. Nigel's flustered manner and rushed speech are very unlike him. Freddy leans forward expectantly, making an encouraging circling movement with his hand.

'And, Nigel, and—'

'So I stood up and went to the window. And I looked into the garden but no one was there. I went to open the window, and then I don't know why, something made me look back at the sofa. There was this white and pink furry thing squished between the cushions where I'd been sitting.'

Freddy's room is suddenly very quiet. Michael can't contain himself.

'Out with it, Nigel, what was it?'

'A poodle. A very old poodle.'

'A very old and very dead poodle,' confirms Freddy quietly.

Nigel nods, eyes downcast.

'You sat on a poodle?' squeaked Michael, 'you sat on the client's pet poodle? You asphyxiated it? You squashed it? You killed it? The family pet?' he screeches accusingly.

'Michael,' cautions Freddy. 'This isn't a Monty Python sketch, much as it's developing into one. It was an accident, not your fault, Nigel, well it was your fault but—'

Freddy looks at the ceiling, breathes deeply and scratches his head, reflectively. He's starting to show some sympathy for the young account executive.

'I like dogs, Freddy and I sort of lost it, then. I was so upset. I couldn't bear to look at it so I moved another cushion over on top of it and rearranged the cushions on the back of the sofa.'

'Are you sure it was dead?' Michael's eyes bulge.

Nigel unconsciously notes Michael's expression.

'Well Michael, its eyes were bulging and staring and its tongue was all swollen and blueish and sticking out and there was this white froth and I'd killed it, poor thing. I was so upset and there was this smell and I started feeling sick, couldn't handle it.

'For a moment I considered taking it with me, I had my sports bag with me, thought I'd sort of lose it somewhere, thought it might soften the blow. But I just got up and left the room, opened the front door and walked out.

'I expected all hell to break loose but it was all quiet. Deathly quiet, sorry Freddy. A bus came by so I just jumped on, got off and caught the train back home. I'm sorry Freddy, Peter, dock my—'

'Nigel,' interjects Michael, 'you have to face up to it. Ring Mr Albreachtson and apologise, say you want to apologise to his wife.'

Freddy raises his hand.

'No, Michael, I don't think that would be prudent at present. When Albreachtson phoned me this morning, all I could hear in the background was this voice screaming, "murderer, baby killer, he killed my baby." At the time, I thought it was their TV, but this explains matters. In the circumstances Albreachtson was surprisingly reasonable.

'Didn't mention the dog, didn't accuse Nigel of anything. Just said he didn't think our arrangement was working, his wife was insulted we'd gone for the cut price angle and had suggested the name change. Evidently, Splendid Funerals was her creation. He said she was rewriting all our material but she'd done that with the last three agencies he'd appointed, anyway. He apologised and put the phone down. So that's it, young Nigel, that's it.'

Freddy carefully pours himself a cup of tea.

'My father swore milk first, my mother said milk after,' he quietly states. 'I'm not sure how you should have handled it, Nigel. Maybe stayed, faced the music, though in view of the manner in which she'd treated you—'

'There was no one around,' mumbles Nigel, sadly. 'It was quiet as a grave.'

'Very apt,' Freddy notes drily.

'And I didn't want to go wandering around the house,' Nigel concludes.

'You could have warned me yesterday,' Michael huffs.

'I left a message on your home phone, Michael.'

'I didn't back until late, forgot to check the answerphone this morning. Did you tell anyone else?'

'I phoned Paul.'

Freddy raises his eyebrows. 'I suppose he found it funny?'

'Seriously funny, he put it. Suggested it was merciful, a sort of euthanasia. Told me it was a shame I hadn't sat on Mrs A, too. Told me to call Michael immediately, which I did.'

'And Nigel, you have to tell Claire and Cynthia the account's gone. They put a lot of work into it. And you don't tell them Mrs Alphabet, I mean Albreachtson was rewriting everything they did, anyway. Don't let yourself off the hook. Just face the music, and Cynthia's tongue and take the blame for losing the business. I'll handle it with the Albreachtsons. And in future remember both of you, I decide whether an account's worth holding on to.'

There's a knock and Paul's head appears around the door. He looks at all three of them, nods, and says sagely, 'may I humbly suggest that at least they'll get the funeral cheap.'

Chapter 57

'Shit storm.' A couple at the next table look towards Paul. He lowers his voice. 'About three months, make that three minutes into a merger, it all starts to fall apart. The smaller shop gets eaten alive, the people spat out like,' he spat an olive stone into his hand and dropped it onto his bread plate.

'Especially if your top guy has gone and there's no support or control. Suddenly, you're on the Titanic wallowing in a sea of piss, a turd iceberg hits you full in the face the moment you step out of your office, a fucking tsunami of Richard the Thirds, followed by an armada of snotty smug account service types from the takeover mob, telling you how to do your job.'

In his vehemence, Paul's usual conversation has lost all semblance of eloquence and coherence. He lets the jumbled words tumble out.

'Fooking good bloody steak, this,' Phil savours, changing the mood. 'Tuscan T-bone,' he rolls the words with relish around his mouth. 'How's the tripe? My Gran used to cook it, with white sauce and onions. I can still smell it. Used to gag just walking past her kitchen. That looks a bit different.'

'Actually, it's fantastic. The tripe works like organic pasta, the tomato sauce is a beautifully judged reduction, pork cheek and crisp nubbins of pancetta, onions nicely caramelised with a subtle undertone of herbs; fuck it, I'm starting to sound like a fucking food writer, still,' Paul raises his wine glass to his lips, is about to swill it down, remembers himself, calms, and takes a sip instead.

'This is fantastic Phil, but you shouldn't have.'

'I promised to buy us tea. That's what Gran called it, never dinner. Lunch was dinner.' Phil's trying to change the subject.

'Paul, your rules, six o'clock, work hat off, fun hat on. And like you said, I'm paying so I get to call the tune,' he says awkwardly.

'Sorry, darling,' Phil raises his glass, 'forget the takeover. We'll discuss it another time: on agency time,' concludes Paul.

'Actually it's bloody good here. Too bloody good for Jonno. He's got no idea about food.'

Fiorelli's is painted in warm orange tones, like a restored Tuscan farmhouse. The floor's red tiled, there are tall vases of flowers, double damask clothed tables, gilt mirrors on the wall. A sinister row of unlabelled medicine flasks of grappa behind the bar has already caught Paul's eye. Now that's a good sign, he thought to himself as they sat down.

'Another bottle of red, Paul? Better get the other half, I'll let you pay for this one. How about something Sicilian, one of those wines from Mount Etna?'

Paul looks up, impressed.

'How do you know about them, you Northern sot, or do they come in a straight glass with a creamy head?'

'There's bottle on't counter behind you, you Southern snob. Got old print of a volcano on it and words Etna Rosso.'

Phil has obligingly lapsed into his Yorkshire accent, which attracts a sniffy look from the couple on the next table.

'Eee oop, need a snake's,' announces Phil for their benefit, lurching to his feet and affording them his malevolent, piratical grin.

Paul smiles graciously, raising his glass to them. His look says we're sophisticates, forgive my uncouth Northern friend.

The news of the takeover has disconcerted Paul and Phil. Freddy's "the news stays in the boardroom" was in vain; their futures are at stake, as Jane knows, and Paul's reading of the Braithwaite's meeting too close to the truth for her not to reveal the full ramifications to Phil.

She'd told him after they'd made love for the first time. It had happened, suddenly, around Phil's flat after work. For once on a Friday night, they hadn't gone to the Feathers. They took a taxi from the office to pick up Phil's car, Jane followed Phil in, he'd turned around the moment the front door closed behind them, pulled her voraciously into his arms and they just about made it into his bedroom, their clothes discarded in a trail up the hall.

After, they lay head to head on his pillow looking at each other, smiling, and she'd said, 'I've something to tell you.'

'Our first pillow talk, eh, loov.'

'Shut up, shaggy. I told Jonno I was going to tell you, he just shrugged, said everyone would know in five minutes, anyway, and went into his office.'

She traced her finger down between Phil's eyebrows and down his nose as she told him.

'Not now', Phil said.

'If I don't tell you now, you'll find out when everyone else does and then you'll ask me why I didn't tell you before and give me that little boy hurt look of yours.'

Phil dutifully gave her his reproachful look.

'And if I don't, you'll be upset because Paul was in the meeting and won't tell you, well not straight away, and you'll be doubly upset.'

So, quietly, she told him.

'Oy, Phil,' says Paul, 'you haven't said anything for five minutes, just chewed on that double fried chip.'

'I were thinking about what we're not supposed to think about tonight.'

'Save it till tomorrow.'

The couple at the next table get up to leave, glancing at Paul and Phil.

'G'night,' says Phil, 'we're sorry if we were, we're caught up in takeover.'

'I can relate to that,' says the man, 'goodnight.'

'Good luck,' says the girl.

'Thank you,' replies Paul.

'Right,' says Phil, rubbing his hands together, 'dessert?'

'No, grappa,' says Paul.

'And more grappa,' concludes Phil.

Chapter 58

Jonno strides into the work-in-progress meeting.

'Morning, troops.'

'Jonno,' says Claire, 'you look positively jaunty.'

'Great haircut,' comments Cynthia.

'Don't encourage him,' pleads Phil.

'I can't get used to the lack of a suit,' comments Paul.

Jonno is wearing his new uniform of jeans and tight black T-shirt.

'I've lost so much weight; my suits just don't fit anymore. And Carol's acting, sort of, well, civilised towards me.'

'Your weekend for the kids, was it?'

'Yes and morning, lads.'

Jonno changes the conversation as his junior creative team wanders in.

'Morning Jonno, Paul, Phil, Cynthia, Claire, Nancy.'

'Very formal, young James.'

'You told me to mind my manners in the Feathers the other night, Claire.'

'Did I?'

'We were a bit Brahms.'

'Alright, let's get on with it, guys,' orders Nancy, the progress controller. 'Jonno, here's this week's list.'

Jonno takes it.

'Oh yes, and there's something new, Nancy. Yet another new product from McBrides. They totally ignored Christine's product development naming strategy document and they're bringing out the range of biscuits; wait for it, called Aunt Maude's.'

'You're kidding.'

'No, they think it makes sense.'

'So Aunt Nora makes the pies and Aunt Maude bakes biscuits?'

'They think it's a brilliant move. Cummings actually asked why we didn't think of the family names angle. Suggested we could even do family product range ads.'

'Uncle George's Spotted Dick, Grandpa's Easy to Chew Pancake Mix; that's probably why we didn't think of it.'

'Anyway they tested it up in Scotland, bought a plant and you're not far off the mark. It's Aunt Maude's Ginger Nuts.'

'Mmm,' pondered Claire, 'biscuits aren't a bad move but bringing another family member into it.'

'If you're going to bring a family member into it, shouldn't it be a male member, so to speak? Uncle Jim's Ginger Nuts?' suggested Roddy. 'Jimmy's a redhead after all.'

'Pretty lame, Roddy. Who do you want to work on it, Jonno?' asks Cynthia.

'Depends on you lot's workload. And who wants it? WhitePage are suggesting radio, and posters.'

'Radio,' says Paul. 'My blind spot.'

'What's the matter with radio, Paul?' puzzles Jimmy, 'you're bloody good at it.'

'Thank you Jimmy but it takes me ages to get my mind round it. All that theatre of the mind stuff. I can never get used to the idea that you just throw away all the other disciplines you apply to everything else and turn everything you know about writing ads on its head.'

'Yeah,' agrees Phil, 'and it's so hard to judge a script.' Jonno nods sombrely in agreement.

'You write a great one,' Paul takes up the argument, 'well you think it's funny as hell, and when you record it, it's flat as a shit carter's hat.'

'A what?' enquires Jimmy.

'It's one of Brian's Aussie expressions. Probably made it up.'

'I reckon radio's great,' enthuses Roddy. 'A thirty foot long hot dog,' he intones in a BBC announcer voice, 'was spotted flying down the Thames this morning. It passed through the arches of Tower Bridge heading towards the Dockland's warehouse of Rowlands Celebrated Hot English mustard. A Rowland's spokesman said, etc. See, you can, well, see it, and it costs nothing in special effects.'

'It's yours, lads, see Christine for a brief this morning,' concludes Jonno.

'Next, Nancy?'

Back in their office after the meeting, Jimmy stares at Roddy.

'What do you reckon, call The Nervous Guy?'

As advertising students together faced with a hard brief and a blank page, they'd resort to calling upon their mythical muse The Nervous Guy for inspiration.

'How would The Nervous Guy approach this?' asks Jimmy.

'When faced with the Aunt Maude brief, the Nervous Guy said, "I'm phoning in sick today".'

'I'm sorry, The Nervous Guy cannot take your message, he's on a mercy dash to Africa, please call back later, said his answering machine.'

'The Nervous Guy is on a yoga retreat in Tibet and will not be back for three months.'

'C'mon, Nervous Guy,' shout Roddy and Jimmy in unison, 'give us an idea. You can do it.'

They fall silent.

'I know, let's have a look at the Orange Grove supermarket dump bin brief first,' says Jimmy.

Three hours later, they sit at their desks opposite each other, chewing on sandwiches. Jimmy's pad is covered in scrawls, Roddy's computer is on screensaver.

'It's a great brief,' says Jimmy, 'biscuits, we know the target, they're sitting there at home listening to the radio, any excuse not to put the washing on, or stuck at their desk in the office, or in the workshop and the radio's on, or in a traffic jam, what would The Nervous Guy say?'

'If you don't mind, I'll sit down with a cup of tea and an Aunt Maude's Ginger Nut and think about it.'

'That takes the biscuit, har, har.' Claire's head appears around the door. 'Actually that sounds good. Is it a line in a script?' She notes their expressions. 'Give me a break just offering a few crumbs of encouragement.'

They both look up at her, coldly. 'Got it, OK, I'll leave you two to it, tea for two as it were, ta ta.'

'I'm going to get a coffee and have a walk around the block,' announces Jimmy purposefully, rising to his feet.

'I know, I know, I'm the writer,' replies Roddy.

An hour later, Jimmy appears back in the office.

'I got you a macchiato,' he says, putting the container down.

'Thanks. What do you reckon on this?'

Roddy clears his throat.

'You'll have to imagine the voices. I'll read it. It's a bit long. Probably need one minute time slots.'

He loosens the knot of his narrow tie and undoes the top button of his Ben Sherman button down. Roddy picks up a piece of paper and running his hand through his hair with a flourish, stands up away from his desk.

'Get on with it then,' prompts Jimmy.

Roddy reads the script, moving his body left and right to suggest different voice sources, while indicating sound effects.

'Good morning, ladies and gentlemen.'

'Good morning, Mr President. Good morning, Mr President.'

'The situation is catastrophic. There's only one thing for it. Mabel, get me The Nervous Guy.'

'Ring Ring sound effect, hello.'

'Is this The Nervous Guy?'

'Oh Mr President, it's you.'

'I've a job for you, Nervous Guy.'

'Aaaaaah.'

'A giant asteroid is heading towards earth at an unimaginable speed and we need someone to get out there and, and, push it aside.'

'Aaaaaah. Slight pause.'

'Are you still there, Nervous Guy?'

'Mr President, do you mind if I sit down with a cup of tea and an Aunt Maude's Ginger Nut biscuit and think about it?'

'Certainly, ring me back. Bye now. Click of phone effect. Everyone, it's going to be OK. You know it's going to be OK when The Nervous Guy sits down with an Aunt Maude's Ginger Nut biscuit, or two. End line, etc.'

Roddy looks up from the script. 'That's sort of it.'

'I get it,' beams Jimmy. 'Genius, thanks to Nervous Guy. He really came good this time. And we have a Nervous Guy Help and Advice magazine column and maybe a comic. I'll start looking at it now. Maybe I can get a real comic book artist, or graphic novel designer interested in a Nervous Guy book. The Nervous Exploits of the Nervous Guy. Because deep down inside, we're all a Nervous Guy and only a cuppa and an Aunt Maude's Ginger Nut, or two, etc.'

Fifteen minutes later, Christine puts her seal of approval on it.

'You didn't show it to me, you showed it to Jonno first.'

'Christine, we will, but all Jonno ever says is, is it funny?' complains Roddy.

'And don't forget to show Clayton before you show it to me. He's got very chummy with Cummings and you'll need him and Brian to sell the campaign in, and to Laura, she's very taken with the silken strine of Bungalow Brian.'

'Golly, you don't make it sound easy.'

'It never is Jimmy, selling a script never is. We've got the hard job. Writing it? You guys have got the easy bit.'

Chapter 59

'Boardroom Seven Occupied,' shouts Bitsa to the agency at large, 'Boardroom Seven.'

'Jesus, right in my earhole, Bitsa.' Phil turns to Paul, 'C'mon mate, aren't you interested?' He enquires mildly. Paul shrugs disinterestedly. 'Above it all, are you?'

Bitsa had persuaded Phil and Paul into the studio to look over the artwork for a Grantham Industries brochure. Interest shifts to the windows, as other agency members casually drift in. Through the main window studio staff can look diagonally across the alleyway into the hostel opposite the back of G and W.

Dubbed Boardroom Seven and home to student nurses and the odd backpacker, new arrivals were unaware of the G and W office diagonally opposite, or that it was a good idea to lower the blinds as they could be seen in their rooms. Over time, agency interest in other people's private lives had palled. It was rude, for a start and staff made their antipathy clear.

But for some reason this morning, there's unprecedented interest. Members of the agency whose business rarely brought them into the studio, congregated. They watched as two blondes, with travel gear and backpacks appear in a hostel room.

They seem blithely unaware, 'or don't care,' as Bitsa comments, that people might be able to see in. The two girls gratefully drop their backpacks and stretch, chatting to each other.

'They're not going to,' mutters Nigel.

'They are,' mouths Bitsa, as the girls slowly unbutton their shirts and drop them to the floor.

'They are.'

The two girls, ever so casually, start wriggling out of their tight denim shorts, chatting to each other as they do so. One pirouettes as she tosses her shorts onto a bed.

'You'd think they knew they had an audience,' says Brian.

'No way,' says Bitsa, 'with the sun at that angle, they can't see us.'

'Paul, Paul, you have to see this,' says Phil, making room for Paul as one of the girls removes her bra.

She appears pleased to be free of it, lifting and caressing a breast. The other girl does likewise, and they both admiringly appraise each other's figures. They look at each other, laugh, and in tandem, push down their thongs with their fingertips,

'Goodness gracious,' exclaims Bitsa, 'just as well I'm not interested in girls.'

One girl suggestively runs a hand over her shaven crotch.

'Too much,' says Nigel, turning away.

The girls turn, bottoms to the window, and bend over.

'They do know,' gasps Nigel.

Then the girls both spin around and stand up. Between them, they hold a placard. On it is lettered, "Happy Birthday Paul." There's a howl of laughter and burst of applause from the assembled G and W staff. Nancy and Jane suddenly appear behind the girls and wave coquettishly across the alleyway.

'You bastards,' says Paul, 'you cheeky bastards, very funny, how did you?'

'Annabel in accounts, getting her staff records up to date for Freddy, noticed it's your birthday.'

'Tomorrow,' says Paul.

'You'd have guessed if we'd done it tomorrow, you crafty bastard. Look now.'

The girls bob up with another sign with "Tomorrow" lettered on it.

'We had bets whether Too Cool Paul would react to a Boardroom Seven call if you were in the studio. And you did.'

Paul shrugs expressively, throwing his hands wide.

'And we knew you were going away Friday, so there's your present.'

'Oh, Freddy's here, Freddy, you missed Paul's birthday treat.'

'Maybe they'll do an encore?'

Chapter 60

There are cracks in the taxi seats, and the windows are grimy. Paul cranks a window down an inch or two. The air smells acrid, metallic, and rubbery. The sky's dull, dark clouds shuffle grumpily past the tops of tenements.

'Wonderful, wonderful,' he mutters to himself.

The Pakistani taxi driver's listening to music on the radio. Paul knew he was Pakistani because the driver had asked him if he was English, then launched into a vehement critique of the Pakistani cricket board before directing muttered invective towards the taxi despatcher.

He catches Paul's eye in his mirror, 'Heard the Sachal Orchestra?' enquires Paul.

The driver grunts noncommittally. Paul feels the surge of energy he always does when he gets in a taxi at JFK to go into Manhattan. When the driver asked which way he wanted to go, Paul just shrugged. He could never remember the names of the bridges anyway.

'It's downtown, please. Soho. Just drop me at Prince and Wooster Streets, thanks.'

The driver returns to cursing the other drivers on the freeway. Paul wishes he'd known Lower Manhattan in the late '50s and early '60s. The days of discovery, Monk at The Five Spot, Coltrane at the Village Vanguard, Ornette at Birdland, a young Bob Zimmerman warbling his way around Greenwich Village coffee shops, Kerouac, Ginsberg, Rothko, mostly a grab bag of names he was only familiar with from LPs, paperbacks and gallery walls.

Names from before Soho became gentrified, Dolce and Gabbana-ised as Bec put it, before the triangle below Canal became Tribeca, and that too succumbed to tourists and the retail imperative. But a long weekend in NYC is always something to be experienced, relished, and savoured; every sight, sound, every smell, every minute.

With the added frisson of meeting someone he'd only known fleetingly on his own turf, in your manor as Bitsa had put it.

'You can't just turn up, Paul,' Perfect admonished him a couple of weeks earlier, 'supposing she's out of town for the weekend, supposing she has people staying?'

'Like the New York Giants?' suggested Phil.

He was duly ignored.

'OK, I'll tell her.'

'No, better still, Cyn can tell her you're thinking of coming over, they're always talking on the phone, she can make sure Becs is in town, gauge her reaction.'

'Oh yeah, as if I'd never said anything? Bec isn't naïve.'

'Still better than if you contact her direct.'

'OK.'

Paul was unaware of Becs' reaction to Cyn's call.

'Really?' Was her one word reply.

'You can do better than that,' was Cyn's riposte.

'I'll be here,' came back from Becs.

'Good,' said Cyn. 'He's a good guy under all that pretension. Great tight bum, too. I'll give him your number. He should arrive early Friday evening.'

'Then just tell him 6.30 Fanelli's,' instructed Becs.

Paul's excited and strangely apprehensive as he gets out of the taxi. He catches his expression in the taxi window and flicks his long hair off his forehead; hefting his dad's old battered and beloved Gladstone bag to the other hand, he pushes his way into Fanelli's. Becs is sitting up at the bar, nursing a beer.

'Do limeys dream of girls in Soho bars?' asks Paul. 'It's possible,' he reminds her.

Becs face relaxes into a smile and she turns towards him, looking at him searchingly, as if this first look will reveal something deep and meaningful. It doesn't.

'Ah, it's you.'

Paul leans forward and kisses her on the cheek.

'You look,' he says, clearing his throat.

Becs turns to the barman, points to her glass and indicates two. Paul slides into the gap next to her.

'There's a couple of empty stools at the other end.'

'No, no, I've been sitting down for hours, it's good to stand.'

'I've been—'

'I wondered if—' they both start talking at the same time and lapse into silence.

Becs laughs. 'Cynth's a terrible liar. Paul's thinking of coming over to see you.'

'I'd already booked the ticket.'

'No, you hadn't,' Becs lifted her chin, looked down her nose at him and poked him in the chest, leaving her finger there.

'Cynth did all the legwork, Perfect booked the flight for you, you lazy bastard, and I'm not even going to wonder if you'd already asked her, or had just mentioned to Phil you were thinking of coming over, and I'll bet Phil asked Cynth to check if I was going to be around and when they found out I was, they told Perfect to book it because you, you diffident git, would never have got around to it and by the time you did, the flights would have been full because it's a holiday weekend. And you'd have just shrugged and said, oh well.'

'Oh well,' Phil smiles wryly, turning to take in the faded photos of boxers on the opposite wall, and to cast his gaze over fellow drinkers who display various degrees of relief and exhilaration at being free for a long weekend.

'Yes, Paul,' says Becs, 'you're in New York. Drink your beer.'

Paul turns back to her and she holds his steady gaze.

'You're as beautiful as I remember.'

'Striking was the word you used to Cynth. Just so it would get back to me. And you practised that line on the plane, probably in the bathroom mirror.'

Paul leans in closer.

'What are we doing for the weekend?'

'Tonight. I'm only free tonight.'

'Then I'd better make the most of it. Where shall we eat?'

Becs takes his free hand. Paul puts his beer down and runs a finger gently over Becs' forehead, lingering to twirl a strand of hair.

'You did that the night we met. It's a gesture.'

'And you wrinkled your nose like that as well.'

'I'm glad you came, Paul, I won't deny I haven't thought of you.'

'And me, you.'

'Not when you're climaxing with another woman, I hope.'

'Ditto. Or bloke.'

'No, yes, we're not the sort of people to admit it, are we, you and me. I got us tickets for the Frank Stella at MOMA tomorrow. And there's a concert in the park Sunday. And I want to try a new Italian in Greenwich Avenue.'

'Just as well I came. Can we get to Balthazar and Odeon? I'm a terrible creature of habit.'

'We've got three days. Let's order a burger here. You don't want to hump that bag around Soho all evening.'

Paul looks around at a man carefully dolloping extra ketchup on his cheeseburger. At a girl, waiting for her date, staring reflectively at the bottles behind the bar while absently disturbing the surface of her drink with a finger. At the faded boxing photos on a wall thick with old paint, the barman pointing out a particular shot, then at his chin to a couple of out of towners obviously enthralled to be included in this particular Friday night scene.

'I'm still here. A nickel for them.' Becs intrudes on his thoughts.

'I was thinking of how I was in here some years back on one of my first trips to New York. I was feeling raw, uncertain, just sitting at this bar, lunchtime early in the week, nursing a Bloody Mary, and all these guys were around me at the bar, construction workers, hard hats, drinking boilermakers and I'm thinking they're obviously off an early shift, they deserve it. Then one of them, the foreman from the way he'd been talking, caught my eye and pointed at my watch.

"Five before two," I said.

"Right guys, time for a shot then it's back on the job."

'And the barman poured them all a shot of Tequila, they all threw it down, and clumped out of the door. The barman turned to me and said, "That building's going up wonky".'

Paul and Becs smile, together. They eat their burgers, down their drinks.

'C'mon, my handsome Englishman,' Becs stills Paul's arm as he reaches for his wallet.

'Home,' she says, throwing a handful of notes on the counter.

'Your place or mine?' Paul raises his eyebrows in enquiry.

Next day, they stand in the snaking line outside MOMA. A light drizzle insinuates itself into their hair. Paul puts his arm around Becs' shoulder as they shuffle forward.

'What next?' he asks.

'In general, or particular? I suggest P.J.Clarkes.'

'No, I mean, with us?'

Becs leans back against his arm, the rain glinting in her tangled hair, and puts her finger against his lips. The couple behind push them forward again. Becs speaks quietly without looking at him. 'Brought your book and reel with you?'

Chapter 61

Michael Michaels looks around the door of the office allocated to Mark Newlands. A short, portly figure in his late thirties stands looking out of the window. He wears suit trousers and worn, burnished, obviously bespoke brogues. Jacketless, his white shirt is impeccable; the sleeves pulled up and held by old fashioned, expanding metal bracelets.

His hair's shiny, black, centre parted, slicked back; he looks, thinks Michael Michaels, like a 1930s matinee idol.

'Aaah,' says Michael.

The figure turns, a dark smudge of stubble on his cheeks, petal mouthed, and fixes small, coal black eyes on Peter. 'My doctor has me say that,' he says amiably.

'Aaah,' repeats a disconcerted Michael, 'Michael Michaels. I was looking for Mark Newlands.'

Mark Newlands purses his brow in thought before smiling brightly. 'Aaah,' he exclaims, 'that would be me.' He gazes quizzically at Michael. 'You were expecting the jeans, were you, the black T-shirt, the baseball boots? Rather the province of Roddy and Jimmy, whom I've just met, nice young lads. Anyway, I thought I might dress in accordance with the outlandish amount of moolah you guys are paying me. And you are?'

'Michael Michaels,' he repeats, sticking out a hand to be shaken, 'I don't expect you to be put on any of my accounts but Freddy suggested you meet my clients, just in case.'

'Yes,' says Grimshaw and Welby's new senior art director, making no attempt to remove his hands from his pockets, 'Freddy said that might be the case. That I won't be working with you.'

Michael looks at him again. 'I say, is that a Cambridge college tie? I seem to recognise it. Christ's College?'

'No idea, old chap picked it up at one of the wife's charity sale dos, wear it to impress clients.'

'Aaah, so you didn't go to Cambridge? Your CV says Cambridge?'

'Absolutely I did, Mickey, absolutely.'

'Aaah,' says Michael again, by now totally confused, a lack of composure evidenced by his pink cheeks.

Newlands plunges his hand into a trouser pocket and pulls out a large white handkerchief. Putting it on his desk, he extracts a packet of Fisherman's Friend from the folds.

'Yes, I did go there, once, school outing to see the colleges. Throat lozenge, old boy?'

Ignoring Michael's tentatively outstretched hand, he thrusts the handkerchief and packet back into his pocket. Newland's left hand stays in his other pocket and continues fiddling around in his crotch, as it has during the entire conversation.

'Anything I ought to know about this client? Name, title, what his company makes? Basic need to know stuff like that?'

Michael thrusts forward a document and a brief.

'This tells you everything, er, Mark.' It was then, the Feathers brains trust later agrees, that Michael made his fatal mistake. 'Er Mark, there is something.'

'Mmm?' Newlands turns back. His expression says, *haven't you gone yet*?

'It's their new marketing manager, he has a disability,' blurts Michaels.

'Haven't met one who hasn't.'

'No really. A really visible one.'

'Then I'll notice it, then.'

'The thing is, he's awfully cross eyed, poor fellow, wears these glasses, tends to favour one side of his head as he talks to you. Sort of leans.'

Michael inclines his head.

'Ever see Charles Laughton do the Hunchback of Notre Dame?'

Ignoring the reference, Michael plunges on. 'We, the agency, don't look at him too much, in the eye, as it were. Try to ignore it.'

Newlands shrugs and rustles the papers.

'Better get on to this, Michael, want to digest it before client appears.'

Fifteen minutes later, the agency team assembles in the boardroom. Mark has put his suit jacket on and looks like the head of an agency, rather than a member of the creative team.

Claire's audience is getting restless. 'Get on with it, Claire.'

Claire was in the meeting. That evening in the Feathers, an attentive audience has gathered around her.

'Anyway, the new guy, Henderson, poor guy has this terrible eye condition. One eye's just slightly wonky, but the other eye looks right into the middle at his conk. He wears these heavy glasses with lenses like milk bottle bottoms.'

Claire has a sympathetic look.

'I thought they had operations for things like that these days,' muses Nigel.

'Maybe, Nige, but anyway before the meeting, Michael had told Mark the agency is very careful not to look at Henderson for too long or refer to his affliction in any way.'

'Well, I would imagine Newlands would take that as an insult. He's not a fool,' comments Jimmy.

'Correct, Jimmy. Well anyway, Michaels introduces Newlands to the client and Mark takes his hand, bends his back so he can look intensely at Henderson.' Claire leans forward. 'Then he pulls Henderson towards him and peers up at him closely, puts his head to one side and then Mark goes cross eyed. Really cross eyed.

'The client's leaning back, trying to remove his hand but Mark's holding on to it, then he suddenly lets go of the client and turns with this chest out, head up, sort of imperious pose, with this proud look on his face; yet he's still, totally cross eyed.

'Then he just relaxes himself completely, turns to the client with this normal, affable look and says, "Mark Newlands. Pleased to meet you Mr Henderson, I'm sure. May I call you Rodney, or is it Rod?"

'And steps back as if nothing has happened.'

'What did happen?'

'Nothing,' Claire continues. 'Henderson acted like nothing had happened, evidently his eye thing makes him pretty shy and reserved but the rest of the client team was sort of a mixture of affronted, puzzled and taken aback. Couldn't work out if Mark was being insulting.'

'Or, if he was being, you know, sympathetic? Knows how Henderson feels?' Suggested Cyn.

The listeners' collective expression is, "who knows?"

'Cyn, our guys just looked horrified. We were aghast.'

'Did anyone ask Newlands why he did it?' Asks Roddy.

Claire shrugs. 'Mark said to Michael afterwards he just wanted the client to feel he was at home, that he was in sympathetic company. Then he says to Michael, "I suppose that settles it, I won't be working on any of your accounts, old boy." Michaels was furious. Speechless. Couldn't wait to run to Freddy.'

'Mark's your mate, Claire.'

'Not any longer.'

'Did you say anything?'

'I cornered him afterwards and said, "Not funny Mark," and he just turned to me, saluted, and said, "Eye, eye, Claire".'

Phil shrugs, and shakes his head with a sour expression, keeping his feelings to himself.

'Fire him, Freddy,' Michael splutters with rage, 'fire him whatever it costs,' he concludes. Michael has given Freddy a detailed account of the meeting.
'It won't cost us, Michael,' Freddy replies, his tone cold, measured, 'Newlands insisted on a contract before he joined us and contracts come with certain obligations.'

Freddy catches Mark as he's about to leave the office. Fists clenched, Freddy is visibly angry.

'Mark, I just talked to Michael Michaels and Jonno. Mocking a client's, anyone's disability, however you might explain, justify your actions,' he pauses for breath, 'Mark it's beyond contempt and in breach of your contract. I could couch it as bringing the agency into disrepute, but it's more than that. What you did, however you might want others to interpret it, was despicable. Go, go now. Collect your things and don't come back.'

'Calm down darling,' Polly says later, 'please. Don't let it upset you. What was his reaction?'

'Didn't say a word. Just looked me up and down, shrugged. I followed him back into his office, he stuffed some stuff into his briefcase, ignoring me, and stalked out. But then he hadn't really moved in.'

Freddy takes a deep breath. 'Darling, you know, you know what really upsets me. No one, no one in our industry at a senior level has ever done anything like that to him before. Never. Agency after agency suffers, tolerates Newland's behaviour because he makes them look good. Good, that's good?'

Freddy exhales, 'Good riddance.'

Polly pushes a large glass of Bowmore into his hand. 'Enough. You did the right thing, the Freddy thing. And I bet all the staff applaud you for it.'

Chapter 62

'Before we start the meeting, Mr Braithwaite.'

Ralph has spent some time thinking how to break the news to his client. Then concluded they'd all have heard, anyway. The disapproving expressions on the portraits of Braithwaite's founders glaring down at him were enough to set the tenor of the meeting. George Braithwaite raises his hand.

'Ralph, Michaels called me while you were on his way up here. I remember our last meeting with some, er, alacrity. I believe the Argent Group from Paris want to take a controlling interest in G and W. Buy you up and absorb your business.'

'Correct. We had a board meeting the other night and Freddy informed us. It was a bit of a shock to have the rumours confirmed.'

'A bit of a fait accompli I would imagine, Ralph. Note the use of French in deference to your new colleagues.'

He casts one of his familiar, beady looks at Ralph. 'Or conquerors?'

'I shall do my utmost to protect your interests, Mr Braithwaite.'

'I'd look after your own first, Ralph. From what I hear of agency takeovers, it's all lovey dovey for about five minutes while their own people settle in, before they put the rest of you out on the street.'

He looks at Ralph for confirmation and continues.

'But you can see what it could mean to us, to the Brewery, and you weren't far off the mark about Cordier. Hmmm,' he nods his head in thought, 'I've had to think clearly about my, er, prejudices. New people, new markets, fresh ideas, a fresh start, all those things Jenny always angles for in our planning meetings.'

'But I always thought, that was why I looked after—' Ralph glances around him, bewildered.

'Yes, so you did, Ralph. But your attitude was always, how I should describe it, defensive. Never proactive. As Jenny is always saying of G and W. And never proactive on your own account.'

Ralph shuffles his papers, takes a breath and turns his gaze back to his client. *Here we go again.*

'It's not my place to be so, Mr Braithwaite, my job is to protect your interests, balance them with those of the agency, until things change.'

'Of course it is, Ralph, of course. But I'd have understood, wouldn't have minded if you'd stood up to me occasionally.'

Oh yes, you would, you condescending, malicious old prick.

George Braithwaite affords Ralph one of the benevolent smiles he saves for his brewery workers.

'Here's a for-instance. You've never once called me George or asked me if you might. Never suggested that in a business sense we might be complementary, act as colleagues. And once you called me Mr B, which I found odious. Nice old fashioned word that, odious, smacks of forelock tipping, trusted worker to boss. I know Noonan occasionally calls me Mr B in that familiar way of his, but I expect that of a creative Johnny, or Jonno,' he smiles thinly for a moment, 'they lack couth anyway.'

Ralph's face has gone white, streaked with pink, muscles taut.

Don't react; don't dignify his insults, not worth it.

Braithwaite recognises Ralph's discomfort.

'No Ralph, I really appreciate, and in many ways, admire your dedication to my business. Selfless, one might say.'

Sneer away, get it over with.

'But that's the point. This is business. Not sentiment. And Cordier have clout, they could offer the brewery a great deal.'

And me too. My turn to needle, he could have a few shocks coming his way. His body language is uncertain, tentative.

'But they're French.' Ralph keeps his voice quiet.

'Yes Ralph, French. A new breed of French; eurocentric French. Not beret and baguette French sneering at our attempts to speak Francais while they flick ash off their Gauloises into that ersatz black stuff they call coffee.'

'But you said—' *Keep needling him, Ralph.*

'Yes, I did Ralph. But business is changing, the beer market's changing, and this way I get access to Europe. Cordier are in bed with Argent, Michaels says. Michaels, oh yes, there's a colleague of yours trying to cover his backside and toady up.

'Yes, Argent is ruled by what you so dismissively call bean counters. Men who know how much things cost and don't countenance the excesses of creative people.'

George pinches his weathered nose.

'And I too am not getting any younger, I have to hand over the reins soon, and anyway the world I knew and loved is passing me by. Yes, there are men up there, fine men, better men than you and I.'

He pauses to cast his eyes up at the Braithwaite portraits obligingly sneering down at them.

'Men who would abhor what I am doing. Like Norris Braithwaite there, who once sat me on his knee and said, "never forget young George, wogs began at Calais, wogs are people who put garlic in roast lamb and serve it undercooked, people who'd take an eyeglass of sweet wine with foie gras before they'd get a pint of Braithwaite's Brown and a pickled egg down their gullet, never forget that young lad".'

Ralph merely stares back at him. Braithwaite looks at him enquiringly.

'Perhaps your receptionist could call me a taxi. There's not much of a meeting left to be had anyway at present, is there Mr Braithwaite? I came up here as a courtesy, to give you the news.'

Ralph gestures at the portraits, 'rather than putting this work in a call report or fax, I wanted to tell you in person about the takeover talks. That's all. The work's been signed off by Jenny anyway, promotional stuff,' Ralph continues. 'I believe you said it was something you didn't have much truck with anyway, dismissed as not in your bailiwick, leave it to Tommy and your staff. And any forward planning discussions on our part are rather extant now, as the French bean counters haven't had their say yet, have they?'

Braithwaite waits a second for the tirade to stop, then looks at Ralph with a small pitying smile.

'French bean, very good. But Ralph, Ralph if you hadn't already been on the train, I'd have saved you the trouble.'

Now you're fibbing. Michaels would have phoned you last night, I bet. You had time to put me off. Too much bother to pick up the phone?

'The cab company know to pick me up in the pub. And I await with interest your reaction to, to beer bottles with designer labels and gold foil around the necks.'

Ralph smiles.

'And I'd turn those portraits to the wall if I were you, Mr Braithwaite. Processed cheese sandwiches on white supermarket bread with a glass of milk might come as a bit of a shock to the eurocentric palate.'

Mr Braithwaite extends his hand.

'Bertram, it's been a pleasure, I am sure,' he says dry icily.

I've always wanted to say this and now's the time.

'No,' he pauses, 'George, one thing I am sure of, it's been something of a pleasure, but it hasn't been a complete pleasure, not since your father died, not for five years it hasn't. And a lot of what I've done for you has been out of respect for him, as well as you and the account.'

Braithwaite appears taken aback, his expression changing, softening, to one of surprise at the mention of his father. Ralph, emotion showing in his voice, heart beating hard, a tic pulsing in his cheek, turns and looks up at the portraits.

'I'd never take your father's name in vain, no, but the French, a buyout? Your dad, Sid, bless him, he'll be spinning in his grave. Goodbye, George.'

Braithwaite is silent for a moment. He looks closely at Ralph and extends his hand.

'Thank you, Ralph, and I do mean that sincerely, thank you for what you've done, over all these years for my family. My father always spoke well of you. Told me you were good for our business.'

Ralph, emotions confused, opens his mouth to speak, shuts it, firmly grasps George Braithwaite's hand and shakes it at length.

'Well, thank you for that, George,' he says uncertainly, 'thank you.' He turns and walks a trifle unsteadily out of the boardroom.

'A pint of bitter,' Ralph says minutes later to the barman in the Brewery Tap. He points up at a bottle of single malt Scotch on the top shelf. 'And a large Ardbeg.'

'It's that kind of day already, is it,' sniffs the barman.

'Paul,' Perfect puts her head around the door. 'Ralph's back from the brewery early and he's upset and a bit pissed.'

'I'll get him out of the agency?'

'Perhaps not a great time for him to be around looking like that, he might say something.'

'Well after what went down the other night—'

Ralph looks up as Paul walks in. Paul eyes him sardonically. He recalls drunken businessmen in films, slumped in their office chair, hair messed up, tie undone, shirt rumpled, rheumy eyed.

'Blimey Ralph, you're a casting director's cliché. Burt Lancaster in The Sweet Smell of Success. You're going home, right now.'

'Can't go home like this.'

'Oh yes you can, old man, oh yes you can. Sonia understands what's going on and you're not expected in here anyway if you've been up north, c'mon we'll get a taxi in the street. Ralph.' Then forcefully, 'C'mon.'

Ralph picks up his briefcase and, feet dragging, follows Paul out. Grace looks up as they walk through reception.

'Ralph's not feeling well Grace, he wasn't in the agency this afternoon and if I hear he was, I'll know who it came from.'

Grace nods, quickly, then angling her head, looks at him questioningly.

'Sorry Grace, apologise. Didn't mean it like that. Keep it quiet for us Grace, please.'

Ralph sways slightly on the edge of the pavement. Paul waves a taxi down.

'How many fucking years have I given Freddy, Paul?'

'Too many, Ralph, too many. Get home, old friend, we'll talk about it tomorrow.'

'Can't talk about it, Paul.'

'We'll see. Waterloo Station, please.' Paul opens the taxi door and Ralph falls in.

'He's OK, driver.'

Chapter 63

The agency team are sombre, uncertain. They stand outside the Dog and Duck, for once forsaking the Feathers so they can talk without people from other agencies wondering why they're so subdued. Even George, walking down Frith Street and seeing them, senses their mood.

'Sorry you lot, mustn't linger today. Got to see a man.'

They acknowledge George with a perfunctory wave and Paul picks up the conversation where it has momentarily paused.

'The problem is, we can't believe anything Freddy promises us. It can all change in ten minutes after the merger's signed and sealed. Michael will be alright with those major earners, and so will you Nigel, you've got a good relationship with our clients. And you, Brian. It's just a case of how long we all stay before we move on.'

'Might be a good thing,' said Jane, 'you can't afford to stay at G and W forever, you guys need to move on, anyway. And you two,' she says to Cynthia and Claire.

It goes without saying that Phil and Jane working in the same office places an unnecessary strain on their relationship and Argent has a strict policy of no couples working together.

'Not worth even thinking about it then,' says Bitsa brightly. 'Part of life's rich pattern, who's for another one?'

There were grunts and nods of assent and he disappears into the pub.

'Are takeovers that bad?' enquires Roddy.

'Well, all agencies have their own mood, tone, their own personality; stands to reason Argent won't change for us.'

'That was what George said,' confirms Jimmy. 'We were coming back from a meeting with Brian and put our heads around the door the other day, thought you might be in here, and got caught by George.'

Brian smiles and shakes his head.

'What's that, Brian?'

'He gave us one of his "I was there" stories,' explains Jimmy. 'You actually wonder if people hear urban myths—'

'And then make them real, use the idea again, relive them?' suggests Roddy.

'The thing is,' says Brian, 'there's one advertising story that became an urban myth right around the world, but my brother was there.'

'Which one was it, Brian?'

'Trevor, you remember brother Trev?'

'I bet he remembers his leaving party,' says Paul, who'd heard the story. Brian looks at Paul, puzzled, shrugs, then continues.

'Trev worked for Hornsby's, a Sydney agency, bit like G and W. One of the partners was real old school, smoked a pipe in the office. Trev said some winter mornings, there was a real nice fug in the room. Like smoke from a barbe. Anyway, the bloke had this rack of pipes on his desk with his favourite old briar in the middle. He was always going on about it, how it had been his uncle's, this old bushie, who'd fire it up and sit on his verandah the moment he got back from a muster.'

'Do we have to have all the Ned Kelly outback stuff, Brian?' Brian dismisses Phil with a look.

'Just setting the picture, Phil, and this was cattle, not your pretty little fluffy bummed sheep. Anyways, the pipe was the agency guy's pride and joy, and one day he comes in and the pipe's gone from the rack on his desk.'

'I think I may have heard this one,' ponders Paul.

'Maybe, but I can vouch that it's real,' continues Brian. 'Anyway, you know the story. The bloke goes nuts, turns his office upside down, but to his credit doesn't accuse anyone of nicking it even though he was a bit offside with the creative department. Kept it to a few black looks.

'Until a few days later, the pipe suddenly reappears back in the rack. The bloke calms down, doesn't say anything, and peace is restored in the agency. All is quiet for a few days, and then this Polaroid shot appears on the office notice board. A close up of a bum, with the pipe stuck up it.'

'Brian,' says Jane, disgusted.

'Stem first, I trust,' comments Paul.

'Anyway, the photo was only up for about five minutes and then it was gone. But enough people saw it for the story to get around. And I've seen it, because I know who's still got the Polaroid.'

'Trev.'

Brain nodded a yes. 'Trev ended up with it. And I think I recognised the bum. Trev and I shared a bedroom, once. So maybe, just maybe, not all urban myths are myths.'

'Like Jonno's piles treatment?' suggests Phil.

Chapter 64

G and W's boardroom is decorated with red, white and blue flowers for the introductory cocktail party. The builders are already in, tearing down old partitions and walls to make the rest of the office open plan. George Braithwaite skirts a small pile of rubble to join the agency staff and clients. Christian Lafond shambles forward, huge paw extended to swallow up George's.

'Christian Lafond, enchante, Monsieur Braithwaite, pleased to meet you, may I call you George?'

'Yes, Christian, please call me George,' he finds himself saying.

Christian ushers Ralph Bertram from behind his back.

'Ralph here has introduced me to your beers, merveilleuse, a true craftsman's product, artisanal, Ralph says it tastes best in the—'

'Brewery Tap,' Ralph offers, looking a little guardedly at his client. They'd parted on such odd terms a month ago. But Braithwaite's gaze is mild, strangely pensive.

'I shall have to come up to your land of, of, the moors.' Christian gestures, 'I love Yorkshire, the rough country, like my home the Bas Pyrenees. But now to business. Marcel?'

Another, younger man in a very stylish obviously bespoke suit steps forward. His English is impeccable as he shakes Braithwaite's hand, and ushers him towards the bar.

'George, may I too call you George? Marcel Gerard, I handle the entire Cordier portfolio for Argent out of Paris, wines, spirits, and what beers we have. And we hope soon to have, to handle yours. I believe the Cordier people have been talking about getting into bed with you, an entente cordiale as it were?'

George Braithwaite stiffens. He'd talked to Cordier, they'd sent a delegation over, he'd agreed in principle to "get into bed" with them, but it was all supposed to be in the strictest confidence. Obviously, Cordier had let it slip to Argent.

'Oops, I have not spoken out of turn? Forewarned is forearmed as they say.' Gerard looks unconvincingly apologetic as he raises his glass in a mollifying gesture. 'You will understand that until anything is signed, Braithwaite's represents rather a conflict of interest with Cordier brands and we cannot obviously talk terms of business until then. Though to be frank, it would be good for your company and for you if with Cordier—'

Ralph kept his face straight. He thought he'd feel an exquisite, if guilty pleasure in Braithwaite's obvious discomfort at being so, manipulated. Instead, he felt sympathy for a man who obviously had real business principles, ones that marketing was yet to corrupt.

Nevertheless, he'd thought Braithwaite had a much thicker skin, born of centuries of immersion in the ruling classes. Perhaps he'd inherited some of father Sid's sensibility? And it also showed Ralph exactly how the French worked. They'd be ruthless.

'Ralph here has already spoken well of your portfolio. We like the traditional nature of it, how you were describing it, Ralph?'

Ralph, working hard to keep his expression neutral, clears his throat.

'Hrrrm. L.S. Lowry. Flat hats, whippets, mufflers, brass bands, factory chimneys, hard work, pride, craftsmen, natural, small batch beers, it prompted a strategy we once considered, but decided—' He'd said enough.

Braithwaite found his voice. 'You'll continue to look after my brand, under any new arrangement, Bertram?'

Marcel answers for Ralph. 'No, no, for Argent the account at present would be as Ralph described it.' He looks questioningly at Ralph.

'Small beer,' Ralph mumbles, guiltily.

'Yes, yes, small beer, an apt expression. No, Ralph is coming to Paris to work on the main Cordier brands there and polish his merde French. His considerable strategic knowledge of the British market will be of great use to us. No, I am confident we can sort out any conflict with Cordier brands, and I hope you stay with us. In the interim, your beers would be handled by our Australian friend, young Brian Arnold. Brian,' he says, raising his voice.

Brian detaches himself from a group in the corner and strides over. Jenny Brownlow hurries to catch up. Seeing them coming, Marcel excuses himself, but not before pausing and taking a long and very obviously appraising look at Jenny.

'Mr Braithwaite, I didn't see you arrive,' she says smoothly.

'This is Brian, Brian Arnold who'll be working on our business when Ralph goes to Paris. I found out this afternoon,' she adds hurriedly.

'Brian Arnold, Mr Braithwaite.'

George Braithwaite has learned one thing from the younger generation in a tortured metaphor from one of his nephews.

When you're a fish out of water, go with the flow.

'Brian, pleased to have you on the business, whether or not, should there be a tie in with Cordier.'

Brian knows George Braithwaite would correctly guess Ralph had carefully briefed him. Even so, Brian has done his own research.

'Pleased to meet you, Sir. Looking into the background of the account, I was surprised to find my great grandfather's regiment fought alongside your great-grandfather's on the Western Front in World War One.'

This insight instantly puts him, the younger man and Braithwaite, the older man, on a working footing. Brian has done his research, yes, and immediately makes it abundantly clear.

It was unnecessary to add that Brian's great grandfather never actually got to the Western Front, being prevented by a particularly nasty accident in a Paris brothel precipitated by youthful over enthusiasm and involving his penis and a broken whalebone in a lady's corset, the full grisly details of which had been consigned to the cupboard along with numerous other Arnold family skeletons.

Brian's grandfather's regiment had made it to the front, though, and that supplied sufficient credibility. In fact, armistice was declared before Brian's great grandfather's legs were out of the stirrups on his hospital bed, and he hobbled back to the family property in central west New South Wales to be greeted as a wounded war hero.

It says much for the Arnold family's resilience and Brian's grandfather's recuperative powers that he recovered sufficiently to father four sons and three daughters.

'Ralph says they do a pint in the Brewery Tap that puts the ice cold dingo wee, as he calls it, that I normally drink to shame, and that I must get up north and try a Braithwaite's for myself. Though he probably says that to everyone.'

'Indeed you must, Brian, *if your new masters can stretch to a train fare,*' George says quietly, suddenly tired of all the ducking and weaving, the fencing that goes with marketing and advertising.

That was the second or third time the Brewery Tap had been mentioned that evening. Ralph has obviously circulated his report to everyone concerned; the Cordier people would probably also use it when they met.

Braithwaite much preferred the English broadsword to the French rapier. For a moment, he saw himself standing on a granite outcrop high on the moors, swinging the huge blade as French soldiers circled, jabbing at him. Perhaps he'd underestimated Bertram's old fashioned principles. Perhaps there was more than mere self-preservation in his approaches of the previous month. Perhaps Bertram had a point, he conceded, when he'd tapped so obviously into the traditional Braithwaite antipathy to the French.

Perhaps there was something in sticking with traditional values, perhaps he'd even made a mistake with his song and dance commercial, and why look abroad when sales in the home market had been the best for three decades?

Looking around him, he sees the obviously ill at ease Phil on the fringe of the crowd, slugging down red wine. Young Arbuthnott, Braithwaite ponders, might come from a very different background but is also true to his northern heritage. Paul approaches.

'Mr Braithwaite, looking at the time, I think there's a train to Leeds in about thirty minutes, and there's always a taxi to be had outside at this time of night.'

'Thank you, er, Paul, yes, I must say my goodbyes.'

Paul looks at Braithwaite and sees an old, discomfited man out of his time, weighed down by centuries of family tradition and heavy-handed paternalism towards those less fortunate.

'Sir, I'd just slip away if I were you. I'll tell Jenny and our French friends you had to go.'

'Right, thank you,' Braithwaite mumbles as Paul indicates the door.

Looking around him, he hurries out. Phil wanders up. 'Jeez Paul, you weren't brown nosing that landed gentry anus Lord of Manor, were you? People like him give Yorkshire a bad name. You'd do anything to sell an ad.'

Paul turns from the door, a sympathetic look still in his eye. He shrugs at Phil.

'You know I wouldn't, Phil. And I wasn't. He might be a boring old prick, but at least you know exactly where you stand with him even if it is knee deep in shit. Let's slip down the Feathers and get a real drink. I'm done tap dancing for the night.'

Jonno opens his front door to Jenny who slips around him into his flat, brushing her lips against his cheek. 'I had enough of the reception, saw you leave, and thought I'd better leave it for an hour, wait till the French had gone. Been up at Braithwaite's, had my overnight bag with me.' She puts the bag down. 'It's starting to rain a bit so I changed into my Burberry.'

'Oh God,' mumbles Jonno, looking at her tightly belted raincoat.

He carefully undoes the top button. Then the next button, working his way down, undoing the belt, throwing the coat open and sinking to his knees. As usual, Jenny is naked underneath. Jenny leans back against the hallway wall, trembling and glances down at the top of Jonno's head as he runs his tongue lightly over her knee and up the inside of a thigh.

'Marcel, mon brave,' she whispers to herself. 'Oh, Marcel.'

Chapter 65

'Phone call for you, Paolo, lady called Christine.'

'Thank you, Maria.' Paul takes the proffered handset and Maria bustles back to her desk by the door of Locanda and her copy of Star. As usual on a Friday, Paul and Phil are the last lunch patrons left.

'Hello, Christine my, my very favourite planner.'

'Paul, it is you, isn't it? You sound a bit Brahms. Paul, yes it's Christine and I had a devil of a job tracking you down. There's a bit of a crisis on Woof, Clayton and Brian and the girls are out at a meeting and Jonno is cloistered with Freddy somewhere. Can you get back here, quickly?' she says in a rush.

'Christine, Christine, may I call you Pie, my little lamb? I'm incommunicado at lunchtimes, devoting my time to protein and the grape, excuse me for a moment.'

Phil's miming hand to mouth movements and indicating Paul's glass. Paul gives a thumbs up. Phil turns in his chair, somewhat clumsily, attracts Maria's attention and holds up two fingers. She bustles over with a bottle.

'Grappa all gone, have a Port, on the house.'

She fills their glasses to the brim.

'Sorry Christine, Phil rudely interrupted us, what was that? It's three thirty, not lunchtime anymore? Sorry, gotcha, Pie, Christine yes, we'll come back pronto, yes.'

The atmosphere in the agency boardroom is frigid. Alan Sergeant has gone to make a phone call, Christine's left with Bruce Wood who's attempting to pull his face into a smile, but is clearly uncomfortable, running his hands through his hair and blinking rapidly.

Suddenly the door bursts open and Phil falls in, followed by Paul. They both look distinctly the worse for wear. Phil is dishevelled, Paul's face is white, with round red clown like blotches on each cheek.

'What ho, Christine, afternoon Bruce,' says Phil loudly.

'No Alan? I mean Sergeant?' Paul salutes, hitting himself hard on the forehead.

'Making a phone call, Paul,' says Christine. 'Just sit down and keep quiet, for once.'

'What about Jonno?'

'Out with Freddy, I believe. Sit down, keep schtum.' She smiles at Bruce.

Phil and Paul slump into chairs. Phil pulls a G and W notepad towards him, ferrets around laboriously in the inside pocket of his leather jacket and finds a Pentel. Taking the top off, he writes on the pad and passes it to Paul, who opens half closed eyes and nods.

The note says, I'm pissed. Bruce looks over at the note and writing one on his pad, tears off the page and passes it to Phil. It says, I'll buy that.

At that moment Alan Sergeant bursts in. As Paul and Phil half rise to shake hands, he holds his up, palm flat, decisively, to still them and sits down, turning his gaze to Christine, who's about to speak. Her mouth sets in a tight line, she's obviously furious the client has hijacked her meeting, and not forewarned her as to why when she'd fielded his phone call.

'Thank you for coming in gentlemen, Christine, a problem,' he says with obvious relish, producing a large manila envelope from his briefcase. He pulls out a still photo from the envelope and pushes it across the table.

'Taken from the first Woof commercial.'

'I thought you liked it?' says Christine quietly.

'Oh, we loved it, at first, didn't we Bruce?' Bruce affects his frightened smile again, eyes darting to the agency members.

'I thought it was great, too, didn't we Paul?' says Phil, looking at each person in turn, mouth pulled into a rictus of a grin that reveals a mouthful of crooked teeth, each one outlined in a grotesque crimson.

Alan Sergeant looks at him, eyes wrinkled in disgust.

'Yeah, we did Alan,' says Paul, his eyes still half closed.

'Well, my head office in Kalamazoo doesn't,' says the client, 'detail, detail, detail they said to me before putting the phone down. And as the rest of the agency appears to still be at lunch, it falls to you two to rectify this.'

Phil blearily studies the photo. It shows a close up of the Woof pack in Annette, the female talent's, hand. He attempts a coherent reply.

'Mr Sergeant, you can't expect any real definition or colour quality when you pull a still off a commercial,' Phil explains, 'I mean, I know the director was using 35mm stock so the definition should be OK and I remember it was slightly over cranked at this point but—'

Sergeant is quick to interrupt and press his point.

'Look closely at that woman's hand Philip. Her middle fingernail's chipped. It looks terrible. It's going to mean a complete reshoot.'

'Reshoot,' mumbles Paul.

'Yes, Paul, reshoot. At the agency's expense.'

Christine rises to her feet. 'I'll get Steve Hayward.'

There's silence in the room while they wait. Sergeant stares into the middle distance, seething, purposely ignoring the two creatives. Paul breathes stentoriously, trying to stay awake. Phil affords everyone his manic grin, and, catching Bruce's eye, gives him a big wink. Steve enters.

'Afternoon gentlemen, a problem, Christine?'

'Good afternoon, Steve,' says Bruce levelly.

Phil shoves the still over to Steve, who remains standing. He picks it up.

'What is it, Mr Sergeant?'

'Steven, Steve, if you look closely, you'll see your female talent has a chipped fingernail. My head office did a frame-by-frame to check this crucial scene, and noticed this, error. They're demanding a re-shoot.'

'Mr Sergeant, Bruce,' Steve was the very epitome of reason.

'I'm hardly going to point out that, on the run, at normal speed, no-one would notice, but—' Seeing Sergeant stiffen and his eyes theatrically narrow, Steve holds up a mollifying hand.

'But I appreciate,' he adds hurriedly, 'that the situation has gone well beyond that. I can see what we can do. I'm sure we can rectify these few frames, but it will mean some extra charges and I'll get you a quote, quickly. We certainly know, now, what to look for when we shoot the rest of the series. A good learning curve. May I have this?'

Steve turns to go.

'Not so fast, man, this will be at the agency's expense.'

'Aah,' says Steve, 'If I remember rightly, and this would be conference reported Mr Sergeant, you gave me Reader's procedural production sheet at the pre-production meeting, and Clayton and I followed it to the letter.'

Steve looks at each person at the table for verification.

'I invited you onto the set for every set up and between takes to check the pack, and Annette's action before we proceeded. We rehearsed every shot with you watching, closely. And Clayton also got you to initial the storyboard before we struck the set and proceeded to the next shot.'

'You didn't,' replies Alan Sergeant, his face looking a little guilty. 'I mean I didn't, not all day. Not me. I had to leave after lunch, if you remember, and delegated responsibility to Bruce here.'

'Aaaah,' says Phil.

'Um,' says Bruce as eyes turn towards him. He visibly shrinks into his tub chair.

'Aaaah, um,' Paul suddenly jerks upright in his seat to mimic Phil and Bruce as it seems the right thing to do, and slumps back again, eyes half closed.

'Bruce is only a junior, I left him in your capable hands, it was the agency's responsibility,' continues Sergeant, self-defensively.

'As I said, Mr Sergeant,' Steve looks towards Christine, whose expression, and a slight nod says, you handle it, 'I can probably rectify this in post-production as that finger is only in close up for a few frames.'

He pauses for a moment for effect.

'And as I got Bruce, myself, Clayton, Paul and Phil, and the girls to pay particular attention to the close ups and most importantly, the cameraman didn't notice it, so it becomes a collective responsibility.

'What I will do though is look in the budget, and see if anything's left, and talk to Clayton, and get back to you. I'm sure this can be sorted out quickly, to all our satisfaction. We'll rectify things with—'

'Kalamazoo,' Christine supplies.

'Yes. Alan, I can fix this to the point your head office can go over it with a magnifying glass. And we do have time before we go to air; we left space in the schedule in case anything like this happened. Like I said, we'll all know better next time. Enjoy your weekend.'

Steve smiles at everyone in the meeting, picks up the photo and strides out. Christine relaxes. She turns to Alan Sergeant, who sits, stony faced. Phil grins maniacally at the client and turns to Paul, who shows every sign that he's slipping into sleep and, potentially, under the table.

'Wake up,' he mutters, 'you dozy git.' He turns to the table. 'Meeting's over, who's coming down the rubbidy. The old rubbidy dub,' he slurs. 'Agency's buying.'

'Shut up. Phil, Paul,' Christine orders. 'Out, you two. Out, please.'

Paul gets unsteadily to his feet, and he and Phil are about to say their goodbyes when Christine puts finger to lips, and ushers them out. She waits till they're gone before addressing Alan Sergeant.

'Alan, I can only apologise for us not helping out Bruce enough at the shoot as he is inexperienced when it comes to making commercials, and when you delegated responsibility to him, we should have all taken that into account.'

She catches her breath.

'And I can't apologise enough for Paul and Phil's behaviour.'

She pauses for a moment. Alan Sergeant's expression is unchanged.

'But if Steve says it can be fixed, then I'm sure it can. Without undue worrying, or any cost to you, we still have the cinema version to do, it's budgeted, and this can be part of that. I'll get Steve to report to Clayton, and ask Clayton to call you A.S.A.P. He'll probably do so tonight, anyway, when he returns from his meeting.'

Alan Sergeant remains impassive; there's little he can say.

Christine coolly continues. 'But, but as Steve said, if the cameraman didn't spot it, in close up, I don't think anyone else would: nevertheless, a mistake. And one we can, all of us, take responsibility for. As for Paul and Phil, again, I really shouldn't have brought them into the meeting, I'm sure they'll apologise.'

Alan Sergeant raises his hand. Christine prudently shuts up.

'I was not impressed, Christine, but they're hardly your responsibility. Still, as to their behaviour, disgusting, I would hope my son would never behave like that.'

If I had a father like you, thinks Christine.

'I'll talk to Freddy and Jonno, Monday, Alan, about their behaviour. Johnstone and Arbuthnott have finished their current assignments on your business, and we do have some other, very able people here. I'm sure Clayton will be only too happy to leave the account with the other two teams. This one is Claire and Cynthia's responsibility, anyway.

'Christine, I'll believe it when I see it. Let's fix the current problem, first. We'll leave it at that, for now. Bruce?'

'If it's OK with you Alan, I'll stay and sort things out with Christine and Steve and see you Monday. And I'm very sorry.'

Sergeant looks at him stonily. 'Monday then, my office at nine.'

Christine and Bruce watch his Marketing Director stride off down the corridor.

'Phew.' Bruce slowly exhales.

'C'mon, Bruce,' Christine turns to him. 'I'm taking you around the pub. I'll concede that is the agency's responsibility.'

Chapter 66

The second Woof commercial shoot is successful. At Freddy's insistence, Paul has hand written letters to Alan Reader and to Bruce Wood, apologising for their drunken behaviour at the meeting, and for the way they'd compromised Christine and the agency.

A salutary lesson, Freddy stated. Paul and Phil had wandered into his office, naughty schoolboys before the headmaster. Freddy's precise tone was at odds with his words.

'You don't hear me fucking swear fucking often Paul, Philip, but when I fucking do, I fucking mean it,' Freddy said in a matter of fact undertone as they stood in front of his desk, shuffling their feet in the pile of the ancient silk carpet.

'No, don't sit down, this isn't a fucking discussion, and keep your mouths zipped just for once, both of you. For once and for all, this is your first, second and last warning, and I've written it down for each of you. So pull your fucking heads in.

'You're my senior team, start acting like you are. I expect you both to set an example for the younger people here, and that doesn't mean lurching around the agency drunk on those days you grace us with your presence after lunch. Got that?'

You knew Freddy was upset when his voice was cold, matter of fact and devoid of emotion.

'I had to grovel, fucking suck client cock on your behalf, Sergeant's of all people. He was surprisingly gracious in the circumstances, actually defended you. Try and look not so surprised, Paul. He'd heard about Argent, fortunately sees some advantages to him in the takeover, so that's another reason I don't want your behaviour to compromise G and W and our relationship with him. Let alone Argent. Next time, you're both out on your fucking ears.

'Now get out and not to boardroom four, five or six, or whatever you call them. And hold on Paul, I want letters of apology to Alan and Bruce handwritten, signed by both of you and on my desk by two o'clock. Now get out.'

Paul and Phil had walked sheepishly into the second Woof pre-production meeting and quietly taken seats at the back. Clayton had phoned Alan Sergeant and suggested that the boys, with all their experience, should also be at the shoot and that Jonno would certainly pop in, too.

Paul and Phil prudently kept their heads down, literally, throughout the meeting as Alan Sergeant darted the odd, contemptuous look towards them. He still appeared to have no idea the concept, or scripts were theirs. Steve Hayward took the clients smoothly through the script, confirming the talent, wardrobe, and the set, which was identical to the first commercial.

'The first three spots all take place in the kitchen, I don't think we'll take Scout into the living room, or out for a walk until next year.'

'When we'll introduce other breeds?' Suggested Bruce.

Paul had opened his mouth to speak, thought better of it, covered it with his hand, coughed discreetly, and quietly apologised.

'Of course, Bruce, good idea, I'll suggest it to the girls,' Christine said with a reassuring smile.

Having ticked off all the other points and got their signatures on the director's shoot board, Steve handed around Cauliflower, the production company's call sheet that listed the crew's, and the Reader and agency members' movement order, as the studio was located just out of London near the Thames.

'Harry Hayward,' said Alan Sergeant as he scanned the sheet, 'a relation of yours, Steve?'

A worried look crossed Steve's face as he scanned his call sheet. There it was. First A.D. Harry Hayward.

'No. Yes,' he replied, nonplussed.

'Which is it, then?' asked Sergeant smoothly.

'Sorry, Alan, yes of course, he's my father.'

'Steve was clearly, "discombobulated"?' suggested Cyn when Paul and Phil gleefully reported on Steve's discomfort.

'Fookin' freaked,' is Phil's summation.

'Jesus,' said Steve, when the meeting closed. 'Dad?'

'I dunno what you're worried about,' said Paul, breezily, 'Cauliflower obviously like working with him, Sergeant has no idea of his reputation, sorry Steve, and anyway your dad's a bloody good first and he'll behave with you there.'

'I suppose so,' agreed Steve.

Chapter 67

Paul was correct. When agency and clients arrived on set, Harry strutted about wearing his trademark black greatcoat, bullet head projecting from the wide bat wing collar. Paul was fascinated by Harry's head, which he likened to a piece of clay moulded by the uncertain fingers of a novice sculptor.

Harry efficiently marshalled the crew, the first scene was set up, and he had Annette, her hands, and Scout the dog, closely scrutinised by client and agency. Then agency and clients settled down at the back of the set.

'Remember guys,' said Steve, 'please, if you want to talk to Johnny the director between takes, do it through me, I want his total concentration.'

Harry's basso profundo voice filled the sound stage.

'Right. You got that track nice and level, Alf?'

'Close as bollocks is to swearing, sir.'

'Does that cupboard door fit nice and tight now, Harold?'

'Like a finger in a bum, sir.'

'Thank you, quiet on set please, everyone we're shooting sound and that includes you, old son.'

Steve raised his head, but Harry was talking colloquially to the standby props man.

'Over to you, Johnny.'

It was smooth a shoot as Paul and Phil could remember. They dutifully stared at the monitor, nodded their approval at good takes and refrained from looking at briefs from other clients or leaving the set to talk to make phone calls. For once, Paul even left the crossword in The Times untouched.

The script worked well, Steve managing to limit the pack shot in the cupboard to three varieties, Clayton citing research that said most women bought an absolute maximum of six pouches of Woof at a time and pointing out the fewer the packs in the cupboard, the bigger they'd appear on screen.

Alan and Bruce, surprisingly, agreed, and Alan said he "felt comfortable enough" to leave at lunchtime to attend a meeting, having first stared disapprovingly at the lavish spread provided by the caterer and raising his hand in a monastic, ascetic, no, when offered food to take with him.

'He's probably off for a spot of self-flagellation,' observed Paul laconically to Phil as they stood in line at the buffet.

It was noticeable that Steve and Harry, having had a close, hand on each other's shoulder, father and son chat at the outset, stayed away from each other and got on with their jobs.

'Clayton, thanks for looking after the clients,' said Paul.

'Just doing my job, Paul,' said Clayton, ever pompous, 'Brian will be along later to take over.'

Bruce was obviously a little out of his depth, tripping over cables, and getting in the way of grips as the set up was changed around. And the moment food was brought out, Bruce moved towards the table.

Phil put out a restraining hand. 'Shoot etiquette, Bruce, crew eats first.'

'Come and sit with us,' Paul suggested when they'd all got a heaped plate of food and led Bruce over to a trestle table where Harry was sitting with some of the crew.

'Is the name Cauliflower significant, Paul?' Bruce had asked.

'No,' said Paul, 'It just means they could hire a girl with a bit of East London in her voice to pick up the phone and say, "Cauliflower 'ere".'

Bruce stared at Paul, uncomprehending. 'Oh,' he said.

Paul moved over to sit near Harry. He'd worked with him before, and they acknowledged each other.

'Busy this year, Harry?'

'Paul, isn't it? Did some pickups for a feature in Canada just before Christmas, skiing thing then went down to NYC for Christmas not easy the director couldn't direct a greased tennis ball up a camel's arse. Or piss into a bucket for that matter.''

'Trifle cold there?'

'They had this blizzard, start of the New Year, you probably saw it on the news here. Bloody snow drifts in the street, yeh high.'

Harry gestured theatrically towards the ceiling with his fork, looking around the table to ensure he has everyone's attention. It was obvious he was about to embark on one of his anecdotes. Phil glanced at Bruce, who was transfixed at the glamour of working with a film crew. Harry continues.

'It's snowing like buggery, drifts are building, but a chap can get a bit stir crazy stuck in his hotel room, so I thought I'd go for a trudge around the block.'

Harry's voice assumed its full, thespian projection, and people at other tables half turned to listen.

'I was walking around the side of the Waldorf Astoria when it hits me, bally wind chill factor of about minus forty. Had ice crystals in my eyebrows, icicles up the schnozz, breathing was like being stabbed in the chest with a bloody bayonet.

'I was about to turn back when I saw this dive bar, one of those sub-basement thingies had just opened and as the sun was almost over the yardarm so to speak, given the weather, I ducked down there.

'It's a long bar, and there's this stubby little barman chappie at the other end setting it up. So I stand there, shaking ice off myself, unwinding the old muffler and he comes waddling up to my end and says in this, what d'you call it, Bronx accent, spoke through his nose, "Whaddya want?"'

Harry pauses to confirm he has the undivided attention of everyone within earshot.

'There's this sign on the wall, try one of our famous Martinis. So I say, "I'll have one of your famous Martinis, please, old boy".

"OK," says he.

'And he mixes one for me. Even leaves the shaker. I take a good suck at it, and I can recommend them, jolly good and finished it. Those Martini glasses are rather shallow after all.

'Well by then, he's back down at the other end of the bar and I indicate my empty glass and he puts down his glass cloth and comes waddling back down my end again.

"Wow," he says, "not so fast, mister, see the sign, only three per customer if you're not used to them, house rules."

'So I say, OK, then I'll try a G and T instead please. He gives a shrug, we agree on a gin and with due ceremony, he mixes me one. I take a sip, it has a requisite amount of London Dry and suddenly the world's looking a whole lot more tickety boo. So I perch myself on a bar stool and start ruminating upon the nature of things.

'I'm stirring the drink with my swizzle stick and I notice the ice. You know it's that funny stuff, looks like a stick of macaroni, hollowed out, and some lumps have a top like the head of a bullet.'

Harry points at his head, drawing a chuckle from his audience.

'I'm sitting there, twiddling a piece of ice on the end of my bally swizzle stick and he suddenly comes marching down the bar again, obviously thinking I'm trying to attract his attention.

"So hey, what is it with you?" he enquires, quite genially, actually. "Whaddya want?"

'I looked at him and said, "Nothing old chap, it's just that I've never seen ice with a hole in it before."

'He rocks back on his heels, cocks an eyebrow at me and says, "You've never met my wife," and stomps off.'

After a moment, Bruce joins tentatively in the general chuckling.

Some crew members, male and female, grimace, slowly shake their heads and cast a look skywards.

Harry rises to his feet and shouts, 'right, everyone back on set, let's shoot this thing.'

Chapter 68

'Great call, Clayton.'

'Well, I live out this way and it's close to the studio and I thought well, you did mention a wrap lunch was customary after a shoot was completed and well, they do know me here and I have this rapport with the maitre'd and—'

'Good,' says Paul, moving towards the table before Clayton can really get into his stride.

A couple of days after the shoot Clayton invited the Reader clients to lunch. The restaurant is in an old coaching inn a couple of streets back from the river, near the studio where they'd shot the second Woof commercial. It's a warm day so they choose to sit at a table in the stone flagged central courtyard where the London mail coach once drew up.

Alan Sergeant arrives early to be welcomed by Clayton and stiffly greets the other agency members as they straggle in. Alan's attitude and body language make it clear he's only accepted the agency's invitation with some reluctance, he's here under sufferance, but if this is the way the advertising industry conducts its business then good manners dictate that for once, he'll accede to G and W's wishes.

He and Bruce are somewhat outnumbered as the whole agency team has, as Brian put it 'found time in their day' as it gives them all 'the opportunity to brainstorm and discuss the next moves.'

Paul has picked up the wine list and is discussing things with the sommelier. Alan Sergeant looks pointedly at his watch. Orders are taken, and the first course arrives.

From this point on, lunch continues smoothly. Paul and Phil prudently show wholly uncharacteristic restraint; after the debacle of the meeting with Reader, they have their careers to think about, and the impending takeover has put them on their guard.

And anyway, with Christine at the table, they aren't about to embarrass her again. Bruce is only too happy to be away from his desk and be given a large, free lunch. Alan and Bruce thank Claire and Cynthia for their diligence on their business, which they humbly accept, thanking Paul and Phil profusely for taking time to go to the shoot on their behalf and not being tempted to tamper with the scripts.

Christine and Clayton are charm itself, Alan Sergeant even sips a glass of wine for appearances sake. Steve is very quiet.

'Steve, you're very quiet,' says Paul, a question implied in the statement.

Steve looks around, nervously.

'I went to make a call and found Dad in the bar. With the studio just down the road, he treats this as his local. And he's had a few G and Ts, I reckon.'

Phil's listening and looks up. A figure in a long black coat appears in a doorway.

'Excuse me,' Phil says suddenly and walks off across the courtyard, threading his way through the tables before disappearing into the main building. He returns some minutes later. 'Harry was about to come over. I headed him off at the pass, told him we were talking business,' he murmurs to Paul.

'Your dad's in there having a snack in the bar, said he might join us later,' Paul passes the message on to Steve who looks up, nervously.

Lunch continues with Steve obviously on tenterhooks.

'Time for a dessert, Alan?' asks Brian. 'You're a bit of a chocolate man, aren't you?'

Brian discovered this early on and has made sure there's a plate of chocolate digestive biscuits on the boardroom table for every meeting with the dogfood clients. He's found Alan Sergeant's soft spot; Alan invariably leaves the agency with a scattering of crumbs on his lapel.

'Well Brian, you could twist my arm,' he concedes, 'the afternoon has just about gone but we have, I believe, put down some good, productive groundwork for next year.'

'I'll contact report it when we get back, Alan,' Bruce dutifully pipes up.

As desserts are brought out, the waiter is followed by a familiar figure in a large black greatcoat, hem almost touching the flagstone yard. He wouldn't have been out of place in the coaching inn a hundred or more years ago. The warm, sultry weather doesn't seem to have influenced Harry's wardrobe. Nevertheless, the combination of heat and alcohol has caused his nut brown face to assume a darker, russet red, autumnal hue.

'Here we all are then,' he booms, 'mind if I join you?'

He swings a chair around from the next table and straddles it.

'Dad,' says Steve, 'fancy meeting you here.'

'It is my local, son. Mind if I?'

Harry spins round again, takes a wine glass from the adjoining table, spins back and pours himself a liberal amount from a bottle of red.

'Cheers, m'dears.'

Considering what happened later, G and W subsequently agreed the saving grace was Harry had been disarmingly docile and well mannered. He just sat there, conservatively sipping his wine and contributing the odd comment to the conversation.

'He lulled us into a comfort zone, it was like waiting for a bomb to go off,' suggested Christine, who'd made a fine job of including Harry in the general banter by eliciting his expertise on shooting commercials.

'Until a bomb did go off, in a manner of speaking,' said Paul.

With lunch almost over, Harry rises to his feet. 'Excuse me everyone, must go.'

Everyone signals their goodbyes, and Steve rises to give his dad a hug. As Steve wraps his arms around his father, anyone watching closely would have seen a fierce spasm of pain cross Harry's face before he hurried off across the courtyard, greatcoat brushing tables as he went into the bar.

The party returns to desserts and conversation. With a warm chocolate pudding liberally slathered in double cream speedily despatched and the last skerrick of molten centre scraped from his plate, Alan Sergeant leans over the table, picks up the cheese knife, and is about to hack off a large lump of fine cave aged Farmhouse Cheddar when something swoops through his line of vision and flops onto the cheeseboard.

The group variously register the intrusion and look up and around the overhanging galleries of the old building, trying to work out where the object has come from. Bruce is first to look at the cheeseboard closely and identify what the intruder is.

'Err, yuck, cack,' he goes, pointing with his spoon.

A pair of voluminous white boxer shorts liberally splashed and streaked a tell-tale brown are draped limply over the block of aged cheddar. One by one, the party rise to their feet, stepping back from the table in repelled fascination. Seeing the commotion, waiters hurry over.

Alan Sergeant stands, mouth open, eyes popping, staring at the offending article in disbelief. Steve is hopping from foot to foot, not sure what to do, looking furtively around, but of Harry there's no sign, save for the underwear which a waiter, head averted, hurries to remove with a pair of serving tongs and a garbage bag.

'I think it's time we all left,' says Clayton decisively, moving to shepherd Alan and Bruce away.

'I'll arrange taxis,' says Paul.

'I have my car,' says Alan Sergeant.

They leave without looking back, awkwardly shaking hands and agreeing not to let one, small, inexplicable incident mar a worthwhile lunch. Restaurant staff apologise profusely, thinking it was nothing to do with the lunch party.

'We'll send the bill on to you Mr Howell, there'll be a significant discount, no need to settle up now.'

Chapter 69

The next day, Steve comes into Paul and Phil's office and sits disconsolately, shoulders drooping, on the corner of a desk. Paul and Phil look up, smiling innocently.

'Neeeow, plop,' goes Paul, throwing his arms wide.

'Pooh er,' supplies Phil.

As Steve is obviously upset, they immediately quieten. For him, this isn't funny.

'Was it Harry, Steve?' Paul enquires quietly.

'Course it was. I called him when I got home. He said he suddenly felt a bit funny, he was caught short, so he rushed into the bar looking for the khazi but there were people in all the stalls. Then he suddenly remembered the bathrooms upstairs. He'd billeted crews up there in the rooms off the gallery, so he ran up there. When he found the lavvy, he says he nipped in, locked the door and was pulling his strides down when he felt the need to fart.'

'With unfortunate consequences?' suggests Paul.

Steve shrugs, resignedly.

'Yes. He took his boxers off and cleaned himself up and for some reason only my dad could explain, well, he pushed the window open and threw them out.'

Paul and Phil could no longer contain themselves and start giggling. They look up as Steve quietly leaves and start giggling again.

'Steve went to Jonno to resign this morning, and as Jonno's taking the day off, Steve left a letter on his desk. Jane told me and,' Phil points at the waste bin. Torn up notepaper is scattered on the top of the pizza boxes and coffee cups.

'Give it ten and we'll have a word.'

Steve's office door is ajar. He's unpinning cards and photos from his noticeboard and tossing them in a cardboard box.

'Are you nuts?' asks Paul.

'I can't stay here now,' says Steve disconsolately.

'Why not?'

'Everyone knows it was my dad.'

'Who's everyone?'

'Clayton, Brian, Christine, the girls.'

'Do they? I doubt it. Even if they suspect, they won't say anything. And I doubt Alan Sergeant is any the wiser.'

'He must suspect.'

'What, why?' asks Phil, 'Sergeant was at the other end of the table, your dad was perfectly behaved, no more full than anyone else, made his apologies and left. And that's it.'

'C'mon Steve, you know the game, just keep a straight face and your mouth shut. Harry's innocent until proven guilty. No one's said a word this morning, and nor will they. No one got hurt, the commercial looks great.'

'Maybe, Paul,' Steve concedes.

'Did your dad say anything else? Did anyone see him?'

'No, in his words, "I did a runner down the back stairs into the car park and scarpered, quick".'

'So, there you go.'

'Spoken to Cauliflower, Steve?'

'No, except to thank them and bring the schedule up to date.'

'Then there's nothing more to be said. If Sergeant brings it up, it won't be with us, it'll be down to Clayton. And his job is to keep the account on track.'

Steve slumps down into his chair, removes his glasses and wipes a hand over his eyes.

'Guys, I've got standards. Professional ethics, it's a personal thing. I let the agency down. The moment they said Brentham Studios I should have thought, twigged it.'

'Steve, Cauliflower use your dad because he's good, not because he follows through when he farts, and decorates cheese boards with his shitty boxer shorts just as the client is making a move on the cheddar.'

Paul and Phil start giggling again.

'No boys, I've resigned and that's it. I left Jonno a letter and—'

'It's torn up in my wastebasket, finito, all over, when are we going to see the cut, the girls will have to come so they're up to speed.'

Steve slowly turns to the overflowing waste bin in confirmation.

'Steve, one word, Kalamazoo.'

'Kalamazoo?'

'Reader Head Office, if they like the spots that's it, game, set and match. It's all Sergeant cares about.'

'I never asked,' says Phil, quietly changing the course of the conversation, 'how did you fix the fingernail?'

'There was a bit of money left in the budget; I couldn't fix it optically but we had a pick up pack shot to do on that Braithwaite's promotion. I piggybacked Woof. Got a hand model in, did a real tight close up of her opening the Woof pack, even tighter than the original. Didn't you notice, Phil?'

'I did wonder.'

'Did you bollocks,' mocks Paul.

'And you?'

'Touché.'

Steve concludes, 'Brian took Bruce out for a drink and confided to him that as his business was so important to G and W, the agency had paid for a reshoot.'

'Clever boy, that Brian.'

'Yeah. Paul, and now the hand close up gives Sergeant something to think about every time we make a Woof commercial.'

Steve replaces his glasses and smiles at last.

'Thanks, you blokes, that's given me a thought. I'll get a frame by frame of the sequence and give Sergeant a copy when we show him the cut of the second commercial. Oh yes, and by the way, Dad says he's making himself unavailable for the next G and W shoot, whenever and wherever that is.'

Chapter 70

'What are we going to do, then?' Phil looks around an office that hasn't changed much since Grimshaw and Welby opened.

He sees scarred desks, and chairs that have survived since the agency bought something a little more practical to replace the old director's chairs, now folded against the wall to be used by whichever guests could squeeze themselves into the office.

There is an old Dexion bookcase, one shelf tilting under its weight of advertising annuals where a mount has been lost, and a couple of Aunt Nora posters on the faded cream walls. The odd page torn from a magazine is pinned haphazardly into the plaster, along with some photographic contact sheets and photos of Paul and Phil on shoots.

It wasn't a place to invite clients, save those who suspected their money wasn't being properly spent and didn't mind treading in the odd discarded pizza box if they were to be reassured by the scruffy austerity.

'Bollocks.'

Paul looks at the ceiling.

'Fuck it.'

Phil looks at him enquiringly.

'We haven't been together long, we're starting to get some good work together, then a big shop not known for their tolerance of the creative muse gets their teeth into us.'

'A bit negative, Paul, we're set like jelly with some of our clients.'

'Phil, we've established a couple of campaigns. Anyone can pick them up and run with the themes, you know that's often the way when a campaign survives into a second year. And clients don't give a tinker's cuss who does their work, as long as it's OK.'

Paul habitually took refuge in the dark, introspective side of his personality.

'Paul, it's like there's a coal cellar under your house and you get in there and close the hatch when anything threatens you.'

'Phil, I don't see my way out. For a start, Argent won't allow relationships in their agencies, not unless you're married and in different departments. Either that or Jane will have to find a job somewhere else or you will, or you and I will.'

'Then we'd better start looking, get the book out there, such as it is.'

'Phil, they've disbanded the G and W board and already started remodelling the agency. I tried to get something out of Jonno the other day but all I got was platitudes. He's none the wiser. He's just getting his marriage together and he's going to be out of a job, or if he's not, he'll reporting to people who couldn't,' Paul shakes his head in frustration, 'fuck it, as of this moment, we'll be just another writer art director team in a big international agency.

'And there's talk, well it's a certainty they're going to absorb us into the Face group, Argent own them, rebrand us Face Argent and that the CD there will come out on top of the pile, when everyone knows Alf Bell hasn't any idea what's an idea.

'And they've got that big design offshoot, where they think they can do ads when they don't even understand advertising. It's like; it's like getting an electrician to do your plumbing just because they work on the same building. Have you ever heard their design CD talk about the role of ads? She doesn't get it.

'Terrific designer, maybe, but you don't design ads, they're not just pretty blocks of unreadable words reversed out of coloured backgrounds; ads are ideas, you still have to have a strategy and write and art direct them.'

Paul's spitting his words out incoherently. He starts balling the pages of his layout pad and hurling them at the already overloaded waste basket.

'I even heard someone in the pub call Jonno an old style CD the other day and it wasn't a compliment.'

'Shite, just because he puts up with people like us who live or die by our ideas.'

'Yes, but the stupid thing is we don't come from the background their guys do. We don't do formulas. We don't have execs who tell us how to do ads. We do the research before we write the ads, not after. We come from little old Grimshaw and Welby that shop in those old offices in Bohemian Soho that's been around a few years, not some glittering, big, international steel and glass and computer ridden ode to architecture, we work in an old style shop where the creatives still go to the pub lunchtimes; look at us, we still work in an office not workstations and have our ideas on layout pads.'

Paul gestures around the untidy excuse for an office.

'Do we look trendy, switched on?' he used the words sneeringly.

'It doesn't matter that we bloody know that it's the idea that counts, and how, not where you use it. Fuck the medium is the message, it fucking isn't.'

'But those guys are going to be our masters if all this goes ahead,' Phil comments morosely.

'True, my sheep shagging friend, true.'

Paul gets up, grabs Phil by both shoulders and shakes him.

'Yes, unless we get out of here pronto, before our integrity and self-respect go down the shitter.'

'Let's get out of here and down Reilly's, I can't stand all that gloating sympathy in the Feathers.'

'No, fuck it, it's our boozer; we go there, we drink there. Go and get Jane and I'll get the girls.'

'It's all happening a bit quickly. Cyn and I were taken around Face Argent headquarters this afternoon and even shown where we'd be sitting.'

Claire speaks quietly.

'It was like they were doing us a favour. All shiny not a spot of character, no pool table, there was a nice shiny coffee machine and no sign of our old pinball machine Freddy said was sent over. All very sharp design, though, I suppose you could get used to it. But then you saw the work on the walls. It's crap, and they don't even seem to know it is. Talked it up like you wouldn't believe.'

'Some of the design work is OK,' says Cyn, 'but Claire's right. Next to it was these ads with these sort of statement headlines that made no sense, or just crap metaphors with people on hang gliders jumping off buildings and talk of your product flying high.'

'So that rumour about the G and W offices being taken over by their media company, while we're absorbed into head office, is true,' Nigel observes.

'Absorbed, like beer into a carpet,' says Bitsa; dribbling a little from his glass for it to quickly disappear into the multi coloured long suffering swirls of the Feathers fake Axminster.

'Very poetic, very Irish, Bitsa,' says Paul.

'I notice Ralph and Michael haven't been in much lately,' says Nancy.

'Well, they're going to be OK, aren't they? On planes and up and down to Paris like a bride's nightie. And Clayton, too, though I know Christine will be having second thoughts and she hasn't been here long.'

Brian joins the group.

'What about you, boy boomerang?'

'Not sure; reckon I'll go with them, then see what it's like though I was in there today after Claire and Cyn for the account service intro. They were explaining their culture to us and they heard my accent and said very nicely they didn't like swearing in the office, they didn't seem to understand Poms swear more than us Aussies and they only ever have a drink after work Fridays and no one takes long lunches even when they're entertaining clients. But that's their culture, I suppose.'

'But it's not how Brian does business, is it possum?' says Claire, giving him an affectionate hug and a kiss on the temple.

'Steady on Claire, that's enough to get you a root down Bondi way, innit,' offers Bitsa.

'You really are a bunch of ignorant Pommy pricks,' says Brian cheerfully. 'Spider pockets too. Not one of you has offered me a beer since I came in and I'm—'

'Dry as a dead dingo's donger,' choruses the group.

'Same all round?' Brian turns towards the bar.

Chapter 71

Paul sits in his flat, looking around the sparsely furnished living room. Through the window a line of stolid, Edwardian red brick apartment buildings march evenly down the street.

He appraises a set of Richard Hamilton lithographs that have risen in value since he bought them; a palm in a plant pot, drooping fronds looking a bit dehydrated; a couple of large, squishy leather couches; a hi fi with a hybrid, valve amplifier, vinyl as well as CDs; an Apple Mackintosh perched on a pile of New Yorkers on the glass coffee table; novels spilling haphazardly from a bookcase. I'm a tick-a-style-box copywriter, he thinks to himself, morosely.

Paul smooths his hair slowly across his forehead and takes a sip of his 18-year-old cask strength Islay malt scotch. Even my drink looks like something out of an Esquire article on the hippest admen of Madison Avenue.

How many would be novelists are there in agencies, he ponders, *happy to take an inflated salary home, knowing full well, however much they kid themselves, that they're totally incapable of sitting down and penning a cogent, literate, graceful piece of real fiction after a day extolling the virtues of dog food? Me writer, me sham,* he says to himself.

Paul's capable of flagellating, eviscerating, self-loathing when he wants, which is often. He's fooling himself thinking what he's doing is real writing, and well he knows it. Listening to the Bill Evans on his hi fi, he wonders just what it would be like to sit at the piano in the Village Vanguard, spinning out chorus after chorus of pure musical argument, the bass player patiently prodding and hinting at new avenues he might explore while the drummer relentlessly drives him on, faithfully accenting his thoughts.

What satisfaction there must be in racing towards the end of a piece, tying up the harmonic loose ends, drawing it to a logical climax, wiping the brow, flexing the fingers, turning to the audience to acknowledge the patter of applause; aware now of the murmurs of conversation, the clink of glasses and then mumbling thank you, thank you, directing the applause to his rhythm section knowing he's actually achieved something; something highly, idiosyncratically *personal.*

And then to turn back to the keyboard wondering if you can better yourself? Paul taps morosely at his own keyboard, tracing a finger absently along the plastic. He's getting his "book" together. Book, he sneers, ad slang for a collection of old ads, assembled to casually impress so one might flick through them in front of an avaricious head-hunter or self-important creative director.

Oh, this one, you remember it, yes well, it did win a D&AD. Hey, that was the year you were on the TV jury, wasn't it? Haven't made it there myself yet, but—

They would both chuckle offhandedly, glow together in mutual self-congratulation.

Paul, your cynicism is degenerating into bitterness.

Bitter: earlier that evening Paul and Phil walked straight past the Feathers and down into Soho where Braithwaite's Bitter was a guest beer in the Dog and Duck. They stood on the pavement among the early evening drinkers.

'Crepuscule with Nellie,' Paul said, looking up at the slowly fading light softening the façades of nearby buildings. 'Twilight with Nellie, a song Thelonius Monk wrote for his wife,' he'd explained to Phil.

'Aye,' said Phil, disinterestedly. He'd shrugged his leather jacket up around his shoulders and looked at Paul, dark eyes intense under lowering eyebrows, "like couple of black sheep on't crag on't moor" as Paul described them.

'Paul, I know we said team, we'd go somewhere as a team, but you're senior to me, you could be creative director, on your own; you'd eat those ponces at Face Argent for breakfast. Or for tasting menu, like, you being you.'

Paul had smiled, ruefully. 'They're not going to give us a look in, Phil, we're enemy. Intruders. They don't want us, just our accounts. I mean, look at us, they've given us space in their building until all the details have been hammered out, but we're losing people already. Kaye, Lois, Sharon, they've gone into their accounts department, Bitsa's lost young Simon.'

Phil looked at him levelly.

'This is not me being bitter,' Paul continued, 'that's fact. Phil, you'll kill 'em in there, they're short of good art directors. I mean, look at the way they're talking to you, already. And I know what you're going to say, and OK, if you get a job offer on your own, I'm going to say to you, take it.'

'Ditto,' Phil had said quietly, and they clinked glasses.

Phil knew Paul didn't look far into the future, didn't see a future for himself, and didn't even want to try. Whereas Phil wanted a measured, sure, well scripted life, a wife, kids, nice place to live, nothing fancy, "don't put on airs and graces," his mum had said when he left for London, reaching up to twist his scarf around his neck and briefly putting her hand on his cheek, "remember you're an Arbuthnott."

Phil didn't see a solid, comfortable family life as some sort of cosy cliché. That's what he wanted. And he was growing closer and closer to Jane. Theirs wasn't just an office romance; the mere fact that they never spoke of the future, yet seemed so natural together, itself spoke of a future together.

Phil couldn't articulate it; he didn't set his sights too high. Paul and Phil said goodnight, quietly.

'Give us a hug, you daft sheep diddler bastard,' Paul had wrapped his arms round Phil for an awkward moment.

Phil responded, then, embarrassed, had disengaged himself. 'I'll take the glasses back,' before they went their separate ways.

Paul looks at his watch and absently picks up the phone. He'd to be outside himself, to be able to see his reaction to Bec when she answers. Then just as suddenly he realises what time it is and puts it down.

He'd couriered Bec a short book and reel the moment he got back to London. He feels faintly guilty, but Phil had brought it up, not him. And maybe a new job in a new country would give him some sort of focus, a new start.

He sloshes some more scotch into his glass, neat, and picks up the TV guide to find something mindless.

Chapter 72

'You've put your hair down.' Jonno's face assumes his hurt look, his tone slightly accusatory, 'is that how you, you dress for a meeting with the French? I saw that Marcel looking at you when we had that get together in the agency.'

Jenny turns away, colouring slightly. She'd put her hair up in a strict bun that morning, then looked at herself in the mirror, noticed she'd adopted her calculating Jenny expression and instinctively let her hair down before joining Jonno in the kitchen.

'Jonno,' she said in a surprised voice, 'you're not jealous, are you? Anyway, it's a meeting with Cordier, I doubt if the Argent people will come over.'

'But the deal's signed, isn't it? Braithwaite has sold out his birth right as Phil so quaintly put it.'

'God, Phil's so prehistoric,' says Jenny dismissively. 'A dinosaur. And I'll have to go back to my place tonight, Jonno, I only brought stuff for today and I have to go up north tomorrow. George is announcing everything to the brewery tomorrow and he wants me to help him—'

'Polish the turd?'

'Exactly, my clever little creative director. So you can go down and see wifey and what does Paul call them, the tin lids, tomorrow.'

'Alright, yes, well enjoy yourself. Do you want me to call a taxi?'

'No, the meeting's in the old G and W building, it's a nice morning, so I'll walk.'

'As long as no one—'

'Sees me? Does it matter? The whole agency knows we've been bonking, shagging.'

Jonno screws his face into an expression of distaste. 'You don't have to put it quite like that.'

'Well that's all it is, and you'd better get a wriggle on, might get called into the meeting.'

'I can hardly be seen coming in with you.'

Jenny shrugs. 'Don't see why not, everyone knows about us, and anyway most of G and W will be getting the chop in the next few weeks; those that haven't done a runner already. And don't give me your hurt, loyal to the troops look, you know it's going to happen.'

'Yes, I suppose so,' mutters Jonno, 'anyway, thanks for coming around last night. And staying. Nice surprise.'

Jenny softens for a moment, looking at him in his blue dressing gown, at his very white skinny legs projecting from below the hem, feet splayed. He thrusts his hands, fists clenched, into his pockets then, wondering why he'd done so, pulls them out again just as quickly.

'You're a nice guy, Jonno, under that pompous creative director skin. Too nice. See you.'

They kiss, Jonno opens the front door and she slips out. For a moment, his gaze lingers on Jenny's lean flanks outlined against her dress. His thoughts stray to the silken pearl French knickers he'd seen her slip into earlier as he walked past the open bathroom door.

'Oh god,' he sighs guiltily, closing the front door behind her.

The building is now unrecognisable as the old G and W offices. New signage is yet to go up but a reception area of steel and glass has been built where Grace's desk once stood. Wiring hangs where new TV screens will soon drive the receptionist mad with indifference as the Argent reel of international commercials plays interminably.

Jenny makes her way down a corridor, following the rough paper signs taped to the walls. Cordier/Argent/Braithwaite's they repeat. Jenny stashes her overnight case in a newly painted office and skirts new, empty, open plan areas before locating the boardroom.

The G and W granite table still holds pride of place, but skeletal chairs of chrome and taut leather are now grouped around it. Brian is carefully pushing down the plunger of a large pot of coffee.

'Morning, Jenny,' he says cheerfully, 'coffee? Our French friends are on their way.'

Jenny takes a seat, noting the number of pads and pencils, and the platter of croissants in the centre of the table.

'Stopped in Old Compton Street on the way in,' explains Brian, 'might as well make them feel at home.'

'Thanks, Brian, we will. Who's coming from the agency?'

'Marcel, and his assistant Charlotte. There'll be a couple from Cordier, and Ralph of course. I just rang Jonno, told him not to bother and that we'd see him later.'

'So we're off and running.'

'Yes, Freddy's still in Paris, I had a word with him this morning.'

Woke the bugger up. He doesn't add, but does grin.

'You're taking Cordier up to The Brewery tomorrow I believe for a courtesy visit. Freddy said I can come up if you need me, but Marcel will represent the agency. If you have any qualms, I'm—'

Brian looks around quickly; there are voices in the corridor. He smiles at her and steps into the doorway.

'In here, monsieurs,' he says with all the tortured intonation common to those Australians and English whose grasp of French is tentative to a guilty degree.

Jenny stands, brushing down her dress as Marcel ushers in a rather mousy girl with glasses in her early thirties followed by two grinning male Cordier executives, both in their late thirties she estimates, one with thinning hair, the other with thick, black hair neatly combed, both wearing grey suits and company ties adorned with corkscrews, bulging briefcases under their arms.

Why do clients always look like clients? Thinks Brian.

He's about to say, 'Ralph not with you?' when there's a loud clatter and a shout of 'fucking painters' before a red faced Ralph stumbles in.

He stoops to rub at a shin.

'Excuse my French, Charlotte, Jenny, how are you?'

Ralph exudes a new confidence, his normal stooped and harried look replaced by square shoulders and open smile. He doesn't even turn and give his characteristic let me escape out of the window look or run his hands through thinning hair now replaced by a closely shaved scalp; designer stubble darkening his cheeks.

Charlotte smiles a wan smile and Jenny reaches across to shake hands with Ralph and the Cordier executives.

'Alain Tracey, Franck Rolland,' explains Ralph.

Marcel steps forward and grasps Jenny's hand. He holds on to it, drawing her towards him, looking closely at her.

'Jenny, it is good to see you, again; to business,' he says, releasing her hand before motioning everyone to sit down.

Jenny looks at him and smiles, levelly, slowly, gazing straight into his eyes. She let her fingers linger in his for telling seconds before taking them away, drawing a nail across his palm.

'This is more a get together, we cannot have a planning meeting until Alain and Franck have seen the Braithwaite's Brewery, got a feel for the product, which we will do tomorrow.'

'Perhaps sooner, in the pub?' Says Alain, rubbing his hands in anticipation. Jenny smiles in confirmation."

'And we can start to see how we will plan and produce the advertising here, and maybe test whether we can introduce such a traditional beer into Europe.'

'Well, looking around Paris, it seems there was a time, around a century ago when the English Bass Ale was very popular among the demi monde and bourgeoisie of Paris,' offers Ralph. 'The Red Triangle of Bass can still be seen in some old café posters and, if I remember rightly, in Manet's famous painting, A Bar at the Folies Bergere in The Courtauld Collection, here in London.'

'A good point, Ralph, perhaps a niche market?'

'Perhaps the advertising might even hark back to then; to the Paris of the 19th century,' suggests Jenny with a thin smile at Ralph, 'nostalgic.'

'But in a forward looking kind of way, perhaps, Jenny?'

'Touché, Ralph,' Jenny concedes.

Alain and Franck look suitably puzzled by the banter and Brian explains, 'we have some concepts, ideas up our sleeves that, er, explore the past. We might revisit them and see if they are applicable or adaptable to a Parisian milieu, to today's café society, even the demi monde, as Ralph suggests, or perhaps prompt other thoughts.'

'I thought what we might do—'

Marcel butts in, 'before lunch, Ralph?' but looking at Jenny.

'Yes, good idea, what we might do is look at Braithwaite's ads over the last five years, give Alain and Franck a bit of background?'

Brian gets up and activates the new, electric blinds at the windows, while Ralph negotiates the new audio-visual set up. As the room darkens so, the large wall screen lights up. As the reel of old ads start, Marcel moves his chair back slightly behind and to the side of Jenny's.

About 30-seconds in, Jenny feels something touch the back of her bare calf. She jumps, coughs, leans forward to pick up her coffee cup as a silk-socked toe gently walks its way up her calf to the sensitive back of the knee, and then caresses it, back and forth.

She moves her leg to the very side of the chair and slides forward slightly in acceptance, as the toe works its way just above her knee and stops there, gently touching. It's impossible, given the position of the chairs, for Marcel to contort himself any further.

Jenny lets her left arm slip over the side of her chair, and moves it behind her, running her fingers under the cuff of Marcel's trouser leg, fingers stroking his shin. She, too, cannot reach any higher.

'Mmmm,' exclaims Marcel appreciatively.

'Yes, that was a rather good commercial, very successful, too,' whispers Ralph, turning around, 'One of the agency's better efforts.'

The reel finishes and Brian opens the blinds. Alain and Franck give an appreciative clap.

'Gentlemen, Charlotte, Jenny will give us a bit more background on Braithwaite's and we'll wander down to Soho for an aperitif before lunch. G and W, as was, has a bit of pull in Soho and we've arranged for one of our favourite pubs to put a keg of Braithwaite's Bitter on for us to sample. Jenny.'

Jenny rises to her feet, smoothing her dress down, and switches on the projector to reveal the first of her slides.

'Charlotte, gentlemen, Braithwaite's Brewery was founded in—'

Chapter 73

The G and W stalwarts are morosely, defiantly grouped in their usual corner of the Feathers. It's not a farewell Soho drink, as some staff have already left. And it's not a move many are celebrating. Grace is taking a holiday; Perfect, who shared some of Ralph's tasks with her, has promised to keep in touch.

Production company members entering the pub, some of whom who haven't contacted Steve Hayward in months, nod and smile their respects knowing that Steve and any G and W creatives who join Face Argent will soon be in reach of clients and accounts with burgeoning TV budgets.

'Fookin vultures,' mutters Phil.

'You'd think he'd have more sense,' says Paul, inclining his head towards a well-known producer on the other side of the bar who raises his glass to them. Steve smiles, sardonically raising his glass in return.

'Mind you. Steve, if I were you, I'd be over there establishing yourself at Face like a shot. Real budgets, international accounts—'

'Shithouse scripts,' interjects Cyn.

'So Cyn really is short for cynic?' asks Roddy innocently, prudently taking a step backwards.

Steve doesn't comment, he's been given a large cubicle in the Face Argent TV production department, and is already experiencing the range of reactions he'd predicted from their producers, which range from friendly acceptance, through quiet deference to his reputation, to outright hostility from those who feel threatened by his very presence.

'Jon Noonan?' enquires a voice, loudly.

The group, and several other patrons turn to the door. A courier stands there, holding a parcel. Jonno raises a finger and steps forward.

'I was told you'd be in here, sign here please, sir.'

Jonno puts his glass on a shelf by the door and signs, 'thank you,' before retrieving his drink and turning to the group, parcel under his arm.

'Well, open it, then,' says Cyn, holding out her hand for his glass.

'It might be personal,' says Jonno defensively, but he, like the rest of the group, has seen the large Big Apple Festival stamp on the parcel.

The Big Apple Festival is the American advertising industry's biggest, and most prestigious advertising awards.

'Oh alright, then.'

He rips open the parcel. It contains their last year's ad awards annual and a festival T-shirt.

'That's nice,' says Perfect.

'Read the letter,' says Claire, eagerly.

Jimmy takes the annual from Jonno and Perfect holds the T-shirt while Jonno opens the envelope. He starts reading to himself. Then sensing the tone of the letter and eagerness of his staff to know what it contains, does so out loud.

'To Jon Noonan, Executive Creative Director Face Argent. Bit premature,' he beams, face flushing, chest puffing peacock-like.

The group crowds in expectantly.

'Dear Jon, as Executive Creative Director of one of the world's fastest growing creative agencies, you'll be excited to hear that the Executive Committee of the Big Apple Festival has decided to assemble a small, separate, select jury of prominent international creative directors to decide upon a world's best for the year, to choose one piece of work that fully exemplifies the standard of work emanating from outside North America.

'Jury members who've agreed to meet in New York so far include Alberto Castagna for South America, Jonty Simmons for South Africa, A.P. Singh for India, with Europe to be confirmed after the D&AD Awards.'

Jonno pauses theatrically for a moment and reaching for his drink, takes a satisfied sip.

'Wow,' exclaims Jimmy, impressed.

'Nice one, Jonno,' says Paul in anticipation.

Jonno clears his throat and returns to his task.

'And representing Asia Pacific Tony Yu from Singapore, Bruce Tompkins from New Zealand and Janice O'Sullivan from Australia.'

'Brother Trev's CD, Jonno,' confirms Brian. 'She's the best. Paul and Phil worked with her in SF. Sorry, Jonno.'

Jonno clears his throat again to draw attention back to him, holding the letter up like a town crier reading an important announcement.

'Jonno, as a senior representative of the UK Industry, we wonder—'

Jonno's voice starts to falter, the volume level dropping.

'Go on, Jonno,' encourages Cyn.

Jonno's voice has gone croaky.

'We, we wonder if you might know the whereabouts of Charles "Crash" Cranshaw, your illustrious predecessor at Grimshaw and Welby,' Jonno's voice is now a constricted whisper, 'as we feel he best exemplifies the qualities we seek of the United Kingdom's representative jurist.'

Jonno's voice dies away. Colour drains from his cheeks only to angrily return as he stares at the letter, willing the contents to change. He stands silently for a moment, looking at it then shakes it, as if it were stuck to his fingers.

'You, you bastards, you utter prick bastards.'

He looks beadily, steadily, around the group.

'What, Jonno?' enquires Claire, innocently.

'It's a wind up, isn't it? A fucking wind up, and you got me, you bastards.'

'One would hope it's a wind up, Jonno,' says Nigel thoughtfully.

Jonno's gaze alights on Paul and Phil, but their expressions say they're genuinely surprised and consternation reigns, segueing to delight as they look back at him.

'It is, isn't it?'

He turns again, to see Claire's back as she makes her way to the ladies, her hand raised in a casual wave, which she then changes, thumb to forefinger and twists her fingers, a hand turning a key. A wind up.

'Claire, Cyn,' Jonno spits.

Cyn has made her way to the bar and turns.

'Large G 'n' T, Jonno?' she asks coolly.

Jonno's expression turns to one of admiration.

'You got me, you two tarts, you got me and it wasn't even you two,' he says to Phil and Paul, slowly, incredulously, shaking his head. 'It wasn't even you.'

Even though he's the victim Jonno, master of the wind up, savours the brilliance of the setup, examining and admiring the devious machinations.

'Your friend, Rebecca in New York, Cyn, and yours.' He turns slowly to Paul, but Paul raises his hands in an "I know nothing" gesture, smiling and slowly shaking his head.

Jonno takes the proffered glass from Cyn and silently raises it in a toast, bowing slightly in acknowledgement.

'I can't believe you did that, Cyn, Claire, where's Claire, it's really asking for trouble.'

Phil looks at Jonno. Six months ago, the pompous, self-important creative director wouldn't have been quite so magnanimous.

'His break up, and the takeover has done him some good,' Jane had commented earlier, 'he's become a little more—'

'Human?' conceded Phil.

His pub audience captive, Jonno continues thinking out loud, 'Cyn, you got your friend Rebecca to get you the stuff, didn't you? I bet she even nicked some headed paper, somehow; you crafty, brilliant. Mind you.'

Paul mutters in an aside to Phil, 'Bec got a gig working on the promos and videos for their awards show.'

Jonno's dark eyes gleam, and the familiar, malignant look scrawls itself across his features.

'Mmmm,' he slowly wags his finger at Cyn in a "watch out" gesture. 'Mmm.'

'Can I keep the annual, Jonno?' asks Jimmy.

'No, you bloody can't,' says Claire, returning from the ladies.

'Aaah, yours is it, Claire?' exclaims Jonno, turning his malevolent gaze on her. 'Claire and Cyn, mistresses of the female product, the washing powders and the shower gels, the tampons and bathroom cleaners, the washing machines and fridges, the new housewives of Face Argent.'

Cyn and Claire look at him, silently.

'Jonno, you wouldn't, that's cruelty beyond a wind up,' says Paul.

They all know immediately what Jonno's implying. Face Argent's whole agency financial structure sits on a bottom line of large accounts that follow the client's dictates to the letter, that offer no creative licence whatsoever, that hew close to unrelenting, old-fashioned, "a woman's place is in the home" formulae.

A word from Jonno to Face management that he has a team skilled at giving those clients exactly what they want and, 'No Jonno,' says Bitsa, firmly. 'Cyn and Claire wouldn't last one client meeting with that lot.'

'Just a thought, just a thought but I'll have others, won't I girls?'

Paul takes a sip of his drink, picks the letter up off the table and starts giggling. Phil takes it from his hand and starts laughing, and then everyone, even Jonno, belatedly joins in. It's a release, a reaction, slightly hysterical, to the unsettling events of the last few weeks.

'I hate to think what Jonno will dream up for Cyn and Claire.'

Paul slowly shakes his shaggy mane. 'Phil, he's got enough to worry about at the moment.'

Phil joins Jane in a corner. Paul turns to acknowledge Brian as he appears at the door of the pub. Paul sees Brian glance at Jonno and quickly look away. Brian joins Paul at the bar.

'Pint, Brian?'

'Yes, I could murder one. Not that we haven't had several already.'

'We?'

'Ralph and I took Alain and Franck down to the Dog and Duck to try the Braithwaite's and can they put it away. Must have livers like sponges. That was before we went to lunch, of course. If you didn't know they worked for a booze company, you'd find out pretty quickly.

'They were onto the wine list at Chambres like rats up a drainpipe. Mind you, they know their stuff. Then we went to the French for afters. I was taking it real slow, got to go out tonight.'

'Wasn't what's his name?'

'Marcel?'

'And Jenny at the meeting?'

'In a manner of speaking.'

Brian takes Paul's elbow and turns him around slightly, so Brian's back is to Jonno. He speaks quietly, confidentially.

'Marcel was sort of eyeballing Jenny all through in the meeting. Actually, it was like a starved shithouse rat looks at a runny Camembert. Or a pommy at a chip.'

Brian pauses to take a long pull at his pint. Knowing how Brian's stories unfold themselves, Paul judiciously keeps quiet. However, to deliciously delay the denouement, Paul suggests, 'Or how brother Trev looks at a meat pie?'

'Exactly. Then at the end of the meeting, Jenny announces she'll bring Marcel down the pub but she has to powder her nose first. So Ralph and the Cordier guys go on ahead. I stay behind because I want to take a quick shufti round the office for some gym gear I thought I'd left behind, but no luck. When I came out, I saw Marcel going into the dunny.' Brian pauses, meaningfully.

Paul shrugs, 'and?'

'The ladies, Paul. I lingered at the door for a few moments; the two of them were in there.'

'As in, Marcel was in, in there?'

'Yeah, sounded like they were trying to demolish the joint. You've heard the Aussie expression, bangs like a shithouse door?'

Brian and Paul share evil grins.

'Didn't hang around, legged it down to the Dog and Duck before it got me excited.'

'Dirty bastards, them and you. How long after?'

'I caught up with Ralph and the guys and Marcel and Jenny turned up about half, three quarters of an hour later. Said Marcel had to get something from the hotel, and call Paris. Alain and Franck didn't mind, just shrugged and indicated they were quite happy in the pub.'

'Blimey.' They turn to look at Jonno.

'Poor sod,' they mutter in unison.

Actually no, it's good, good, it's good, thinks Paul.

Jonno sees they're looking over and indicates they should join him.

'Good meeting, Brian?'

'And lunch, Jonno, and aperitifs, and afters. Left Marcel bedding down the account with Jenny.'

Paul winces at the innuendo.

'So Marcel was there.' Jonno's face darkens, 'and Jenny's still with him?' His jealousy is transparent.

'It's in her interest to stick close to Marcel and Cordier, Jonno. And in your interest,' Paul casually points out.

'Mine?' asks Jonno suspiciously.

'You're the CD on the account, you're responsible for the last Braithwaite's campaign, the Argent guys like it, you've got to look after yourself a bit at the moment.'

'Oh, yes,' Jonno concedes. 'Suppose so.'

'Politics Jonno, politics. The Cordier account's a biggie. As Ralph said, Braithwaite's is small beer to Argent. But you've proved you do the sort of work Face like.'

Jonno's eyes narrow.

'Jonno, that's a fact, and anyway you can piss all over the Face crowd but only if Argent say so and back you.'

Jonno looks reflective, then smiles, 'imagine if you pulled a wind up at Face.'

'They wouldn't understand, Jonno,' says Brian. He gestures dramatically. 'It would go straight over their heads, whooshka.'

'Put Tabasco in their piles cream and they'd sue you.'

Jonno has the good grace to laugh and riposte.

'Send someone on an expensive wild goose chase and they'll—'

'I'll get them in,' says Brian.

'Seeing Carol and the kids tonight, Jonno?' Paul quickly puts in.

'Oh yes, thanks, Paul. Scrub the drink Brian, I'd better get on my bike.'

Chapter 74

Next Monday morning, the G and W people wander into the Face Argent building in Holborn. There's a large sign on the front of the building.

"It's time to get the G and W out of Soho."

'Blimey, is that the best they can do?' says Paul to Phil, screwing up his face in disgust. 'Could at least have let us write it.'

Jane tightens her grip on Phil's arm. They'd met for breakfast in Soho before making their way across town.

'C'mon you two it's not bad, give them a chance. At least they're trying.'

'Very,' grunts Phil.

They walk into a large, high ceilinged marble foyer and amble towards a series of gates like a cross between a tube station and airport security. At the reception desk, a large man in a dark suit swiftly stands.

'Excuse me, are you from Grimsby?'

'Grimshaw and Welby,' supplies Jane amiably.

'Oh sorry, yes, I have to give you your security passes. Did you bring identification?'

'Blimey, what is this?' reacts Paul, irritably.

'Paul,' cautions Jane, 'he's only doing his job.'

She looks reproachfully at Paul.

'Yeh, but we weren't told.'

The three approach the desk where the commissionaire is now going through a list. Paul and Phil obligingly put their driving licences down on the counter, Jane adds a Visa card. The man picks out three cards from a box and hands them out.

'Now if you could all sign for them, just use them to get in and out of the building.'

'Thanks,' says Phil, 'sorry if we were a bit shirty, James.'

Phil has read the commissionaire's name card. James smiles, obviously unused to being called by name.

'That's OK, sir.'

'James; me Phil, Paul, Jane,' indicates Phil as they turn towards the lifts.

They go through the barrier and take the lift to the ninth floor.

Michael Michaels precedes them. He knows where his office is, a cubicle in a line of equal sized boxes along a wall. At least there's a fine view across the city to St Pauls. He'd come in the previous week for "orientation".

His pedantic, obsequious, defensive, client-is-always-right attitude suits the Face corporate mentality, where fresh ideas and creativity came a long second behind endless research and focus groups and management assessment of ideas. Whereas at G and W, unless there was a legal, ethical or tactical reason, Jonno was sole arbiter of the creative work that went to client.

There's a scattering of envelopes on Michael's desk, left neatly tidied after last Friday's orientation. There's even a boxed bottle of Chivas Regal with a card.

'Oh, a welcome, that's nice of them,' Michael says to himself, self-esteem bubbling in his chest.

He looks around to see if any of the other Face people, Face Faces, as he has *cleverly* dubbed them, proudly including himself and dutifully arriving on the dot of 8 am, can see what he's doing.

Michael nods and smiles in acknowledgement as two suited figures wave as they walk past. Michael points at the box and raises his eyebrows, but they have gone.

Michael carefully selects an envelope, opens it and reads the card inside.

Sorry Michael, really enjoyed working with you. It's signed, *Cynthia and Claire.*

Michael flushes and looks around furtively. No one is watching. He unfolds a sheet of layout pad. On it is scrawled, *Nah, brother, that's cruel shit, innit. The bastards. Best Bitsa.*

He pulls the card off the box of Chivas. *Michael, we had our differences but no one deserves treatment like this, least of all you. Regards, Paul and Phil.*

Michael's vision blurs. His shoulders shake as he opens yet another card. *Michael, they said the good guys would go first. Commiserations, you taught me a lot, thanks Nigel.*

Now Michael is angry, indignant. His left eye is twitching, madly. He steps out of his office, turns one way and then the other, unsure what to do. He sees Roddy and Jimmy standing idly by a partition on the other side of the floor, looking across at him. Roddy waves his hand, beckoning him over. Michael doesn't want to talk to them. He storms off down the corridor, trying to look purposeful.

In the corner is the main boardroom. A sign on the door says Meeting in Progress. Michael pauses for a moment. From inside he can hear voices, one of which he identifies as Freddy's. From behind him, he hears Roddy's urgent voice calling, 'Michael, Michael.'

Ignoring Roddy, Michael throws open the door. Grouped at the end of the table are the senior Face management and Freddy Grimshaw. Confronted by a shaking, obviously unsettled figure with a hurt, angry expression they look up, surprised.

Sir Francis Eccles MP, Group Chairman, raises his heavily jowled head, clearly affronted by the intrusion. Trevor Kane, the MD turns, face questioning as does CEO Janice Edwards who lifts her glasses from the table and puts them on. Thin, weasel faced CFO Charles Driscoll looks up slowly from a sheaf of figures.

Freddy is first to react, rising to his feet. 'Michael,' he asks, 'Michael, what is it?' There's silence for a moment. 'Michael, are you alright?'

Had Michael Michaels at that moment thought rationally and coolly, he would have seen the genuine surprise and puzzlement around the table. But as Freddy confirmed later, Michael had already totally lost it.

All he sees is indifference and annoyance at his interruption.

'You bastards,' Michael snarls. 'You cold hearted bastards, and you, of all people, Freddy, after all I've done for you, you bastards. You couldn't even face me.'

The group sit there, startled.

'Michael,' says Freddy, alarm in his voice, 'what is it?'

But Michael, noting their stunned reaction turns, stops for a second, and stumbles out. Freddy turns to the group. 'I'd better,' Sir Francis waves him dismissively towards the door.

Freddy hurries out, to see Michael stomping down the corridor only to stop suddenly at his cubicle, point at his desk, and slump, grasping the doorjamb.

Freddy slows as he reaches Michael and puts a hand gently on his heaving shoulder.

Michael is shaking with anger, trying to contain himself as interested faces appear over partitions and secretaries, newly arrived at their workstations, pretend not to look. Freddy shepherds Michael into his cubicle, sits him down and perches on the side of the desk to obscure the view of onlookers.

'They, they, I thought the bastards had,' Michael, shoulders slumped, gestures towards his desktop.

'What, Michael?' Asks Freddy, 'what am I, what are they supposed to have done?'

Michael gestures at his desktop, and looks forlornly at Freddy. It's as clear, clean and anally neat as he'd left it the previous Friday. He tugs open a desk drawer and retrieved a couple of tissues from a box and dabs at his eyes.

Then his body stiffens, and he raises his head, his eye starts twitching madly again and his face sets in an angry expression as the full import of the situation begins to dawn on him. He thinks back to Roddy's urgent call as he stormed into the boardroom.

'The childish, stupid, the irresponsible, the,' he says to himself, the volume of his voice growing.

'Freddy, those stupid juniors have—'

On the ninth floor, Paul and Phil stroll towards their new office, grudgingly stopping to accept the waves of welcome and warming to the handshakes from art directors and writers; though it's noticeable that the degree of welcome varies, as Steve has gleefully reported.

Jimmy and Roddy are at their office door, jumping from foot to foot and looking very worried, Jimmy occasionally glances towards the lift doors. They both start talking at once.

'We've really done it, fucked it, messed it up, put the kibosh on it.'

Paul puts his fingers to his lips and he and Phil walk into their office, gesturing for Roddy and Jimmy to follow. The boys follow them closely, agitated.

'Roddy, explain, what is it?'

Roddy's silent.

'Jimmy, what have you done?'

'It's, you know all the wind ups lately?'

Paul and Phil both nod, slowly.

'We pulled one, just for the laugh, on Michael.'

'Michael?'

'He'd been getting us to rewrite our copy again and again, saying it was the way they did it at Face, and it's been upsetting Nige as well, and we didn't want to bother Jonno, so we thought we'd have a laugh with him.'

Jimmy pulls some crumpled cards from his pockets and hands them mutely to Paul and Phil.

'We didn't mean—'

Paul raises his hand to still them. Phil and Paul read the cards, swapping them, and start giggling.

'Fuck, he didn't fall for this. It's a bit transparent, innit, as Bitsa would say?'

'I suppose you believe what you want to believe,' Phil suggests, 'fuck you'd better get down there and explain before it all goes pear shaped and Michaels starts—'

'Too late, he already has,' replies a forlorn Jimmy.

'What d'you mean?' asks Phil, voice growing concerned and serious.

Roddy pulls at the scarf looped casually around his shoulders. He'd spent some time deciding on the right balance of wardrobe for his first appearance in his new agency.

'The big wigs were holding a management meeting and Michaels jumped in there and sounded off at them.'

'We tried to stop him.'

'You could hear him all down the corridor, shouting at them, calling them heartless bastards, or something.'

'Jesus,' says Paul, alternately appalled, amused, impressed and angry.

'I don't know whether to be appalled, amused, impressed or angry. Probably all of those, fuck, you didn't think it through, did you?'

'We'd had enough of Michaels,' says Jimmy staunchly, defensively.

'What do you think Jonno's here for?' Demands Paul. 'Or me, or Phil? Creative is king at G and W. We'd have had a word.'

'Bit late now,' says Jimmy, morosely.

'Yeah,' says Paul. 'Mind you, you'd think Michaels would have acted a little more, you know, thought it through, how to handle it.'

The four of them stand there for a moment. The phone rings. Paul hesitates a moment then picks it up.

'Paul Johnstone.'

'Paul. Freddy, get down here and bring Jonno, if you can find him.'

Phil mouths something at Paul.

'Jonno's out doing a recording, Freddy.'

'Then you'll have to do.' He rings off.

'Freddy,' explains Paul redundantly as he puts the phone down.

'We'll come with you,' says Roddy. Jim nods agreement at the offer.

Paul, Roddy and Jim walk down the corridor to Freddy's new office. They glance across the open plan area in the centre of the floor to Michael's cubicle. Empty. Paul knocks on Freddy's door, an unnecessary gesture as Freddy can see him over the frosted glass panel that extends halfway up the window. He beckons and the three sheepishly enter.

There's no antique silk carpet, or large desk. The furniture is perfunctory modern, following the skeletal stainless steel, glass and chrome motif that characterises Face Argent.

'Soulless, impersonal,' as Phil deems it.

The three stand in front of Freddy's desk.

'I'm tired,' says Freddy, 'of these practical jokes. And seeing you, Jimmy and you, Roddy have come down with Paul, I can see you're accepting responsibility.'

Freddy looks at them, his face set, stern. He taps his fountain pen on the desk blotter, the sole remnant of his G and W office.

'I suspect, actually I've no doubt that, somehow, you persuaded Michael that he has no place here, that his job has gone.'

There was quiet for a moment, as Freddy looked at the three. The two boys' faces are downcast.

'And I must assume you weren't party to this Paul, for even you would have seen the stupidity of it.'

Paul looks steadily, slightly sadly back at him.

'I'm not interested in the mechanics the damage has been done.'

There's silence. They all knew whatever Freddy said to Face management would make no difference. He no longer has any power, or influence. He's emasculated, the word he used to his wife Polly and that, in itself infuriates him. He's out of the place. He'll take "gardening leave". He'll agree not to do anything in the field of advertising, or approach any of his old clients for a couple of years.

He no longer has any authority. In the eyes of his new bosses, Michaels displayed weakness, instability, a lack of judgement. He's a hysteric, insulting, couldn't handle pressure or adversity. No matter what the circumstances, he hadn't shown any amount of the "strength, the backbone, the degree of personal fortitude we demand at Face Argent" as Trevor Cane acidly put it to his fellow board members.

Though the sad fact is Michael is perfect for Face Argent, their style and approach to account handling and clients. Freddy emphasised this when he explained Michael had been under a lot of pressure lately, misinterpreted a situation, thought he no longer had a job; it had sounded weak, lame, and the more he pleaded for Michael, the more Freddy realised he was demeaning himself.

Michael was an important member of the G and W team but had, as everyone agreed, "blown it". Whether his clients would support him, whether they'd stay with Face if Michael were no longer handling their business was debatable. For the moment, it's best that Michael isn't seen in the Face offices.

All this flew through the heads of the trio in Freddy's office. Freddy swung his chair towards the window and spoke without looking at them.

'Roddy, Jimmy, and you Paul; once upon a time, I hired someone called Crash Cranshaw, invited him into Grimshaw and Welby with open arms and in doing so drew anarchy into the agency. Those were the days when, and I've heard you, Paul, state it, "creative was king."

'Unfortunately, many of our clients didn't agree and left us, and with them many good G and W people had to go, too, much as I tried to cut overheads and keep them.

'It's only due to the efforts of people like Michael Michaels in attracting and holding down our bigger yet more boring clients that you creative souls still have the licence to do as you please on some of the other accounts, and to behave in a louche, or irresponsible manner.

'No, scrub that, I went into bat on many occasions for many of our more lateral and creative concepts because I believed they were, and are what's best for advertising, our clients and the consumer. But the fact remains, we couldn't and wouldn't survive without the Michael Michaels of this world.'

Paul, Jimmy and Roddy stand stock still, listening.

'So, I don't care how much you like Michael, you may hold him in contempt, but in a way he guarantees your jobs and it's the solidity of his accounts that gave, that give you lot the springboard to go on to bigger and brighter things. Most probably now, elsewhere.'

Freddy spins to face them.

'Michael could, maybe will still have a career here, in fact the chagrin is he's the best suited of all of us for this place.'

Freddy pauses, calming down, his voice less forceful. He runs his hand across his face and draws breath.

'Jimmy, Roddy, at the moment you two have put his livelihood in jeopardy, without harming your own one skerrick. Perhaps you'd like to explain that to Mrs Michaels?

'Anyway, hell, you're young, you're still in thrall to the glamour of your job, you thought you were bullet proof and who cares or gives a fuck what account service do, or think?'

Roddy and Jimmy stand quietly, wincing as Freddy's words bite home.

'Had you talked to Paul first, I've no doubt he'd have said this isn't a good time for pranks, however you feel about account service in general or Michael in particular. You, no doubt Paul, might think it faintly amusing as it exposed Michael's sensibilities, but you at least understand the politics of advertising and where your bread is buttered.'

Freddy pauses again, in turn looking at the three.

'I just spent fifteen minutes defending Michael to the principals of Face without, it should be said, any success at all. Thanks to you two, the jury is out where his future is concerned, and what's left of G and W's reputation has suffered accordingly.

'If you Jimmy, and you Roddy think you have a future here, get your heads down and carve one out. And don't fall on your own swords, it'll do you no good to resign, that'll just be three careers lost through one stupid, irresponsible prank.'

Freddy makes a curt, dismissive gesture. 'Now get out, all of you.' Freddy rises to his feet. 'Actually, Paul, I want a word with you, let's get out of this designer nightmare and get ourselves a coffee somewhere. You've no doubt tracked down the local gun barista.'

Chapter 75

Phil positively bounces his way up Jane's front path. His habitual approach is an uncoordinated shamble but it's a lovely, balmy Saturday afternoon with a cosseting warmth to the sun. He greets a neighbour doing some pruning and rings a tattoo on Jane's front door.

She appears instantly, putting a finger to her lips and forcing Phil backwards as she gently closes the front door behind her.

'Now't wrong is there, love?'

'Mum's gone to bed with a headache.'

'Well then—'

'No, it's worse than that.'

Jane kisses Phil gently on the lips then links her arm through his. 'Let's walk down the pub.'

On the way, she tells Phil what happened.

'Aunt Glad suddenly appeared this morning. I was out getting some shopping. Evidently, she'd heard Lily was starting to get out of the house and suggested they went into town for a coffee. Mum says she was up for it, but the moment they got in Aunt Glad's car, Glad started fussing. You know, "now you're going to be alright, aren't you, Lily? Don't hesitate to tell me if you feel funny." That sort of thing.

'And Mum said Glad's erratic driving and running commentary didn't help, either. Mum says she only just got her to stop at a zebra crossing where this old dear was already halfway across the road. Lily was a bag of nerves even before they sat down for coffee. Then it was all Aunt Glad asking loudly, "you're looking a bit peaky, love, have you taken your pills? Oooh, you don't take pills. I thought you'd be taking pills for a condition like yours," and Lily's trying to shush her.

'Lily said she was just relaxing and starting to enjoy herself when the waitress came up and Aunt Glad started confiding in her about Mum, and Mum said everyone else could hear and all the nosey heads were turning, you know the sort of sniffy crowd you get in those tearooms and Aunt Glad's all, "Oh, isn't she's doing well, well you are, aren't you Lily, what a love," Mum does a great Aunt Glad imitation, "suffers from that phobia, don't you Lily, scared of leaving the house, what d'you call it, but looking at her, you wouldn't know it, would you?" all that sort of stuff, and Mum's too nice to tell her to shut up. Mum said she just smiled at everyone until they looked away.'

'Sounds like she was coping well?'

'She was, but then of course, the more she starts enjoying herself, the more Aunt Glad's worrying Mum might flip and it's all, "drink up Lily or Jane will wonder where you are." Mum pointed out she'd left a note, but Glad's up on her feet and, "come on Lily, let's get you home," like she's some sort of invalid so Mum's out of there and back in the car and Aunt Glad's driving gets all the more erratic on the way home.'

Jane pauses for breath and plunges on. 'Mum couldn't wait to get out of the car and back in the house: which Aunt Glad took all wrong of course. Just as well I was home by then. Mum just came in, shaking her head and rolling her eyes. I suppose it was funny in a way.'

'No wonder she got a headache, but mebbe it's really positive. Isn't it? Lily's reaction was normal. Because she didn't react, she didn't have an attack. Your Aunt Glad pressed all the wrong buttons, but still Lily's alright. And what's so wrong with a lie down on a Saturday afternoon?'

He nudges Jane and nibbles her ear. She narrows her eyes at a recent memory, 'as long as it's not in the back seat of your car, again.'

Chapter 76

The G and W remnants have found themselves a pub. The Nine Bells is small, hidden down an alley, a warren of dark higgledy-piggledy rooms, nooks and crannies, uneven floors, gnarled wood, pitted mirrors and worn bars; it looks much as it must have three centuries ago.

Nominally a haunt of the legal profession, Paul and Phil have quickly become regulars and the rest of the crowd has followed. Even Clayton has joined them. Though Paul suspects Clayton, the favoured son of an old farming family with considerable holdings, his sculpted hair and bespoke suits and shoes, handkerchief flowing from his top pocket, feels very much at home among the silks and solicitors who frequent the front bar.

Unwinding after a couple of Friday night drinks, Paul asks Clayton how he felt it was going for him at Face.

'Same clients, same problems, same opportunities, Paul, not been offered any of their clients so far but putting my irons in the fire with Cordier. And I'm not forgetting you boys. Did drop a bit of a gooly today, though. You, you, haven't heard?'

'Nigel, carrier of all good tidings, hasn't graced us with his presence yet, Clayton and nor have the carriers of all scurrilous goss, the girls. And unless they've heard something and it's not as if we have that much contact with the Face aches yet, no. And nor are we likely to.'

Paul knew Clayton liked things explained at length. Clayton looks around. There are just the three of them in the small bar.

'Goodo, well yes, no, maybe not.'

He clams up as if he hasn't said anything.

'C'mon, Clayton, it's only us, do tell, especially if it's funny. We won't repeat it, it's your story.'

Just for a moment, Clayton's pompous façade cracks. He becomes the naughty ex-public schoolboy, the Clayton who once stirred his boss's tea with his penis.

'Well, you know, you know how it is.'

'Tell us.'

'I was walking along the exec floor just after lunch and I felt the need to pootle.'

'Pootle?' enquires Phil.

'He means fart,' explains Paul.

'Oh.'

'Yes, well, I was walking along the corridor, as I said, and Charlotte, Trevor and Janice's PA, was pushing this trolley covered with files towards me. You know how we're all shuffling offices around. Anyway, it meant I would have had to backtrack, or flatten myself against the wall to let her pass.'

Paul and Phil, used by now to Clayton's endless obfuscation, patiently wait for him to go on.

'Well, what I see just ahead of me but the door of one of those boardrooms they use as viewing theatres. The door is ajar and it's dark in there.' Clayton pauses for effect.

'I time it so just as Charlotte reaches me, I'm able to back into the room as I greet her. Which, while giving her the opportunity to pass me by, also affords me the opportunity to pass wind, to—'

'Drop your guts.'

'Absolutely, which I did, chaps, I must admit at great, rather satisfying and I must say noisy, length.' Clayton pauses and exhales at the memory.

'And?' prompts Paul.

'Well that's it, Paul, I'm suddenly aware of all this rustling and shuffling and the lights come on in the room. I'm sort of framed by the door and there's the whole of the Boost Petroleum account team in there, looking at me, aghast. They'd been watching a reel of commercials.'

'Fantastic, Clayton, great, that's really funny,' react Phil and Paul. 'What happened next?'

Phil's voice dies away as Cyn and Claire enter the pub, attracting glances from the legal fraternity in the front bar.

'Have we missed something?'

'Clayton was telling a joke,' says Paul dismissively, 'it wasn't that funny.'

'No,' agreed Clayton, 'more an anecdote really, about, mmm, my days at university. What can I get to drink for you delightful creative ladies?'

Chapter 77

Jane emerges from the cubicle in the ladies' loo at Face, wiping her lips with a tissue. There's a thin, acrid taste in her mouth. She hurries to a basin to splash some cold water on her face and fix her makeup. She'd felt nauseous on the train on the way in and only just made it into the office toilet before she threw up. A middle aged woman is looking at her in the mirror.

'Feel better love, you're from G and W, aren't you? Jane, isn't it?'

Jane nods.

'I'm Felicity. From accounts. Heard you in there and thought I'd better hang back see if you're OK.'

'Thanks.' Jane is genuinely touched. Felicity, short, plump, motherly, with dimpled cheeks, has a warm and solicitous manner.

Felicity continues, 'it gets better love, after the first few months, well it did for me with my first, but you'd have been told that, wouldn't you?'

She continues, ignoring the perplexed, and then slightly shocked look dawning on Jane's face.

'Pop in and see us, Jane, anytime. Felicity. Gartner. See you.'

She bustles out. Jane turns and leans towards the mirror, looking at herself closely. 'I'm not?'

She was late with her period. Had missed one, in fact, but then her periods had been irregular, all over the place ever since she'd come off the pill when she left her flat to move in with Lily. Hardly worth taking them, she'd thought.

But then, belatedly, she started again as her relationship with Phil became more serious. *I can't be.* Over the last couple of months, *the expression of our romance* as she explained it to herself, had changed. She'd never been *sexually adventurous*, in fact her partners up to then had been, *inept*, would be the word she used.

Clumsy, shy, immature, however as she admitted to herself, however much she'd read about sex, or had become aware of it, she'd never been with anyone who was particularly *good at it*. For instance, she'd never enjoyed cunnilingus before she met Phil. And her attempts at fellatio had been awkward and unsatisfactory, at best.

But as she'd become more comfortable and more trusting with Phil and realised that at times sex can even be funny, that you can laugh about it, they'd become a lot more *adventurous*. Yes, that was the word. And Jane had discovered a delicious, unexpected *frisson* in having sex in places where one might be discovered.

Against a tree in the local park, in Phil's car, and once against the kitchen sink, Lily upstairs, with Phil's hand over Jane's mouth to stifle any involuntary gasps and cries.

'Makes a change from washing oop,' as Phil put it.

So now, with the other women at Face taking her nickname of Perfect at face value and probably thinking of her as rather prim and straight laced, she could sit at her desk, smile in a perfect manner and think, *how little you know.*

Phil ambles, shambles, into Jane's office, looking every inch the art directed art director with his designer leather jacket and tousled just-the-right-length mop of hair.

'Morning, Philip,' says Jane brightly, formally, 'what can I do for you?'

She glances quickly through the goldfish bowl glass out at the junior account execs and assistants in their cubicles on the open plan floor. Her relationship with Phil's not generally known, not that anyone has shown any discernible interest. Jane shares her small office with the other senior PA, Charlotte, who hardly ever seems to be at her desk.

'OK?' enquires Phil. 'You look a bit peaky.'

'It's the air conditioning here, not used to it.' *Phil we need to talk, but not now.* 'Jonno's off being briefed on his new responsibilities. He's inherited Alf Bell's groups since Alf's elevation,' Jane flutters her hands like a bird taking wing, 'into the Face Group Executive CD stratosphere.'

'As long as Jonno can handle the politics.'

'He'll be OK. But it'll be pretty full on. I heard Scotty what's-his-face talking about absorbing Jonno into the face culture, how his Braithwaite's ad showed he was halfway there.'

'Culture? There's now't. They bain't got enough to turn pot of yogurt sour.'

Phil is purposely keeping well away from Jane's desk, absently jockeying the drawer of a filing cabinet in and out as he talks.

'Phil,' warns Jane, 'please.'

'No one can see, eh oop, what's this?'

Phil pulls a folder from the drawer and keeping his back to anyone looking in, opens it against his chest. It's tagged Grimshaw and Welbeck Personnel. Personal Assessment. Phil pulls out a sheaf of papers and shouldering the drawer shut, starts leafing through them.

'Phil,' warns Jane beseechingly.

'Insulting buggers. You seen this?' His face registers anger, and then morphs into an evil grin.

'Phil, that's Charlotte's cabinet.'

'Get this,' he reads, 'Paul Johnstone. Senior Writer, question mark. Anachronistic, nihilistic, creative, known to speak his mind to clients.' He guffaws, throwing his head back. His voice then takes on a quietly outraged tone. 'Borderline alcoholic. Responsible for the Aunt Norah freezer campaign, question mark, question mark, question mark.' His voice becomes incredulous. 'Then it says, no, no, one thousand times no. Bloody underlined. Fook 'em.'

Phil carefully studies another assessment.

'What do they say about you?'

'Doesn't matter, fook it.' Phil starts systematically tearing the pages into small pieces. 'Does that window open?'

'About six inches. Try pushing it.'

Phil walks casually over to the window and pushes, hard. The window grudgingly pivots the six inches. Phil tears the pages into even smaller shreds and stuffs them through the gap. At this height, the wind whipping around the building quickly disperses the G and W files creating an unseasonal flurry of white flakes.

Paul jams the empty folder back into the cabinet. Jane signals an urgent go, go. Phil does so, inclining his head back around the door and waving a finger.

'Seeing as Philip Arbuthnott is, I quote, talented tick, surplus to requirements question mark, he'll be in boardroom Nine Bells.'

Chapter 78

Phil looks up from his lunchtime pint as Paul wanders in from a McBrides progress meeting.

'And how was your morning, my hirsute heathen?'

Phil drains his pint. 'Buy me a drink and I'll tell you, Mr Nihilistic, fooking anarchic, and I'll tellyou.'

Phil is about to explain his morning discovery when Jane walks purposefully into the Nine Bells and into the back bar. Phil looks up from his Scotch egg, and Paul discerns something from Jane's expression.

'Hello, Jane love,' he says, finishing his pint. 'I need to get some stuff for home so I'll love and leave you two lovesick lovebirds and see you back at the morgue.'

'Drink?' asks Phil.

'Just an orange juice, please,' says Jane, giving Phil a peck on the cheek. She settles onto the bar stool next to him, straightening the collars of his jacket. Jane waits until the drink is in front of her. Phil, intuitively, says nothing, waiting for her to speak.

Her expression is open, yearning, eyes wide, as if hoping for something. He looks at her expectantly, taking her hands.

'Phil.'

'Love?'

'Phil, I think I'm.'

'What?'

'You know.'

'You don't mean?'

She squeezes his hands even tighter.

'I've missed a period. Or two.'

'Pregnant?' Phil seeks to keep his voice low and contain a range of emotions as they course across his face. Surprise, alarm, excitement, happiness; he settles on a mixture. 'Fook. Fook, fook, fook, fook,' he says with mounting, protective bantam cock pride.

'Yes,' says Jane, surprising herself, 'yes that would be what did it. Well, one of them.'

She's still gripping his hands tightly.

'You want to keep it, don't you?'

She nods, shyly, eyes downcast then looks up steadily into his.

'Yes', she replies, 'yes, if you do.'

'Yes,' Phil says, then frowns for a moment as if questioning his own answer. His mind is racing. Lily? Where would they live? Did he want commitment, but he'd already decided that some time ago.

'Yes,' he says, 'you know that I love you, fook, there's a lot to think about.'

'Mmm. Yes,' says Jane.

They sit quietly for a few minutes, Jane looking at Phil closely, moving her head to see him from different angles. Finally he speaks. 'Lily.'

'I didn't tell you,' she quickly replies. 'Sunday,' Jane flushes slightly, obviously pleased. 'I'd popped down the shops as Mum said Julian might be around for tea and could I get some of his favourite biscuits.'

'Euro Nobs? Sterling Custards? Dollar Creams?'

Jane ignores him.

'When I got home, Mum wasn't there. House was empty, I panicked, even looked in the garden shed. I ran out onto the front step and Mr Edelmann—'

'The old guy who lives opposite looks like Einstein?'

'Yes, him, he appeared on his front step and shouted across, "Lily's over here." 'I hurried over, thinking something had happened, but he's smiling, holds up a hand, you know, like it's OK, and leads me into the house. There's Mum in the front room, cup of tea and a piece of fruitcake. Happy as Larry she is, should have left you a note, she says.

'Then Mr Edelmann jumps in. "I saw your mum, Lily, on the front step after you went out, and she invited me over for a cuppa." Then he gives me this huge wink. "So I said to Lily, why don't you come over here? I'm waiting on a call from my daughter in Germany. I can't eat a whole fruitcake on my own." So over Lily comes.'

'So the crafty old bugger wasn't really waiting on a call?'

'No, we'd talked about Lily, he being a neighbour since Mum and Reg first moved in, good friend of Dad's actually, used to play chess with him, and he knew about Mum's problem, so he thought he'd help. And he did. Proved that she could be—'

'Independent,' confirms Phil.

'Aye, but let's take it slow, two steps forward, one step back. Best not tell her you might be, you have checked?'

'No, I will, but I know, and Mum'll guess, soon enough.'

She links an arm through his, pulls him towards her and says, 'Eh oop, Phil,' and kisses him gently, pressing her chest against his.

'Eh oop, they're getting bigger already,' he whispers thickly in her ear as he puts both arms firmly around her. 'Tha's mine, Jane Saunders.'

'All four of me?' she murmurs in his ear.

Chapter 79

Sunday in The Engineer. Paul is reading The Observer and enjoying a quiet pint when an expensive perfume intrudes.

'Afternoon, Paul.'

Paul, ever the gentleman, folds the paper as he stands and indicates a chair.

'Jenny.'

'Mind if I join you, Paul?'

'Not at all. Drink?'

'V.A.T if I may, thanks.'

Paul goes to the bar. Chance meeting engineered at The Engineer? Whatever. We'll see.

Jenny stirs her drink. Exhales. 'Paul, Cordier, Braithwaite.' She looks levelly at him, 'I'm up there three days a week at present. Mr B won't tell me what's happening?'

'Jenny, I've no idea. It's not my account anymore. Sorry. I just cover the meetings for Jonno.'

Paul's thinking rapidly. Tell it like it is. Just be straight.

At work on Monday, he reports to Phil. Jenny knows we see right through her. Probably vice versa. Knows you're seeing Jane, Jane sees the schedules, you talk to Jane and pass them on to me.

'So, I'm dead straight. Told her Argent was coming over, execs and wives, including Marcel, she was onto it like—'

'A seagull on a sick prawn, as Bungalow would say,' Phil supplies, deadpan.

'Dead right. "Couldn't get me a schedule, could you, Paul?" Even batted her eyelashes. Almost blew my Observer onto the floor. "I'll owe you one," she says. So this morning I go to Jane, explain Braithwaite's want to know Argent's schedule, told her to clear it with Ralph and give Jenny a heads up.'

'Um,' says Paul, pondering. 'More of a leg over with her. Could be a way of levering her off Jonno. I saw the way Marcel held her arm the other night as he shepherded her into the Argent crowd. Like hwe wanted to souvenir it.'

Chapter 80

Jonno settles back into the couch, his son Jack nestled in his lap. He catches Carol looking at him and colours slightly, his hand on the drowsy boy's forehead.

'Mmm?' she enquires.

Jonno raises his head and looks directly at her, then around the sitting room, and back.

'Thank you,' he mumbles.

'I was going to say I did it for the kids, but seeing you here,' Carol looks aside.

Jonno has the sense not to say anything. He shifts with difficulty, the dead weight of a now sleeping child on him. He manages to leverage himself to his feet, hefting his son up so his head flops on Jonno's shoulder. He shuffles out of the room, taking the child to bed.

Carol watches him go. Jonno has changed. She'd said it to Jane the other Monday morning, when Jane had called to ask if Jonno was with her as a meeting had been brought forward, and he wasn't picking up his phone. Jane had prudently kept her counsel when Carol commented Jonno seemed chastened, humbler, a nicer bloke.

'Not that I'll trust him again for a long, long time,' she'd quickly emphasised.

'Yeah, well,' Jane felt awkward, 'the takeover has shaken him, upset all of us,' she suggests, searching to deflect the conversation, knowing where it's going.

'Jane, I shouldn't ask, puts you in an awkward position but—'

'No really, it's not for me to comment but as far as I can see, it's over Carol, definitely over.'

Jane pulls at a thread on her sleeve, waiting for Carol to speak. She had brought an old cardigan to work; it could get cold in Face's air conditioning.

'I know that Jonno put you in a difficult position, Jane,' Carol is straightforward, 'and I just wanted you to know that I didn't for one moment think you were covering for him.'

Jane keeps silent.

'Anyway—'

'Thanks for saying it, Carol. And anyway, Jonno's not as, what's the word, duplicitous as that.'

'No, you're right,' Carol's laugh has a slightly harsh tone, 'Jonno wouldn't know how to be crafty.'

'No,' laughed Jane. 'And those haemorrhoids would have slowed him down a bit.'

'Haemorrhoids?'

'I think he suffered a bit from the takeover, the worry. Sorry. Forget I said anything.' For once, Jane's flustered. 'I'd better go Carol, my new masters approach. Goodbye.'

Jane quickly puts the phone down.

Chapter 81

It's 9 pm. Jenny strolls past Alistair Little's eponymous Frith Street restaurant. It's full. She turns back, goes in, smiles at the manager on reception.

'Good evening, madam.'

'Good evening, I don't have a reservation but if you could squeeze one—'

The girl surveys the crowded floor and her book, grimaces, 'I'd normally find room for a walk in but tonight—'

Marcel materialises at Jenny's elbow. 'Excuse me, Jenny, if I'd known you were down.'

'Marcel, I had no idea you'd be in here. You're with?'

Their expressions don't match their astonishment. Both faces acknowledge Jenny has arranged this.

'Jenny, Jenny you know I am here, you want to see what my wife is like. You must meet her.'

'No, I have to get ready to go north again. I've seen perhaps a little bit too much of you already recently.'

'A little bit? Double entendre is a French expression, Jenny.'

Marcel grasps her elbow, 'Jenny, I have asked Mr Braithwaite to release you for familiarisation in Paris prior to joining us.'

Jenny, jostled by departing diners, tears her arm away.

'Speak tomorrow, Marcel, your wife is,' as she turns to leave, Jenny raises her hand to still the manager's offer of a seat.

Marcel goes and sits down.

'Who was that?' enquires his wife in clipped tones, 'your new London floozy? You are well suited. Your darkness.'

In striking contrast to her husband's, Josephine's looks are Nordic, glacially so. Slim, hair white blonde, blue eyes, skin translucent, ski jump nose, her curved neck "a black run", as skier Marcel tortuously describes it, her pronounced collar bone "a precipice I once slipped over".

'Jenny Brownlow, Marketing Manager Braithwaite's Brewery, a company Cordier are thinking of acquiring. G and W is, were, their agency.'

Josephine fondles the collar of her Chanel jacket. 'What's the English expression, getting into bed with? She is talking to you while studying me. And I can see your wandering eye even with your back turned.'

'That is why, my love, I have a beautiful wife.'

'To drive you to distraction?'

Marcel picks up his wine glass, Josephine raises hers and they click them in a toast.

Chapter 82

Monday morning, Jonno appears by Perfect's desk.

'Morning, Jane.'

Jane pushes back from the desk.

'Jane? Wasn't I perfect enough last week?'

'You were perfect, Perfect Jane.'

He smiles. His shirt is neatly ironed, sleeves crisply creased. He stands very straight, shoulders back, his smile threatening to crack his face. Gone is the slumped, hangdog look of the last few weeks.

'Carol suggested that it was demeaning not to call you by your real name.'

'Carol? This wasn't your weekend with the kids. You're not?'

Jonno leans forward eagerly, in his happy puppy pose, as Cyn puts it.

'I took the kids out for burgers Friday night and Carol invited me in to put them to bed. And then she offered me a drink and we got talking, and she said she had enough spaghetti sauce for two, and we had a couple of drinks with dinner, and she said you'd better not drive home now, not in this rain.'

'But it hardly sprinkled all weekend.'

'I know, then she said the bed's made up in the spare room, and about half an hour later, she came in and asked if I had everything and I said I could use a goodnight kiss.'

Jane raises her hand.

'Too much information, Jonno. I just wondered who ironed your shirt like that, so—'

'Trial period, you know,'

'Well, you—'

'Behave, I will, I promise,' says Jonno, turning decisively into his office, with a little jump and click of the heels.

Chapter 83

Paul lets the crowd coming off the tube carry him up into the street. He looks around; these city streets have always teemed with people going about their business.

He imagines muddy alleys, the breath from harried oxen, a jumble of buildings, small ragged kids dodging through the crowd, street sellers, prostitutes and business men in high hats, women in long dresses decorously avoiding puddles; the eras and ages jumble and mix in his mind as he's jostled along, stepping out the hurrying flow and into the foyer of the Face Argent building.

He nods to James on the reception desk as he always does, unwinding his muffler and extracting his pass card from a top jacket pocket in the one movement.

Paul notes wryly how many of the crowd waiting for the lift go through the ritual of unplugging their ear buds and switching off their Walkman, or ostentatiously checking their new house brick of a mobile phone before acknowledging workmates.

He smiles a hello to those to whom he'd been introduced and shuffles into the lift, full at this time of the morning with people from other departments and subsidiary companies on other floors. Christine's waiting for him in his office; he'd taken a call from her before he'd got on the tube.

'Perfect timing,' she says as he walks in, indicating a takeaway container of coffee, 'haven't got time to go out for one.'

'That's OK, Pie.'

Paul switches on his computer, waiting for her to speak.

'Confidentially, Paul, I've had a couple of leads, touch ups, from people on the Argent planning board. Freddy tells me they're going to make me some sort of offer and I'll be mad not to listen, but I'll have to tell them what I feel about the standard of creative work my strategies are being put to.'

'Pie, G and W's views on creativity are extant. Strictly between you and I, Phil saw some staff assessment files and I'm well out of the loop.'

'G and W staff assessment?'

'Just creative, as far as Phil saw before he trashed them.'

Christine reflectively licks froth from her top lip.

'I like working with you, Paul, and Ralph and Clayton come to that.'

She grimaces.

'I heard about Michael.'

'Sad,' says Paul.

He smiles, looking up as Phil enters, pulling his messenger bag over his head as he says, 'You heard about Bitsa yesterday?'

'No,' they both say in unison.

Perfect appears at the door with a mug of tea.

'Your morning brew, Mr Arbuthnott, sir.' She bows, putting it on the corner of the desk as Phil indicates, and nodding 'morning team' at Christine and Paul.

'Well,' says Phil, 'Bitsa's lot have been integrated into the new department, and Bitsa has some big Face stuff to look after. There's this campaign going into the South China Morning Post, evidently, and Bitsa has it all under control, you know, being offhand and casual as usual to account service and their guys start getting all officious, not used to production people talking back. So the account director, what's his name?'

'Hugo Chamberlain,' interjects Christine, 'has a couple of big accounts out of Hong Kong.'

'That's him, the short, smarmy guy, uses a lot of glue on his hair, looks like a transplant, his head, not the hair, anyway yesterday, Bitsa's on his way out to one of those supplier lunches, they're all after him now he's here, and Hugo's harrying him all the way out to the lift to see some proofs, and Bitsa's going "not now, it'll keep until this afternoon, I'll show you after lunch," and Hugo's really getting the Tom Tits and Bitsa's just pushing him off, you know, and he's trying to get in front of Bitsa, stop him getting to the lift.'

'Not unreasonable,' comments Christine.

'No, it wasn't. Bitsa's being a prick, he knows all the job timings. Anyway, they get to the lift and Hugo dodges around in front of him, like it's a game, to stop Bitsa getting in the lift and Bitsa's trying to ignore him and lift door opens.'

Paul and Christine listen expectantly.

'So, it's lunchtime, isn't it, and the lift is absolutely packed, like chapel, it's full. So Bitsa steps back a bit and sees the lift is full and so does Hugo. So Bitsa leans forward, grabs Hugo by shoulders, pulls him in't his arms, kisses him full on the lips, spins round and pushes him backwards into the lift and goes, "not now lover, I'll see you tonight," and gives him a little wave as the lift door closes on him.'

'He certainly knows how to make friends, Bitsa, hope that Hugo guy isn't homophobic.'

'That's the whole point, he is, he knows Bitsa's gay and has been making his distaste obvious. You know, nasty little snide comments round the office, jokes with his sycophant mates behind Bitsa's back. Imagine how Hugo would like another bloke kissing him full on the lips. He'd have really hated it. And a Jamaican Irishman? The gits a right wing racist arsewipe as well.'

'Chamberlain's lucky Bitsa hasn't stuck one on him already, then. Probably waiting for an opportunity. No, scrub that, Bitsa's bigger than that. I'd like to believe he doesn't care what they think,' observes Paul, 'but it must get to him, sometime.'

'Bitsa's got mates everywhere,' says Phil. 'Probably already putting out feelers.'

'No,' says Christine, 'you both underestimate him. Bitsa's drawing a line in the sand. Putting their execs in their place. He'll be the best production manager they've ever had and they'll see that in the bottom line. But who knows how long he'll hang on without his friends?'

'Yes,' says Paul, sharing a glance with Phil.

Chapter 84

'What's the weather like?'

Becs holds her phone up to the window. There's a crack of thunder.

'Wow, and lightning and raining, too?'

'Yes, it's spitting,' says Becs, sitting down and pulling her kimono around her.

'What are you wearing?'

'My kimono, why?'

'Show us your tits,' says Paul.

Becs obligingly opens her kimono and closes it again.

'Oh,' says Paul, 'I've gone all weak at the knees. Just think, one day we'll actually be able to see each other as we talk.'

'You could at least have shaved before you called me.'

'How do you know I'm cultivating a laddy look? It's Saturday and I'm having a lazy day. Done my laundry etcetera and I can't tell you how fanciable you look.'

'That's because you can't see me. Oh, by the way,' she says, her manner purposely offhanded, 'you're in with Bros.'

'Bros Brothers? The agency?' Paul asks, excitement creeping into his voice.

'Yes,' mocks Becs, raising her voice to a Paul like squeak. 'It seems the madder they become, the more business they pick up. Everyone loves their Britishness. I met Grahame and Bert at a function the other week and told them about Phil and the files and what Face said about you.'

'Are you sure that was OK?'

'I knew one of them worked at Argent's NYC office a couple of years back and didn't last long. And the fact that Face called you anarchic.'

'Don't forget nihilistic.'

'Probably said as much to them as your ads do. They want to talk, maybe make you an offer and I don't think they bullshit.'

'Should I come over?'

'Grahame said to ring him, and I'd make it quick, like Monday, the head-hunters are circling.'

Paul loudly kisses the phone.

'Errgh, I can't tell you how horrible that sounds. I think they caught on that you and I—'

'A long distance item; ships that don't pass in the night? Bec, I don't know why it's easier to say it when we're talking like this,' Paul pauses, drawing breath, 'but I miss you, and I've thought about it and feel awfully unfulfilled and therefore insecure in my life and I need something different and new, and you.'

'Jeez, Paul, how long did it take you to compose that sentence? You need an editor. I'm putting the phone down before you say anything else that isn't anarchically and nihilistically Johnstone P. 'Love you, my limey lover, and I don't say that to too many men. Well, not this early. And certainly not to a Brit. I've faxed you Grahame's personal number. Don't forget to call him, Monday. And don't forget to bung on that awful accent of yours.'

Paul smiles. 'I'll tell Phil tomorrow. He's been a bit strange lately, seems all excited about something, very protective towards Jane, all of a sudden.'

'Paul,' spoken quietly, 'let's think about us, for once. Ta ta, toodle pip.'

'Yeah,' agrees Paul, 'let's. Cheerio, my dear.'

Chapter 85

'Michael,' Paul speaks to Michael Michaels' disembodied answerphone, 'Paul Johnstone, it's none of my business but I've written you a letter to send to Kane and to Edwards, one to each of course. Copy it exactly as is or not at all. Handwritten, mate. Please resist your normal temptation to rewrite everything. I put it in the internal post to you, didn't want it near a fax machine.'

Paul had thought it over. There was no way Michael could walk straight into Trevor Kane or Janice Edwards office, he had to pave the way, somehow get them in a receptive frame of mind and a letter, properly couched, was the best way in. I mean, he thought, who sends hand written, personal letters anymore? Very disarming.

He'd sat at home, poured himself a large Auchentoshan, "a breakfast whisky" the wine merchant had called it, and carefully composed the screed. Not grovelling. He penned it in classic Michaels-speak.

The other morning, the victim of a crude practical joke, I displayed in the most unfortunate manner that my deep attachment and dedication to the job can sometimes stray into an emotional area; one that I would never reveal to my clients but one to which in a moment of weakness and bad judgement I subjected you, my new colleagues.

It was a salutary learning experience and I must apologise for my offensive behaviour and language. I will only say in mitigation that affecting a smooth transition for my clients from Grimshaw and Welby to Face Argent has not been without its difficulties, but they have all now come around to recognising and welcoming the perceived strengths and benefits of this new relationship.

Trevor/Janice, they say that any advertising job is a constant learning curve, and this incident has made it clear to me. I can only hope that you can see fit to look beyond this unfortunate episode, and fast forward to the future successes we might enjoy, together.

I am, respectfully,
Yours and etc.
Michael Michaels.

Paul put the letter in an envelope with a covering note suggesting Michael was not far behind the letters in person, when they were delivered. I'll be proud of myself if they buy that constipated tosh, Paul admits to himself as he gleefully sloshes another scotch into his glass.

Chapter 86

Friday lunchtime, Roddy and Jimmy stick their heads around the door of the Dog and Duck, looking for Paul and Phil. They'd wandered back to their old Soho haunts, perhaps unconsciously to give themselves a little reassurance; they both felt more comfortable back on familiar ground.

As they confided to Ralph the previous night in the Nine Bells, they hadn't realised how deeply they'd absorbed the culture of G and W, the way things were done, attitudes and approaches to work. And how things were diametrically different at Face Argent.

It was this, they suggested, this that had put them off kilter, which had dulled the checks and balances that should have stopped them pulling their prank on Michael Michaels.

'You pulled a stupid stroke,' Freddy had mused. Mind you, I do sympathise to a certain extent. You creatives would feel unsettled, at the very least.'

Ralph put his pint down on the bar. He moved the glass around slightly, noting the light coming through the old whorled glass in the room divider gave the faintly cloudy beer a warm, amber glow. He put a hand lightly on the worn wood.

'It's often zinc in old Paris bars,' he mused quietly, 'sort of a pitted, dull silver, leaden.' Ralph collected his thoughts. 'Anyway, you're a silly pair of blighters, but Michael did overreact. Maybe we all are, at present. Overreacting.'

'Or overacting?' suggests Jimmy.

'Very perceptive, Jimmy, yes, that too. Or posturing, at least.'

The following lunchtime, Paul and Phil announce they must go to a "studio" in Soho. Jane had quietly suggested every creative tell her where they are, so she can "keep them in the loop" and this is where Jimmy and Roddy follow them. Now, in the familiar bar, Roddy turns to Jimmy.

'They'll be in soon.'

George emerges from the scrum at the bar.

'Lads, lovely to see you. No Paul and Phil? Let me buy you a drink.'

George looks at them, his manner quietly sympathetic.

'Pints? The Young's is good today.'

'Thanks, George,' Jimmy and Roddy nod.

They've come to realise that, as the bright, young new generation creative team anticipating a digital future, they were going through exactly what Phil and Paul experienced when they'd first come into the business, and George, too, all those years ago.

Roddy, and Jimmy feel they're different, want to act differently, do things differently, look differently at things to the dinosaurs of previous decades but have been drawn inexorably into the cycle that is advertising.

'Cheers, lads,' George hands them their pints and picks up his own. 'Have they put you in the too hard basket yet?'

'No, we're sort of hanging on in, George, sticking to our own accounts, you know, keeping our heads down de dum de dum.'

Roddy and Jimmy feel awkward, they'd always thought themselves different to George, and now realise they aren't.

'I was thinking,' says George, 'Looking at you two, I was thinking of my first day, or was in second, in advertising. It influenced the whole of my career. My attitude, everything, just as working at G and W has for you, I can see.'

Roddy and Jimmy nod, encouraging George to continue, for once.

'Anyway, well I was taking the mail around at J. Walter Thompson in Berkeley Square and it was around four pm on a winter's afternoon and getting dark and drizzly. I was up on the eighth floor, I think it was the eighth, must count the floors next time I'm over that way and I was delivering stuff to this art director, and I put these magazines on his desk and just as I'm leaving his office, he came in, he was in a rage, tearing up layouts and throwing them around.

'Well, I'm the new boy, fresh out of school, and I sort of go to sidle out and he says, "hey, what's-your-name, what's your name?" and I said, "George." He says, "right George, follow me," and we go up the fire stairs to the top floor, I think it's the ninth, anyway it's the TV department and Richard, that was his name, Richard, heads straight for the door to the roof and this woman shouts, "you're not allowed out there," and Richard takes no notice, it's just, "come along, George" and we're out there on the roof and it's all cold, and dark, and slippery and puddles.

Richard goes to the parapet overlooking Berkeley Square and looks over. He gestures for me to follow him and I'm looking down on the front steps, I think there was some sort of a cupola over it. These figures appear from under it looking for a taxi, and this JWT guy, he didn't have a coat on, must have been the AE, is signalling for a taxi and these other blokes in coats, must have been the clients, are grouped on the pavement. Richard looks at me and says, "piss on them, come on, piss on them," and he unbuttons his fly, gets his cock out and pisses over the edge. So I did, too.'

'Did it?' Enquires an equally appalled and enthralled Jimmy, 'hit them?'

'Well, you know from that height, and it's raining, and there's a breeze up there, I doubt it, maybe the odd drop. Anyway, Richard puts his cock away and turns to me and claps me on the back and says, "It's the thought that counts, isn't it, Georgy," and I said, well I think I said, "If you say so, Richard".'

Roddy and Jimmy stand there, looking at George reflectively. George takes a pull of his beer.

'Aaah. What I'm saying is, well I'm not sure what I'm saying. It taught me that some people are passionately involved in their work, and really believe in it. But in our job, there will always be those philistines who, how do you put it, disrespect us and what we can do that they can't and you have to stand up for what you believe in.

'I was always well-mannered, saw the other person's point of view, tried to rationalise their position but now I reckon I was often too, giving. You two have to stand up for yourselves at that joint. Don't let them absorb you, take you in, take you for granted. This is a hard enough business to work out what's right and what's wrong and maybe G and W do, did, things which were wrong for their clients but they did more that was right, stood up for what they did, and believed in it.' George takes a breath and sucks on his drink.

'They gave the consumer good ads. Didn't insult their intelligence. And you two have to do that. This has come at a bad time in your careers. If you get an offer, take a good look at it. And you can always ask me what I think.'

'Thanks, George.'

'Yeh, well, I know you probably think of me as some sort of advertising dinosaur.'

Jimmy and Roddy's eyes flicker in acknowledgement and embarrassment.

'I am. Look at me, dressing like a 30-year old at my age, and listening to the music I do. But anyway,' George looks at them affectionately; they're him, many years ago.

'Drink up, it's your shout, and Paul and Phil will be in soon.'

But Phil and Paul are sitting at the counter of an Italian restaurant on the other side of Soho. Phil tilts a tumbler of wine.

'I dunno how you can eat that.'

'You should try it', said Paul, twirling a strand of linguine in a puddle of squid ink. 'I mean if you can eat cow heel pie and deep fried Mars bars.'

'That's Lancashire and Scotland not Yorkshire,' Phil corrects him.

'Anyway,' continues Paul offhandedly, 'I phoned New York this morning and spoke to Grahame and Bert Kingston.'

Phil tilts his head in astonishment.

'The Bros brothers?'

'The very two. They're interested in both of us but—'

Phil pauses, a baby lamb chop on the way to his mouth as a waiter tops his glass up. 'Thanks.'

He turns to Paul. 'You were going to mention Lily, but it goes further, deeper than that.'

He puts the chop bone down. 'You'll know soon enough. Jane's pregnant.'

Paul leans back from his food and peruses Phil, raising an eyebrow.

'Yours, I trust?' he says, smiling.

Phil points at his eyebrows. 'You'll bloody well know it is when it's born, won't you?'

Paul leans forward and grasps Phil's shoulders.

'Congratulations.'

'Ey oop, watch my wine.'

Paul prudently decides against making any gratuitous comments about safe sex. It's all too late, anyway.

'So, you did the deed, old son, eh, up the duff, bun in the oven.'

'Aye, reckon so,' says Phil quietly. A serious note creeps into his voice, 'and we want to keep it.'

'Wouldn't have expected anything else.' Paul lowers his voice as the girl sitting next to Phil snatches a quick glance at them.

'Maybe not the conversation to have here, but it does rule out NYC doesn't it, what with the Arbuthnott tribe and Lily to think about.'

Phil confirms it with a nod of the head.

'Well, I think we should adjourn to The French and celebrate, better call Jane and warn her we won't be back.'

Paul suddenly looks serious.

'And tell her to warn Roddy and Jimmy not to drink too much if they're going back to the office.'

'I think they've got some Orange Grove radio to brief into a studio this afternoon.'

'They're learning. Anyway, it's fantastic, and I'm pleased for you and Jane, and you'd better tell her I know.'

Phil looks sombre. 'Mmmm, it's not as if we live together, or anything.'

'Phil, it'll work out. Get on the blower to Jane. I'll get the bill.'

Phil puts up his hand. 'Hold on.'

'No, I insist. And by the way, New York with you would be twice the job,' Paul says awkwardly as he picks his trilby up off the counter, 'twice the job. Not that there's much Yorkshire pud in Manhattan.'

Phil raises his eyebrows sardonically. 'Or sheep to shag.'

Chapter 87

The streetlights had come on and seen from the windows of the fourth floor Paris apartment, a glowing, caramel dusk is washing over the sandstone facades of the houses in the square, soft, through the branches of the chestnut trees.

Jenny straightens her clothes, tucking her blouse in, smoothing her skirt and pushing it down; then retrieves her thong from under the coffee table. Her bottom still smarts where Marcel slapped it before entering her as she knelt on the chaise longue. Marcel appears from the kitchen, hair ruffled, shirt still untucked, with two gin and tonics.

'Well, that was a bit—'

'Vite? Quick?' grins Marcel.

'We'd hardly got in the door. Getting the day out of our system, were we?' she enquires waspishly.

'I did not hear any complaints.'

The French cockerel puffs his chest feathers; Jenny smiles, accepting the drink. 'Non, vraiment, Marcel mon brave, that wasn't what you heard.'

Marcel ignores her purposely mangled French. 'I am hungry,' he announces.

Jenny observes him, raising an eyebrow.

'Just because you fucked me doesn't mean you can buy me dinner,' is her smooth rejoinder.

Marcel shrugs.

Good line, went straight over his head. Whooshka, as the agency guys would say. He's a bit full of himself.

Funny, for all Marcel's French manliness? Bravura? When it comes to making love, he isn't a patch on silly, British, bumbling, boyish Jonno. Still, looking around the apartment with its faded can't-remember-which-Louis-era furniture and art she didn't recognise, a girl could get used to it. Better get used to it, she thought, pragmatically.

As she left for Paris George Braithwaite had instructed her to "get close to the Frogs". And she had, even if her boss had meant Cordier, not Argent. Jenny straightens the cushions on the chaise, which she'd fully expected to collapse given the centuries of wear and ferocity of Marcel's thrusting, coupled with their combined weight.

Coupled with, I like that.

'Leave it,' commands Marcel, 'the maid will fix everything.'

'I hope she's discreet.'

'Jenny, I am allowed to bring my clients home,' Marcel replies somewhat pompously. 'And Josephine, she will be in Lyon until Monday.'

'Lyon's only hours away.'

'Her mother is very—'

'Domineering?'

'If that is the word. Where do you wish to eat?'

'La Coupole?' Jenny says it innocently. 'Is that not the place you frequent?' *With your wife? And where you meet your friends?*

'Jenny, it is hard to get into at short notice in the evening, all the American tourists, those early eaters.'

'We'll go later then. They know you *and your wife, and her parents* very well there. You can try.'

Marcel bows, slightly, putting down his glass, picking his jacket off the parquet floor and moving towards the phone. 'As Madame insists.'

'We will share the mushrooms, I will have the pigeon, you want fish so you will have the Hake, and we will share the rice pudding. And a bottle of red? A Gaillac, I think.'

Jenny looks around the bustling dining room. They aren't at La Coupole as 'they did not have a table tonight,' explains Marcel.

I believe you, thousands wouldn't.

'Please, no, really, this is great,' says Jenny, as the last of the early tourist diners are ushered out by ebullient staff and noise levels rise as locals take over and the restaurant relaxes. 'I'm not familiar with Basque food, but it all looks terrific. And I'm hungry, now.'

'You will like it,' replies Marcel, putting his hand on hers.

Now you wouldn't have done that at La Coupole.

She leans forward, looking into his eyes as he strokes her wrist. Jenny smiles coquettishly at him, gently works her toe up inside the cuff of his trousers and runs it sharply down his shin. He flinches.

'Oops,' she says, keeping her eyes locked on his, 'didn't have time to take my shoe off.'

Chapter 88

Phil nudges Paul and points. The windows of The French are open, and though the lunchtime crowd had dwindled, there were still some drinkers left at the bar. Paul pauses by the door.

'It is, isn't it?' says Phil.

In the corner of the bar stand the Kingston brothers. Short, solidly built, snub nosed, their round shaven heads and stubbled faces almost identical. They both have Arsenal scarves above their American motorcycle jackets. They wear jeans and boots. "A caricature of each other" as Mark Newlands had once offered, as he flicked disdainfully through an advertising magazine.

They appear to be permanently, almost cockily grinning. Their body language is engaged, upbeat, constantly on the verge of sudden movement. Bert is slightly shorter than Grahame. Or is it the other way around? They both grasp glasses of pastis, as if this were de rigeur in a bar called The French.

They'd been out of London for some ten years now, arriving in New York via South Africa before starting their own agency. Paul didn't hesitate. He walked around the pavement drinkers, in The French's other door, and straight up to them. Phil followed close behind.

'Grahame? Bert?'

'Ah, here he is, Paul Johnstone, the Noel Coward of advertising. Your PA said you'd be in here, it being Friday afternoon, but it took some getting it out of her.'

Grahame indicates Bert, then himself. 'Him Bert, me Grahame. How do.'

Paul shakes hands with them and steps aside to introduce Phil.

'Bert, Grahame, Philip Arbuthnott.'

'Ah, the talented member of the duo,' says Grahame.

'Spoken like a true art director. How d'you do, Grahame. Bert, how do.'

For all their similarity in looks and outlook, while Grahame is creative, Bert's an account executive, trained as an accountant. It's the reason the agency's financially sound and prospers. Bert is conservative and allows no excesses on Grahame's part.

'I'm a tight git wot runs a tight ship,' he'd explained to Paul the previous Monday.

The four stand there for a moment. 'I'll get 'em in,' says Phil.

Grahame and Bert look Paul up and down. They both bob on their feet like middleweight boxers.

'Don't think you're the reason we're in London today,' says Grahame, ticking points off on his fingers.

'It's our mum's birthday, we've business to see to and most importantly.'

'The Arse are at home tomorrow,' says Phil, handing a glass of red to Paul.

'Cor, an educated northerner,' says Bert. He turns to Paul. 'Let me guess, you've been talking this lunchtime, Paul's been thinking how he'd like to get over to NYC to see his girl, guys like you don't want to be and shouldn't be,' he waves a finger, 'at Face Argent for more than ten minutes, so what's the story?'

'Lay off bro, we're in their manor, and you're carrying on like a clockwork watch.'

'No,' says Paul. He looks around the bar but there aren't any advertising or film people he knows left in there, and of those left no one's taking any particular interest in them.

'Bert's right, Grahame. You know very well I'd like to join you, and I told you it would be hard for Phil to leave London at the moment.'

Phil looks surprised, Paul hadn't actually warned him he'd talked about his position. Paul caught Phil's reaction and looked at him as he spoke.

'Actually, I suggested it might be a little difficult for you, Phil, and that we'd have to talk.'

Paul defers to Phil who speaks up. 'Let's get to the point. I'm flattered you'd think of me, but I can't leave London at the moment.'

Phil points to their glasses. 'Do you want another of those things?'

'No, I'll get a bottle,' announces Grahame, 'The Ricard's just a bit of a custom when we come to back to London.'

Paul looked round the wall at the gallery of autographed, faded publicity photos of pre-second World War French music hall, vaudeville, theatre and film personalities, all smiling brightly, yearningly, putting on their winning faces, people who had to grab their chances if they were to advance their highly insecure careers.

There was nothing to be gained in playing hard to get. Bert's a moneyman, Grahame knows what people are worth, and they all know Paul has little stomach for a future at Face Argent. Of course, Paul could hang on and play politics with the best of them but if he had to do so he'd scorn himself, it was below him.

'You're going to lose one of the best writers in London, Phil,' says Grahame, quietly, art director to art director.

'Aye Grahame, he's a right toffee, stuck up prick but you Londoners need each other.'

'Enough, Phil,' Paul interjects, affectionately. 'Not now. Where are you two staying?'

'With Mum and Dad. We can't pull any hotel strokes with them.'

'And it's cheaper,' says Bert, deadpan, finishing his brother's sentence.

'Let's get business over. We're here until Tuesday, here's our London number, Paul. Give us a call, we make you an offer and bingo.' Grahame scribbles a number on a business card and hands it to Paul.

'Right, let's get in a bevvy or two. Mum's cooking dinner, we can't be late.'

Chapter 89

Alan Sergeant and Bruce Wood stride through the door of Face Argent, negotiating the various tubular stainless steel sculptures that ring the reception desk. A receptionist stares at Alan and Bruce vapidly.

'Alan Sergeant and Bruce Wood of Reader to see Clayton Howell.'

'Clayton Howell?' The receptionist looks puzzled.

'G and W?' offers Bruce.

'This is Face Argent, Mr?'

Alan Sergeant bustles forward. 'Clayton Howell was with Grimshaw and Welby.'

'Aah,' a degree of comprehension creeps into her voice. 'The agency we bought. And Mr Reader, you're here to see?'

'No, I'm Alan Sergeant of Reader and we're here to see him.'

'Who?'

'Whom. Him. Clayton Howell.'

Bruce prudently takes a step back.

'May I tell Mr Clayton who you represent?' the receptionist asks, brightly.

'Mr Howell's expecting us, we have an appointment with him,' says Alan, an edge creeping into his voice.

The girl studies an appointments book in front of her and spins it around to them.

'If you'd both like to sign in here, first.'

'That won't be necessary, Joyce,' says Brian Arnold, sidestepping around one of the sculptures.

'But Brian, every visitor has to sign in.'

'These gentlemen aren't visitors, Joyce, they're clients.'

As if on cue, a Woof dog food commercial appears on the TV screen on the wall behind her desk, where a loop of the agency commercials is silently playing. Brian points to it and she turns around to look.

'Oh, I haven't seen this one.' She watches it then turns back to Bruce and Alan.

'Is that one of yours? I didn't realise we had any dog food clients.'

'Well, we do now, Joyce,' says Brian, gently.

'It's clever that commercial; the way you put speech blurbs in for people who watch TV with the sound off,' she bubbles to Bruce.

There's silence for a moment, interrupted by Trevor Kane who strides into the scene, hand outstretched.

'It's all right, Arnold, I'll take over. Bruce, Alan?'

'Alan, Bruce,' Bruce corrects him.

'Trevor Kane, MD of Face Argent. Welcome to the fold. The real world of advertising. Advertising as it should be.'

Alan Sergeant's cheek muscles twitch noticeably as he shakes Trevor's hand.

'Alan, Bruce, I'll leave you with Trevor,' says Brian.

'Thank you, Arnold.'

'Actually Trevor,' says Brian over his shoulder as he moves away, 'it's Brian. Brian Arnold.'

Trevor Kane's eyes narrow, theatrically. The trio stride off up the corridor.

'No Clayton?' enquires Alan.

'Sent him off to Paris.' Trevor speaks over his shoulder. 'Thought you should meet me as I'm the MD, peer group as it were.'

'But we have some budgetary specifics to discuss with Clayton, Trevor.'

'Ah, you're with Face Argent, now, Alan, we do things a little differently here, as you'll discover, to you and your company's benefit. And I thought we ought to get to know each other, chew over the big picture. Young Arnold can do the detail stuff with Bruce, here.'

'I believe its Brian, Trevor, Brian Arnold,' corrects Bruce.

'Aah. Of course, er, Bruce, we're not yet familiar with the juniors we inherited from G and W.'

Trevor surreptitiously checks his watch and ushers them into the boardroom.

An hour and ten minutes later, Alan Sergeant makes an uncharacteristic gesture, he buys Bruce afternoon tea.

'Leaf tea, Bruce,' he says, lifting the lid of the teapot and peering in.

'True tea, proper tea, made properly tea, made with care tea, not a tea bag, not a quick contemporary make do, the real thing.'

Bruce squints, concentrating hard as Alan looks back at him, urging him silently to understand the metaphor.

'What you're saying, Alan, is that Face Argent—'

'Precisely, Bruce.'

'But Alan—'

'I know what you're going to say. G and W equated with rudeness, creative arrogance, offices badly in need of organisation, a sometimes offhand attitude, a certain laissez faire when it came to budgeting. And they gave us advertising that, at first, you and I didn't buy. Didn't immediately, appreciate, is perhaps the word.'

Bruce nods seriously, because he feels he has to.

'And?'

Alan inclines his head, inviting him to contribute.

'Ah, well Alan, they did, they always seemed to take our products, well, very seriously. Especially Paul and Phil. They even seemed to,' he grimaces as if in apology for what he's about to say, 'really like our products. Own them, sort of, as if they were theirs, not ours.'

Alan nods encouragingly.

'And they believe in what they're doing, I can see that going through my meeting notes. And they fight for their work. Even if they look like they do most of it down the pub. And Christine and Cynthia and Claire are very clever, I think?'

Bruse has opted for a cappuccino. He looks to his boss for confirmation before slurping and acquiring a froth moustache. Alan takes a nibble at his Friand. 'In France, this is called a Financier, Bruce. Because the shape resembles a gold brick. Pure almond meal, no added flour.'

'And G and W is the Financier to Face Argent's Friand?'

'No need to take the metaphor too far, Bruce, but in a manner of speaking, yes, I suppose so.'

'But I thought?'

'Bruce, I'm well aware you may think of me as a little stiff, old fashioned, and that's true. I was brought up in a certain manner, trained in a certain way. I might be a trifle conservative but what I see is that my attitude and approach gets us a very high standard of work out of the agency.'

'But Paul and Phil?'

'I wouldn't say as much to their faces, but our sales figures prove they do a good job for us. And my daughters love the commercials. The only down side being they want me to get a dog.'

'But the work's Claire's and Cynthia's, isn't it?'

'They have nothing to do with it. It's Johnstone and Arbuthnott's. Yes, Bruce if you haven't worked out, that obnoxious pair do all our TV work, whatever they and Freddy want us to think. You don't think I'm taken in by the agency's shenanigans, do you? I've been in the business far too long. Anyway, the girls gave themselves away at the shoot, the way they kept referring to the scripts as if they weren't familiar with them.'

Alan takes an appreciative sip of his tea.

'Whereas you could see Johnstone was hanging on every word. Spent half his lunchtime talking to the director discussing the dialogue. Anyone could see that.'

'But what about the incident in the restaurant, after?'

'Appalling Bruce, absolutely appalling. Disgusting. Obviously that Hayward character, it was written all over his son's face. I knew something was up at the pre-production meeting when what's his name, Steve, reacted to his father's name on the call sheet. But that wasn't the agency's fault. They were all as obviously shocked as we were.

'And much as I disagree with the profligate way in which G and W generally conducted themselves, we did get some valuable work done at that lunch. And at least they didn't reward themselves in underhand ways, and, and I'm sad to be talking of them in the past tense.'

He puts his cup carefully down on its saucer and pauses for a moment, thoughtfully.

'Got to knock another agency into shape now, hmmm, and I wonder Bruce if I have the energy. Hmmm,' he recovers his previous chain of thought. 'Where was I? Oh yes, and G and W was genuinely pleased to have lunch with us, until,' The underpants incident replays itself in his memory. 'until just as I happened to be reaching for that rather fine aged cheddar cheese…'

Bruce nods, face suitably scrunched in disgust.

'Mind you, Bruce,' Sergeant continues, a sudden gleam in his eye, 'when I recounted the incident at a dinner party the other night, the other guests couldn't get enough of it. Appalled, disgusted, that was their reaction and yet they were absolutely rapt. Wanted all the details. Twice. Fascinating thing, human nature,

Bruce, they were repelled yet enthralled. Human nature, so predictable. And it proved to me once again that being involved with the advertising industry is a little more interesting than, say, being an estate agent. The dinner party host's profession,' he explains.

Alan again sips his tea appreciatively, savouring it.

'One can get bored talking house prices and double glazing and one's children's academic achievements.'

Bruce is perplexed; he'd never heard Alan open up like this before. He'd have taken notes, but felt it was a trifle gauche.

'You see, Bruce, they say that clients don't really care who does their creative work, but I do, which may come as a surprise to you. And I doubt Face Argent can carry our two campaigns across into the next phase in a satisfactory manner.'

'But Paul and Phil?'

'I don't see them lasting there.' He flicked crumbs off a lapel.

'They'd have to change their manners, and habits. Ill-mannered creative drunks, both of them.'

'Maybe that's the price of talent, Alan?' Bruce suggests.

Alan cocks his head at the unexpectedly profound insight from his normally callow assistant. Bruce nods sagely.

'And maybe if; maybe they could hand our business over to the girls. You might suggest it, Alan, fresh viewpoint; we could make it clear we knew about them all along, were playing them, and had the upper hand as it were.'

'Good thinking Bruce, bold, and by the way, I've no idea why they thought they had to get that receptionist, Grace, to flaunt herself in that manner before us. Mind you,' he ran his tongue over his lips a trifle lasciviously, 'she would certainly brighten up Face Argent, or whatever they call themselves.'

He briskly collected himself.

'Finish that coffee, Bruce, I've got a train to catch. And, err, you have a froth moustache,' he indicates with a thin smile.

Chapter 90

Ralph pauses at the doorway of the restaurant as patrons burst from it, cameras in hand. Sonia had joined him in Paris for the weekend. Ralph appraised her in the light spilling through the open door, a handsome, ash blonde woman in her forties. Simone Simon, he thought. Or was it Simone Signoret, the one with the fantastic eyebrows?

'The trouble with travel and restaurant guides, Sonia,' he says, eyeing the American tourists grouped on the pavement, 'is that everyone in the world gets to know about every restaurant, and then prints an ill-informed opinion.'

'Are we going in, Ralph? Much as I find the pavements of Paris alluring a glass of the jumping grape—'

'Umm,' opening the door and looking inside. 'Oh, ah, good gracious, you remember I told you about Jenny and Jonno?'

'That rather sordid affair?'

'Well,' his words are lost in the swirl of noise that greets them, the aromas, the clatter of cutlery, declamatory voices at the bar.

'Ah,' Sonia breathes it in. 'I could get used to this.'

The maître d' greets them and confirms their reservation, swiftly leading them through the throng of diners at the closely packed tables. Ralph pauses by a seated couple, a darkly handsome, wavy haired man and a younger, thin, hawkish, Italianate woman. The man swiftly removes his hand from the woman's before rising as Ralph greets him.

'Marcel, fancy finding you here.'

'Paris is a small town, Ralph. And finding you here is a testament to our, and your good taste, also.'

Ralph nods in agreement.

'And Jenny, no, please don't get up. Marcel Gerard, Jenny Brownlow, my wife, Sonia Bertram. Jenny's with Cordier, Marcel's at the agency with me.'

The maître d' hovers as introductions are effected.

'We'll leave you two.' Ralph and Sonia are whisked away to the back of the restaurant.

They settle in their seats and order drinks. Sonia adjusts her napkin. She studies the menu studiously.

'They were holding hands. Isn't she the one, is she, are they?'

Sonia glances at the blackboard specials high on an architrave, and then down at the couple.

'At a guess, yes. Don't look, don't bother about them, we're here for us, my love,' says Ralph. 'He's Argent, she's client, why shouldn't they have dinner together?'

'Why not indeed?' answers Sonia magnanimously, 'and why shouldn't they hold hands and play footsy? Or is it crutchy?' she continues, noting Jenny's slumped posture and calculating how far her foot must be stretched under the table.

'Are they? Oh, well for your information Sonia, it's all over with Jonno, who's back with Carol. So, thank goodness, matter closed.'

'And my Machiavelli has now seen something maybe useful to his cause—'

'But this is Paris, my love, they do things differently here.'

'True but wives tend to react in the same way the world over, Ralph, if only to maintain the upper hand. And I will have that glass of champagne.'

'It looks like we might be getting a bottle sent over from their table, my dear. Just a guess, of course.'

Chapter 91

'You're absolutely not the sort of bloke I ever go out with.'

Claire jumped slightly as she felt warm breath on her neck and the brush of lips over her tattoo before her jacket is draped over her shoulders.

'Ditto,' agrees Brian Arnold.

'So why did you ask me?'

She steps down into the alley outside the Nine Bells. The steps are worn, bowed by the feet of drinkers over hundreds of years. The pavement had been re-laid after the Second World War, but it, too looks worn down by the sheer age of the city.

The buildings leant over to look at them, windowsills eyebrows on ancient faces. Claire turns as Brian joins her.

'Because,' he says, awkwardly, avoiding her gaze as he smiles and looks around him. 'Because I like that you're, you.'

'Is this how you sell ads? You can do better than that.'

Claire links her arm through his. Brian effects an exaggerated Australian twang.

'OK Sheila, because you're tough on the outside and soft on the inside. How about you? You said yes.'

'I'm not entering a verdict yet, until we know each other. And that's not biblically.'

'OK.'

'Actually, you're the nice sort of Aussie. The old fashioned, laconic—'

'Jeez, Claire, enough. Let's just enjoy an evening together. Shall we work our way West and eat?'

They emerge from the alley and Brian waves down a cab as he speaks.

'Spanish OK?'

'If we can get in.'

'If we can't, we'll just have to find somewhere else,' he says as the cab stops and he moves to open the door for Claire and to direct the driver.

Chapter 92

'Where d'you reckon they'd have stood?' ruminates Phil, sitting down on the grass.

There's a single tree, its canopy full, next to a bowl of land gently sloping into a copse, tawny grass lying flat, hiding from the unseasonal heat.

'Who?' asks Jane, settling herself beside him with a slight exhalation of breath as she instinctively favours her stomach.

'Duellists.' Phil cocks a finger, 'Bang. This is the Heath duelling ground. Close to Kenwood House, but far enough away I suppose. They must have parked their coaches up on the road and walked in. No, they could have driven down a track. Wouldn't have wanted to carry a body out.'

'Don't be macabre. How long ago was this?'

'Couple of hundred years. Paul brought me here when I first came to London, and he reckoned: hey relax, Lily will be OK, she promised me she'd phone if she needed us. That's better.'

Jane leans back, her face softening as she looks up into blue sky.

'Paul reckoned there was a craze for duelling around the end of the 18th century and there was even a list of twenty six insults that could spark a duel between gentlemen.'

'Men. Typical,' comments Jane, archly.

'Yes, evidently right here in 1836, some dandy was shot in the neck when the other chap's musket ball ricocheted off his outstretched wrist, and all he did was shout to him, "are you satisfied," and the other one said, "yes," and they called it a day.'

Jane shakes her head in wonder at the male ego and the stupidity of it all, and they both settle back.

'You couldn't count the shades of green,' observes Jane.

'Aye,' says Phil, 'you can see what inspired Constable.'

'And John Keats. I'm getting to love London, Phil, I'd hate for us to leave it, not now.'

Phil plucks a blade of grass, and chews on it reflectively.

'You look like one of those peasants in the paintings.'

'They had it tough, those buggers, wasn't all, what's the word?'

'Bucolic. No, seriously,' Jane raises herself on one elbow and looks down at him. 'Phil, we need to settle things. I'm going to try and move within the Face organisation, perhaps into IT. I'm not bad with computers,' *as I proved when I got into Trevor Kane's and Human Resources' hard drives and erased the G and W creative assessment file, but Phil doesn't need to know that; he'll only fret,* 'have you spoken to Paul? He won't stay at Faceache, but you can, you're by far the best art director there, word is.'

'On Jonno's desk?'

'He leaves me stuff out to read.'

'The best art director at About Face,' Phil muses, 'and Fish Face, Pig Face, Fuck Face.'

Jane ignores him and continues. 'Jonno reckons they'll keep the remnants of G & W people with our current accounts, give Michael Michaels access to some of their creative people for the more clunky stuff; by the way, they're going to give him, Michael a second chance. He grovelled his way back in, wrote some cringing begging letters, and—'

'Leaves me without a writer if Paul goes.'

'Will he?'

'Reckon so, and quickly if the Brothers have anything to do with it. So, I'll have to find a writer quick smart. Shit. Shit.'

Phil sits up and tugs the grass stems he's been chewing from his mouth, spitting out the remnants.

'Let's not ruin a lovely afternoon. Time for tea for me, you and Caleb.'

'Polly.'

'It'll be a boy. Ultrasound will show it, won't it?'

Jane stood and stretched.

'Phil, how about we act all old fashioned and don't find out. Just wait till the birth.'

'Aye, it'll at least stop the oldies speculating.'

'And knitting.'

Phil allows himself to be pulled to his feet, puts his face close to Jane's and looks closely into her eyes.

'Say, eh oop darling, tha looks like tha could use a pint of Boddies.'

'Eh oop, what's that supposed to mean?' she looks puzzled as Phil takes both her hands.

'That means the big test, a weekend away from your mum while we go and see mine. Before young'un gets too obvious.'

He inclines his head down at Jane's abdomen. She looks apprehensive for a moment.

'We'll speak to Julian and the neighbour across the road, he fancies your mum.'

'Mr Edelmann?' Jane leans back to look suitably affronted, then grins. 'Actually, Mr E's a lively old bugger, lots of fun.'

'We'll hop on't train Friday night, no, we'll make sure Lily's OK first. We'll go early Saturday morning, get up there lunchtime.'

'Then you can go to football or whatever with your dad and leave me to chinwag with your mum.'

She looks at him appraisingly.

'OK,' suddenly decisive. 'OK, we'll put it to mum tomorrow. Julian's coming to lunch and I promised you'd be on your best behaviour.'

They stroll off across the duelling field.

'Right, I'll come straight out and tell your brother I were right out of order last time and I'm sorry but I were only rude to him because he's such a pompous prick.'

Phil suddenly walks away from Jane.

'Six, seven, eight,' he counts his footsteps off, spins on his heel and extends his arm, 'bang.'

He blows on his fingertips.

'Silly to get to ten and let other bugger fire first, eh?'

Chapter 93

'Cyn, Claire, Trevor Kane would like to see you both.'

Jane looks quizzically at the couple as she conveys the request.

'Probably wants to rap us on the knuckles for our impertinence in the research meeting the other day,' explains Cyn. 'Fancy going to the trouble of testing the crawling with germs ad with a bunch of consumers when its already boosted sales. Probably shouldn't have suggested post research was a fucking waste of time: which it was.'

Jane raises her eyebrows and diplomatically retreats.

Claire ponders. 'I'd have thought a talking to was Jonno's responsibility?'

'Well, he's away, and none of the senior creatives here are familiar with our work. And they probably haven't sorted out the department pecking order yet.'

A couple of minutes later, they stroll into Trevor's office.

'Ladies, come in, Cynthia, Claire take a seat. Tea, coffee?'

'No thanks Trevor,' they both demur, 'and I'm Cynthia, Trevor, she's Claire.'

'Ah, my apologies, all these new faces; right, ladies, I won't beat about the bush as I'm not one for going around the houses, but I've, we, the board, has come to a decision.'

Claire smiles: not in anticipation of what the board's decision might be, but to confirm Trevor's natural expression is that of a large man with a small, irritating insect constantly buzzing just off the end of his nose. Clearing his throat and linking his hands in front of him to indicate the gravity of the moment, Trevor continues:

'It's not without a degree of soul searching, heaven knows, but Face Argent have decided to offer you both redundancy, as you are both surplus to the creative department's current needs.'

Claire sits silent. She suddenly feels hollow, disappointed, sick, "sort of violated" as she explains later. It's my fault, she feels, I've let myself down and G and W down.

Cyn bursts out, 'You're firing us?'

'No, Cynthia,' replies Trevor, smoothly, 'redundancy, it's an unfortunate, the natural fallout, the flow on as it were, of a takeover.'

'But what about our accounts? You don't have a female creative team who,' her voice trails away.

She looks at Claire, who is close to tears.

'Indeed, no, and Jon, Jonno your CD, made that point very winningly to me the other day. Almost convinced me. Came in to discuss creative staffing with me and made the point very strongly just how useful you were and would be, how you were perfect for so many of our accounts.

'How, uniquely among his teams, you took direction from clients, how you understood household and feminine hygiene products, were brilliant at jingles and vignette commercials, and strong adherents to concept research; indeed he suggested you were a throwback to those times when the great female teams selflessly, yes selflessly, his word, tackled whitegoods, brown goods, washing powders and those other more female oriented accounts but—'

The fat toad. Cheeky bastard, mutters Claire, an admiring note in her voice.

Trevor continues, 'however, given your obduracy in a recent research meeting, much as I admired your creative director's defence of you, I didn't believe a word of it. So, sadly, we have decided to absorb your accounts into the existing Face Argent structure, which in itself is grounds for redundancy.'

Claire has regained her composure. She looks puzzled. 'In itself? There's something else?'

'Yes there is, ladies, because, of the quality of your work there's no question. However—'

Trevor stiffens his shoulders. The insect at the end of his nose is obviously buzzing loudly.

'As you know, we do not allow relationships between staff members, although we do make allowances for married couples but only if they are in distinctly different parts of the organisation, and are of different genders but seeing as you two have, are, reputedly—'

'Have, are, reputedly, what? Excuse us a moment, Trevor,' Claire rounds on Cyn, incredulous. 'Have you been, are you fucking Brian?'

Cyn's mouth falls open. 'Of course fucking not. Claire, you moll, have *you* been fucking Brian? You haven't.'

They both, for a moment, totally forget Trevor whose head swivels back and forth like a spectator's at Wimbledon.

'Well almost, just about, I am thinking of it,' Claire concedes, demurely. 'It has crossed my mind, severally. But fucking doesn't constitute a relationship. Sorry Trevor, you were saying?'

Cyn looks at her, jaw slack, a smile creeping across her features. The gravity of the situation is forgotten, for a moment.

'Ladies,' Trevor regains their attention. 'Ladies,' Trevor, puzzled, forges on, 'it's the nature of your personal relationship, with each other that has attracted the board's attention.'

'Our what, our personal relationship? Hang on, Trevor, you think we're an item?'

Trevor's discomfiture at even broaching the subject is obvious and Claire plays on it.

'Trevor, the board has determined that we're *vagitarians,* that we're in a *lesbian* relationship?' Cyn emphasises the words, to Trevor's obvious distaste and embarrassment.

'Not that it would be any of your business Trevor if we were. Think about it, if we were lesbian, and we were cohabiting, living together, we'd be discussing work all the time, not turning our brains off at 5.30 like those clueless automatons in your creative department.'

'Yes, Trevor, it's none of your fucking, and I use the word advisedly, fucking business but actually no, we're not.'

Claire, vehemently, icily, 'we're not fucking each other much as we like, in fact are very fond of each other. So that is a definite no.'

Claire sits back in her chair. Cyn is now angry, spits her words out.

'Yes, Trevor, I do, have had fleeting relationships with other women, and men, but Claire and I, no.'

'No Trevor, no, we don't sleep with each other,' Claire confirms, noting embarrassment and outrage are now mingling on the other side of the desk.

'We're not what you might call in your blatant male, what's the word, sexist, misogynist manner, carpet munchers, we're not muff divers.' Face reddening Claire pauses for breath, 'what gave you the idea we were in a lesbian,' she emphasises the word once again and gratifyingly sees him flinch, 'relationship.

And so what if we are? What's wrong with that? What business of how and who we both sleep with is yours? Where on earth did you get that idea?'

Trevor clears his throat before replying.

'Well we all, I, the management, we assumed—'

'That just because two women work as a team, they're in some sort of relationship?'

'Well,' mutters Trevor limply.

'Well, what?' Claire is clearly getting upset, 'is it because I look a bit butch, is that it Trevor, muscles here and there?' Claire flexes a bicep. 'Cropped hair?' She points at her neck. 'A tatt? And because Cyn's a little bit petite, preppy and fluffy pretty?'

'Hey, steady on Claire,' admonishes Cyn.

Drawing on Trevor's totally awkward body language, Claire's starting to relish the whole situation.

'Did you ask Jonno, Trevor?'

'Yes I did, indirectly.'

'And?'

'He seemed to find it amusing, but then realised the seriousness of my enquiry and said he didn't think so, and that anyway he didn't delve too deeply into his staff's shenanigans, his word, as it wasn't any of his business unless it affected their work.'

'Then what?"

'If you must know,' Trevor started to dig himself in deeper, 'Janice and I had a chat, and she said that in her experience, creative teams sometimes got very close. I believe in the 1970s, an American agency even encouraged it among their staff, they called it, "kiss kiss, bang bang".'

'What would Janice know, that dried up old prune?'

'Darling, don't get upset.'

Cyn flutters her eyelids at Trevor and moues. 'Assumption, Trevor, as my old production manager used to say, assumption is the mother of all fuck ups. And you and your board have just fucked up. Big time. Unfortunately, Claire and I don't fancy each other. Excuse us for a moment though.'

She turns to Claire, who, simmering, has brought herself back under control.

'Are you really thinking of having a scene with Brian? Establishing a Bondi beachhead, as it were?'

'Well,' Claire demurely confirms, 'I am working on it after hours, of course, Trevor. And weekends.'

Claire slowly starts to stand up.

'Sorry Trevor, but you can understand why we're upset. Yes, we do accept your offer of redundancy, but given the way the termination has been put to us, and the board's reason for it, my lawyer will want to look over the terms very carefully. And I shall tell him we want an extra emollient for defamation on Face Argents' part. And for the record, we wouldn't want to work for a bunch of sanctimonious, misogynist, sexist—'

'Narrow minded pricks,' concludes Cyn. 'And you can stick your agency right up your ugly tight little arsehole. That's after you've pulled the hair out of it.'

They stand, and Trevor does too. He's apoplectic. 'Get out,' he says, finally forcing the words through his teeth, 'get out of my office and my agency immediately. I'll have security—'

But the two girls are already going out of the door. They turn and demurely curtsey, in unison.

'Vagitarian?'
'Made it up. I was livid. His attitude.'
'Oh.'

'The girls have gone,' reports Jane to Phil and Paul. 'Came straight out of Trevor's office, asked me for one of those boxes we used to move the agency, and left the office. Security was lurking. Said they'd be down the Nine Bells, and please would you tell everyone they'd been fired.'

'Fuck me dead. Better get down there, they'll be upset. Freddy doesn't know?'

'Isn't in, yet. And I haven't seen Clayton or Christine.'

'Jesus, it's all happening this morning. Have you done the deed yet, Paul?'

'No, seeing Alf Bell this afternoon. But I'll call Freddy,' says Paul, putting his computer to sleep. 'Keep him up to date. So much for the pizza campaign for today, just when we were getting somewhere. Not that Freddy can do anything,' he says as an afterthought.

Chapter 94

Paul knocks and sticks his head around the door of Alf Bell's office. The new plate on the door not only has his name in full, Alfred "Alf" Bell but the title Group Executive Creative Director.

'Come in, Paul,' says Alf, indicating the chair in front of the desk.

'Thanks, Alf.'

Alf favours the look of the new age techno nerd, creative director; long, tousled, curly hair, round glasses, a neat V-neck jumper and crisp white shirt. The spare glass desk, large computer monitor, and array of other hardware proclaim I know things that you don't know. But his look is wary, guarded, and almost apprehensive. Paul's reputation as a writer and pure ideas man precedes him.

'What can I, we, do for you?'

Paul looks around the office. It's large, with a couch and conference table with a half dozen chairs. It smacks of ostentation and ego. Certificates from small and specialist advertising award festivals, several of which Paul is unfamiliar with, are grouped on the wall. The big shows, D&AD, The One Show, The Big Apple Festival, and Cannes are conspicuous by their absence. Alf sees Paul looking at them.

'Got a few.'

'Yeah,' says Paul, 'well done.'

Paul pulls an envelope from his pocket. Alf's name is written on it in brown ink, with Paul's characteristic flourish.

'My resignation,' Paul casually announces. Lounging on the chair as he almost insolently flicks it onto the desk. 'One month, though I'm prepared to go before that.'

An array of emotions flits across Alf's face, relief foremost amongst them.

'Philip's not?' Alf looks past Paul as if he expects Phil to amble in.

'Oh no, definitely not, on the contrary.'

Paul and Phil have carefully discussed Paul's exit strategy.

'No, Phil's really happy here. And so am I, great accounts, great possibilities, but we always said we wouldn't stand in each other's way,' he says blithely, as Alf winces slightly, before his expression became more calculated. How can he turn this to his advantage?

'It's just that I've had an offer,' continues Paul, 'Bros. The Kingston Brothers.'

'They're not opening here?'

'No, the New York office.'

Alf visibly relaxes.

'Aah, New York. Always wanted to work there, but Face insisted I stay here.' The inference leaves his importance unsaid.

'I'd always set my heart on it, and now, I am.' Paul shrugs exaggeratedly.

'Paul, sincerely, I wish you well.'

'Well, Phil's got our accounts properly under control, and I'm sure you can find him a writer, come to think of it, he's the sort of guy you might consider working with.' *I can't let this opportunity slip.* 'Shame about Claire and Cyn, though,' he shrugs offhandedly without any inflection, 'but shit happens, I'm sure the clients will understand.'

'I'm sure they will when the account directors explain to their clients.'

'Explain what?' Paul manages to look genuinely puzzled.

'About their relationship.'

'Eh?'

Alf puts on a responsible, corporate face. 'They're lesbians, and we don't allow interpersonal relationships between staff members. Not that it bothers me,' he adds hurriedly.

'They're Axminsters, Alf? Who says?'

'Trevor said they owned up to it. They protested so much that they weren't that he judged—'

Paul's whole mien changes, his expression hardens, he laughs harshly.

'C'mon, Alf, Trevor says? Who the fuck's Trevor to say? And how dare he make judgements or pronouncements and meddle in his staff's personal lives? Fuck it, Alf, it's none of your, our, my or the agency's fucking business. And I mean fucking, because they're not.'

'Unfortunately, Paul,' Alf adopts a mollifying tone, 'it is agency policy.'

'Agency policy to do what? No, no one thousand times no, it's not, it's an excuse to get rid of who the Face board see as potentially disruptive elements. Anarchic, nihilistic, even.'

Paul takes a punt. Phil hadn't had time to read the assessments of the girls so Paul goes for a smorgasbord of possible allegations.

'I can hear the board now and were you in the meeting? Disruptive, argumentative, prone to intemperate outbursts, drink to excess, have no respect for authority, especially males in authority, Sapphic tendencies.'

Alf's face colours, confirming Paul has guessed correctly. This makes Paul even angrier, his voice becoming vehement, loud.

For the benefit of any employees listening in, especially any girls, as he explains later.

'Anyway, they're lesbians? Aren't? Maybe? Were? Sometimes? Only on Fridays? What on earth does it matter? They're one of the best creative teams in town, regardless of gender. And they work their tits off. They'd have made you look good; you Alf, personally, think of that? Your name on their campaigns as creative director?

'Alf, don't buy into this corporate boardroom politics shit, creative directors are supposed to support their people, you've got a good rep round town, you're respected, you're better than this, Alf, better, much better. You could be one of the good guys.'

Alf looks at him, speechless, blinking behind his glasses.

'Forget it, I'm out of here, why should I care about you and this shithouse agency and its ridiculous policies. See you, Alf.'

Paul goes to slam the door, thinks better of it and walks out, closing it gently. Shocked and intrigued faces in the office quickly turn back to their desks as he stalks off down the corridor.

Chapter 95

Friday, and the G and W leftovers gather in the Feathers for a farewell drink with Cyn and Claire.

'Readers, Friendship, McBrides.'

Christine and Clayton walk purposefully into the pub, stand in front of the group and announce themselves with three client names.

'Readers, Friendship, McBride's,' repeats Clayton. 'It's enough to start an agency. 'And isn't this the staff standing right here?'

'It is, right enough, Clayton, I think they'll do,' confirms Christine.

Conversation is suddenly stilled.

'What? Clayton? Christine? Are you serious?' enquires Nigel. 'You are.'

'You bloody are,' repeats Paul.

'They're not kidding. Are you?'

'Hold on, and am I hearing this right? An agency, and bankrolled by?' asks Bitsa, doubtfully.

They all look at each other in turn, confused. Clayton and Christine just stand there, smiling at the general reaction.

'We're serious,' confirms Clayton with uncharacteristic brevity.

'Freddy? Is this Freddy?' suggests Cyn.

'Wow no, not for one second Cyn,' replies Christine. 'He mustn't suspect a thing. He's on a two year exclusion clause on the buyout. Gardening leave. Mustn't get a sniff, we can't compromise him.'

'Of course, silly me.'

'Mind you, he's appalled by the way we've all been treated, and maybe after we've established ourselves would agree to chair us, if we all agreed, on a part time basis.'

'And no,' Clayton butts in, 'no, as Bitsa has correctly discerned,' Clayton assumes his normal, formal, pompous patrician pose, 'finance was the first thing I looked at when the proposal was made, and since then I have made promising inroads with friends in the city.'

'Whoa, whoa, Clayton, Christine you're getting a bit ahead of yourselves here,' cautions Paul.

'Yes, whose proposal, whose idea is this?' demands Phil.

Christine and Clayton exchange a look.

'You two? Well, good on you,' says Claire, raising her glass.

Christine slowly shakes her head, no. 'It wasn't us.' She looks around the expectant faces, prolonging the moment. 'It's Alan Sergeant,' she affirms quietly.

'Sergeant? Bollocks. You what?' Phil exclaims incredulously amid general astonishment and expletives.

'He called me last week,' explains Clayton. 'Said he was worried that he wouldn't be able, in his words, to drag the same level of commitment and creative expression out of Face Argent that he's become used to, grudgingly, from G and W.'

Paul bursts out laughing, pure wonderment in his expression. '*Field Marshall* Sergeant? Blimey, what a turn up, wonders will never cease.'

'He suggested Reader might have to look elsewhere, at another agency, unless we could collectively come to some other arrangement. He emphasised collectively. When I responded positively, I must admit cautiously, he even suggested the account and creative teams he wanted working on his business should he have to look outside Face and something eventuates.'

'In other words he stipulated,' Paul shakes his head in wonderment, 'goodness gracious me.'

'No, not you Paul,' Christine gently appraises him, 'Cyn and Claire.'

'Well he would, wouldn't he, he thinks we do his work.'

'No, Cyn, he doesn't,' again corrected Christine. 'He took me aside after the last shoot and commented, quietly, that for a team who hadn't actually written the ads, Paul and Phil seemed unusually involved, especially when he expected cool detachment on their part. Just smiled that slop bucket smile of his and walked away.' She nods to Paul.

'I'm stonkered, flabbergasted.'

'And he'd already made it clear he knew very well where the flying underpants came from, but he didn't take it personally. All he and Kalamazoo are interested in is what ends up on TV, not on a cheese platter: and the sales figures after the ads run.'

'I'll never look at him the same way again.'

'I don't think you'll be looking at him at all, Paul,' says Clayton.

'Point taken, Clayton, but McBride's?'

'Face were in the Aunt Nora's pitch,' observes Nigel, 'Cummings has already seen what they're capable of or aren't. Clayton just has to play on that, don't you? They're not about to move the entire account so quickly, they might leave a bit at Face Argent, maybe even some of the design stuff, takes the onus off us, but they'd at least give us the lead agency role, after all, they've already stated they want the same people on their business.'

'Well observed, Nigel,' says Clayton.

'And Friendship?' Enquires Phil.

Claire puts her drink down, raises her hands and interlinked fore fingers. 'Christine and Angela Ainsworth,' she explains. 'Freddy's masterstroke.'

'And legacy, we hope, Claire.'

'The big stumbling block up front is that Face Argent would make a far better offer to all these clients than we can; they'd cut their margins to get them to stay.'

'We've already been through all that, Phil,' says Clayton, putting on his serious face. 'We'll just have to make sure we have some compelling reasons for them to come with us and not some other small creative shop.'

'Better the devil you know, Clayton,' says Cyn.

'Well Clayton, it's just your cup of tea,' states Nigel, 'stirring stuff, I'd say. And hot.'

Clayton looks at him questioningly for a moment, but Nigel's expression remains blandly innocent.

Phil shrugs. 'Go for it, you two, we're all sitting tight. But I'd tell all't clients on the q t how Claire and Cyn were fired and for what reason. Even Sergeant would understand injustice of that. Hardly the behaviour you'd expect from a top advertising agency.'

'We'll need affiliations,' ponders Bitsa.

'No more so than when we were G and W,' says Christine.

'Great name for an agency,' says Paul, 'G and W, readymade brand and advertising philosophy, G and W lives, make G ampersand W, I can see the logo, office in Soho, tab at Locanda, dum de dum, I'll register the name for you tomorrow.'

'Grace'll have to get the school uniform out again,' says Phil. 'Nah, only joking, Paul.'

A familiar smiling face is seen peering through the frosted glass in the pub door.

'Schtumm, everyone, here comes Freddy.'

'I've just had a thought.' Brian had stood quietly on the periphery of the group. 'This isn't so much a leaving drink for Cyn and Claire, but a staying drink; and just as they were off—'

'Like a sick prawn in The Simpson Desert,' finishes the group.

Later, much later, Paul and Phil find themselves in a corner of the bar.

'Well that's it then.'

'Suppose so, but it's fantastic if G ampersand W gets off the ground.'

'No, you and me. Just as we get something going.'

'Phil, think of Jane and the sprog. You'll make a great creative director, it's a big step up, share of the action and you're not a nasty, backbiting, malicious bastard like me.'

'Paul, you'll be OK in NYC. There'll be a lot of Scorpios there and most of them in the ad industry.'

'You've noticed.'

'Have to find yourself a French and a Feathers. Big call.'

Paul looks around at the familiar, comfortably worn surroundings.

'There's a few. Fanellis, for a start.'

'I'll miss you, you poncy Southern shitehawk. And Laurie and Beryl send their best wishes.'

'You make them proud of you, you big lummox. And don't look at me with those four pint eyes and go sloppy on me.'

Paul puts down his pint and looks at Phil questioningly.

'And no, I don't want Glorious as a leaving present.'

Phil looks taken aback. 'How dare you. Never even crossed my mind.'

'Only kidding, but it's just the sort of thing Bitsa would think of. The difference being we know Glorious actually fancied Trev.'

'Bitsa? Any man who can pour a double dark rum into a pint of Guinness shows a complete lack of judgement. C'mon, I've had enough. A well greasy kebab is calling.'

'How about a vindaloo with a pint of Kingfisher?'

'You've twisted my arm.'

Chapter 96

There's a knock at the door.

'Who could that be?' Asks Jane, grinning, 'I thought Julian had a key? I'll get it.'

She levers herself out of the sofa, but Lily's already halfway to the door, primping her hair and removing her apron. Phil sees Mr E out of the window. Mr E peers in and gives a thumbs up to Jane as she settles back down into the sofa. They hear the front door open, and Mr Edelmann's voice, 'Hello Lily, I apologise. I hope I am not late, you said around one?'

'No, er, Jonas, that's perfect.'

Lily, looking slightly flustered, puts her head around the sitting room door before sidling in guiltily with Mr Edelmann in tow.

'Er, Jonas, you know my daughter, Jane and this is Philip.'

'Lily, I have only known Jane since she was a baby, I changed her nappy when your Reginald decided he didn't want to. Jane, don't get up, and Philip, we have met.'

As he bent over to kiss Jane's hand, Phil was again taken by Jonas's uncanny resemblance to an elderly Albert Einstein, from the mischievous grin to the mane of white hair.

'I have brought a bottle of wine, not from the old country, well it is from the old country but from the off licence in the High Street.'

'It looks right handsome to me,' says Phil, 'but reckon a beer first, eh, Jonas?'

'I'll get that,' says Jane, 'C'mon mum, kitchen. Is Julian joining us?'

Lily's answer was lost as they left the room. Jonas mumbles a word under his breath.

'Sorry?'

'Pillock, that Julian, in your language, Phil,' says Jonas dismissively, settling himself in Reginald's armchair.

'Like Jane, I've known him since he was in nappies, flash git, as they say in the TV shows. Him and his Porsche, won't even park it in the street, scared it'll get vandalised.'

He quickly stops as Jane brings two beers before disappearing back into the kitchen.

'Well, chin chin,' he says, 'prost, bottoms up or whatever, here's to you and Jane and the babooshka. Cheers.'

Phil's mouth falls open as Jonas continues on cheerfully, 'Jane looks so well, positively blooming,' he pats his stomach.

'You noticed,' says Phil, incredulous.

'Of course, I've had three wives, not that I was married to all of them, and four children. Lily suspects, I think, but she's waiting for Jane to say something.'

There's a shriek from the kitchen.

'Either the penny has dropped or she has dropped something,' Jonas observes evenly.

Phil has gone bright scarlet. Jonas' voice takes on a resigned tone. 'Ah, and here, just as we have something to celebrate, is Julian. Oh, and the car. We are honoured.'

Phil looks out of the window. A yellow Porsche Carrera has parked by the front gate. Julian emerges, wearing his pink shirt and tartan golf trousers. Phil and Jonas listen to the conversation at the front door.

'Julian.'

'Afternoon, mum, finished golf early, one of the blokes had to rush off.' Pushing into the hall, 'Mum, you look all excited.'

Jane's voice from kitchen, a warning note; 'Mum.'

They enter the sitting room.

'Oh, Phil.'

'Julian, how are you?'

'Mr Edelmann.'

'Jonas, Julian, call me Jonas.'

'Yes, Jonas.'

Hands are cordially shaken. Jane enters, sharing a quick glance with her mother who smooths her hair back, colour returning to normal as she calms down. Lily smiles fondly, reassuringly at Phil; her hand touches his shoulder as she moves across the small room.

'I'll set another place for lunch and put on a few more potatoes. I'm sure the joint will stretch to five.'

'Nice trousers, Julian, what do the Scots call them, trews. You've been golfing?' asks Jonas.

Phil relaxes, audibly. Jane perches on the arm of his chair, her hand on his shoulder. As Phil later reports to Paul, 'Jonas picked up my baton and ran with it. It was like some relay race. All I had to do was watch.'

'I've never really understood golf, Julian, hitting a small white ball around the countryside. What did the American, George Twain say?'

'Mark Twain, Jonas. He said, I think, that golf was a good walk ruined. Something like that.'

Julian smiles, attempting to be amiable. He obviously feels some antipathy towards Jonas and his friendship with his mother but would be the first to see the advantages of a neighbour who watches out for her and so lessens his sense of responsibility even further.

'Of course, of course, Julian, Mark Twain. A term used when they measured the depth of the water under a Mississippi riverboat. You have brought some wine with you? Your nice golf club stuff? That pink one is agreeable. Light perhaps, but agreeable. I have brought some wine made in my country, it is a bit rough, full bodied, tannic, but fits with my mittel European persona.'

Jonas does it purposely, thinks Phil, to satisfy Julian's expectations and prejudices. Just as I play the uncouth Northerner, he admits to himself.

'Good round today, Julian?' asks Phil.

'Yes Phil, shot an 86,' replies Julian warily.

Phil feels Jane's grip on his shoulder tighten.

'That's good, what's that 14 over par? Playing to your handicap? Not easy.'

'Well yes, Phil, thank you.' Julian's tone is still wary.

Phil smiles.

'Well, Jane and I brought a bottle of red, to go with the beef, so that should be enough, what with you driving. Red rag to a bull, a Porsche and coppers.'

Julian's eyes narrow, he shifts nervously. Phil smiles up at Jane, moves his beer bottle to his other hand so he can squeeze the hand on his shoulder. Lily bustles in, still apron less.

'You're all alright for drinks? Jane, you'd better come and help.'

'Mum.' Jane looks around the room. 'I'll tell them now.'

She takes a breath and stands: 'I'm pregnant, Phil and I are going to have a baby.'

For a second, Julian looks annoyed, big brother protective, stares at Phil who smiles back, easily.

'Well, congratulations, you two,' he says finally, flatly, flapping out a soft hand to Phil, who shakes it.

'What, where, when?'

Phil answers, voice firm, decisive.

'Julian, it's not for months, yet. We'll get a flat in town and move in together, soon. Don't worry, trust me, I'll look after your little sister.'

Lily is beside herself, hopping from foot to foot.

'We should have champagne, me going to be a grandmother for the first time.'

She looks at Julian reproachfully.

Julian suddenly stands, dragging the Porsche keys from his pocket.

'There's an off licence down the road. Coming, Phil? You can watch out for parking wardens.'

Chapter 97

Freddy walks jauntily down the corridor of the executive floor at Face Argent, a man relaxed, a weight off his shoulders, though noting with a distinct pang how few G and W staff members are still at the agency. He pushes open the door of the boardroom. This was to be the last Face Argent, FA, Sweet Fuck All board meeting he'll attend, as he said to Polly that morning.

'Keep smiling, keep your powder dry, Freddy,' she'd advised.

The quartet in the boardroom looks up as Freddy walks in. Sir Francis Eccles MP, Group Chairman raises his leonine head, clearly affronted by the intrusion. Trevor Kane, the MD turns, face quizzical, as does CEO Janice Edwards who lifts her glasses from the table and puts them on.

Thin, weasel faced CFO Charles Driscoll raises his head slowly from a sheaf of figures. Exactly the same reactions, Freddy amusedly notes, as when Michael's had stupidly burst in to confront them. It had already been decided that as Freddy's clients were now being absorbed into Face, with its philosophy and ways of working, G and W's influence was waning, and his attendance at meetings was now a mere courtesy rather than a requirement.

'I'm superfluous to requirements,' as Freddy put it to Ralph and Sonia at dinner on a recent trip to Paris when he'd "signed the agency away" as he'd put to his reflection in the hotel mirror, bitterly swigging down a nightcap of scotch.

'The board had obviously been deep in conversation,' Freddy reports later in the Feathers, 'they stiffened when I walked in, their expressions hardened.'

Trevor Kane is first to speak.

'You knew about this didn't you, Grimshaw?'

'You may still call me Freddy, Trevor. About what?' Freddy enquires amiably.

'He engineered it more like,' says Janice Edwards, removing her glasses with a curt shrug of the head.

'Problem?' enquires Freddy, his mind racing.

'Three of your old clients, I should say our clients, have all contacted me in the last 48-hours to say they're reviewing their arrangements before formally signing contracts with Face Argent.'

Freddy looks puzzled.

'Which three?'

'Readers, Friendship, McBrides.' Charles Driscoll waves some letters at him.

'Well, I certainly haven't had any contact with the principals of those clients in the last fortnight,' states Freddy curtly. 'That's telephonically, by mail, fax, or verbally,' *or carrier pigeon,* he lists pedantically, swallowing the last bringer of news.

'In fact, this morning, I was going to confirm your suggestion that as I was now fully surplus to requirements, I should formally resign. But it now appears you might need me to talk to them on your behalf.'

There's quiet for a moment. Then Freddy speaks again, looking at each of the Face board in turn.

'However, given the way that you have treated some ex staff members of G and W who worked with those clients, I'm not sure that my heart would be in it, and given that I've not spoken to those clients for a fortnight anyway, nor have they attempted to contact me,' Freddy pauses to let his words resonate, 'then as they're now your clients, it's something that you have to deal with yourselves. I might be able to advise you as you're perhaps unfamiliar with the personalities involved but,' Freddy raises his hands in a "what-can-I-do" gesture, 'But what can I do?'

Again, there's silence. Freddy, sensing he has the upper hand, turns his back on the silent board members and walks across to the sideboard to pour himself a cup of coffee. He returns to the table and Trevor speaks, stiffly.

'You might, on behalf of Face Argent, ask them what they're doing.'

Janice speaks. 'But that, Trevor would be an admission of weakness on our part. And however Freddy puts it to them, it might drive them further away.'

'True, Janice,' Freddy says quietly and firmly, 'the facts are you did not, for one moment, talk with me or my clients up front, openly, when the takeover was mooted. Nor did you consult with me, informally, or my management group, on the best way to handle this takeover in human terms. Both with my clients, and my staff. I emphasise my as they, we, were still Grimshaw and Welby.'

He takes a sip of coffee.

'I was told many members of your staff went out of their way to make my staff welcome on a personal level, the banner on the building proved that, but the whole thing has been handled in an appalling manner. It was a takeover, so, you just took us over.'

Freddy pauses, coffee cup halfway to lips and looks at each of them in turn, again.

'Did you just expect my clients, some of whom have been with me for many years, to just walk in the door and say thank you for your munificence. For so generously,' he searches for the right term, 'appropriating them? I can't think our friends across the channel would be too impressed.'

Charles Driscoll slaps his hands on the table.

'Dammit man, you must have known something was up?'

'Charles,' admonishes Trevor.

'No, Charles, I didn't, nor, and perhaps I should have, nor did I warn you up front that some clients might feel unhappy with being so peremptorily informed of their new business arrangements. I'll admit that, after years of running an agency, maybe I just felt freed, that you'd taken over, and it was no longer my responsibility.

'Also, I never had any great personal ties with these clients. We weren't drinking or golfing buddies, I left that to my very able senior executives. Have you, did you talk to Ralph, Clayton, and Michael?'

The three look at each other.

'No, we thought we'd speak to you, first.'

'Why me? Would it not be, or have been better to consult them? Informally, in a civilised manner? Up front, as you should have immediately the takeover was confirmed?'

Freddy suddenly gets angry. Affronted. He puts his cup down.

'You assume I have something to do with my clients' recalcitrance, don't you? You impugn on my integrity. I gave you my agency, I gave you the results of 40-years of hard work, 40-years of fighting for good advertising, not dross. You insult me.'

Charles Driscoll half rises from his seat, jaw and fists clenched. Then subsides back into his seat. Freddy continues, 'Janice, gentlemen, I will not talk to *my* clients as it was your responsibility from day one. You did not consult with me so we might mutually put them in the picture. As far as I'm concerned, you showed a complete lack of trust in my ability to help you effect a smooth takeover and that was because you wanted my clients and not my staff. Here's my personal resignation from the board of Face Argent,' Freddy pulls a crumpled envelope from his pocket, smooths it and lays it on the table. 'Good morning.'

Freddy composes himself, picks a chocolate digestive biscuit from a salver on the table, nibbles it appreciatively, and takes another for good measure before walking out and shutting the door behind him.

Chapter 98

'Kickable stools,' says Bruce decisively, nodding his head with a serious expression.

'Hang on, Bruce, bit early, haven't even had me coffee yet,' says Phil amiably. 'And there are ladies present.'

Claire raises her eyebrows and look around the Reader meeting room. 'Where, where are they, Bruce?'

'The ladies or the stools, Claire?' enquires Cyn.

With Claire and Cyn no longer at Face Argent, Alan Sergeant has called a project meeting in his office. 'In this instance,' he informed Christine, 'I would like Claire and Cybrnthia to be involved. I believe though they are still being paid until the end of the month, and would like them to be present with, perhaps, the future in view.'

Given the situation, Clayton and Christine have made it very clear to the rest of the team that Reader must be serviced diligently, on a day to day basis. 'We want to keep them onside so let's all be on our best behaviour, however much it means you have to kowtow to Alan and Bruce.'

Phil puts down his coffee.

'Sorry, say again, Bruce?'

Alan Sergeant jumps in.

'Kickable stools,' he enunciates with great precision. 'Kick-a-ble stools. They're Bruce's pet project for pet dogs. Perhaps you'd like to explain, Bruce, amplify matters for the agency?'

Alan is relishing the moment and puts on his most malevolent smile. Bruce clears his throat.

'Our scientists and food technologists have been working on a day to day dog food formula that benefits dog owners.'

The agency looks at him expectantly. Bruce has the floor. His mien becomes even more serious.

'The one thing most dog owners dislike is picking up doggy's do's after their dogs have done. Even though the fines for not doing so can be quite prohibitive. Excuse me Claire, Cynthia and the more, well, runny it, the pooh is, the less owners are inclined to try and pick it up.'

Claire and Cyn nod sagely in agreement, grimacing sympathetically while simultaneously biting their tongues. Phil jumps in.

'Yes Bruce, I haven't got a dog, but I must say some of the residents of Camden are not that good at picking it up.'

'Don't assume anything, Philip. Strangely enough, it's not the nature of the demographic, it's a very personal thing, where some owners prove to be more responsible than others.'

Alan Sergeant smiles to himself. Obviously, ex G and W staffers have been instructed to tread on eggshells where their old clients are concerned. They were, as he reported to his wife later, 'being sickeningly obsequious. Risible is the word I normally apply to their attitude, but not today.'

'So,' Bruce continues, 'this is why our chaps have come up with a brilliantly apposite solution, an agent in the dog food, a stiffener as it were that renders a dog's faeces,' he looks around expectantly.

'Kickable,' says Cyn. 'So one might pick them up easily, even when tempted to irresponsibly kick them into the gutter.'

Claire winces. 'I'm not going to see all these constipated dogs crouched down the local park am I, Bruce, straining like crazy with their tails stiff, ribs showing and eyeballs out on stalks? The imagination boggles.'

'Claire,' replies Bruce, 'very perceptive, you've picked on the very stage the development is at. The degree of hardening agent.'

Imagine, Cyn thinks, what normal people might think of this conversation? The hospital staff up the street, for instance, who spend their day saving lives?

'Must also depend on the size of the dog, and the breed, the genetics,' muses Christine.

'And the serving size?' Offers Phil.

'I have to say,' Alan finally speaks, 'that I find the lack of jokes on the part of the agency somewhat disconcerting. But then Paul isn't with us.'

'Kickable stools,' says Phil. 'If we do any ads, will those be the words we use?'

'May be an awkward phrase,' agrees Claire.

'How about pickable stools, pickable upable?' contributes Cyn.

'I shall be copyrighting kickable stools,' says Bruce defensively, 'as my contribution to the creative direction.'

'Ah, so you've been kicking it around for some time, Bruce?' enquires Christine, brightly.

Had this been a G and W meeting, thinks Christine, it would have degenerated into crude, hilarious mayhem by now. But clients do tend to take their new products somewhat seriously.

Phil, in his new creative director elect role, and without Paul to egg him on, says quite soberly, 'Bruce, if we were first in't market with this product, would we get first dibs on words? Could we sort of make them ours?'

'Exactly, Philip, other entrants into the market would be loath to use the same terminology as ours, which is why Alan has sanctioned my seeking to copyright the phrase.'

Cyn was having difficulty not laughing. She could see Bruce's notes, his meeting prompt sheet, with words like apposite, rendered, sanctioned, prohibitive, and faeces underlined. Cyn settles for a friendly smile.

'Thus we might use supplementary phrases like doggy do's or poohs?'

'Poo and poohs is the territory of nappy and baby wipe manufacturers,' states Bruce.

'Toe punt that terrier turd,' says Claire. 'Sorry guys.'

'Boot that Boxer bum burger,' says Nigel, 'side foot that staffie shite, let's get it out of our systems now. We could even have a promotion, how far can *you* kick a stool?' he declaims.

'Don't leave behind what your dog's behind leaves,' contributes Claire, sagely.

'C'mon, guys,' admonishes Christine.

Alan Sergeant waggles a warning finger. 'Up to this point, I was happy to be free of Paul Johnstone's contribution and influence,' he says, resignedly.

'Sorry, Alan, Bruce, excuse my youthful enthusiasm, but I know,' Nigel quickly changes tack, 'but I know what it is to pick up after your dog. Our council supplies these plastic poo bag dispensers and they use words like pet waste.'

'They shilly shally around trying not to offend anyone,' agrees Christine, 'when words like turd are traditional, satisfying.'

'Sturdy,' agrees Claire. 'Good word, sturdy. There you go Bruce, there's your slogan. For sturdy turds.'

'I think there is room for movement, as it were,' continues Christine, 'into research among dog owners. Though kickable stools is a safe option, it is somewhat cumbersome. But we'll see. And the product might never—'

'Get off the ground?' suggests Claire.

'Fly?' suggests Cyn. 'Take off?'

'Exactly. Apt metaphors, ladies. Now let's move on to other business,' says Alan decisively.

'That's another word they use, business,' concludes Nigel.

Chapter 99

Freddy walks into the Feathers. He's surprised to see Clayton, Christine and the nucleus of his old team grouped at the bar. He stands, rocking back on his heels.

'A reception committee. What's all this? Well?'

The remnants of G and W staff stand in a tight cluster, serious, awkward.

'Freddy, we need to talk to you,' says Clayton, obviously designated the spokesperson.

'I thought I was coming in to talk to you?'

Phil walks over from the bar and hands Freddy pint. Paul appears from the gents.

'Hi, Freddy.'

'Paul.'

'Well?'

Christine nods to Clayton, who clears his throat.

'Well, Freddy, we couldn't say a word to you, couldn't compromise you; protocol.'

Paul speaks. 'Clayton, stop faffing.'

'Hardly your business anymore, Paul,' Clayton ripostes.

Paul nods in acknowledgement. Christine takes over.

'Freddy, Freddy,' she pauses for a moment, 'Clayton and I were approached, well actually it was suggested to us that we form an agency.'

Christine pauses, as Freddy's expression forms the quizzical question, who suggested?

'Believe it or not, Freddy, we were approached by, of all people, Alan Sergeant. He called it self-interest. So we hope you don't mind,' she rushes ahead, 'so if you don't mind we want to, should we go ahead, Freddy, well we've decided, we'd like to call the agency G & W. That's G ampersand W.'

Freddy stands there, emotion flooding into his face. He composes himself.

'You've, well, bloody fantastic, amazing. What can I say? Good on you,' His voice is cracking, 'and you've the clients onside? Well, of course you have, that's why I'm here. And I really shouldn't be.' He looks around him. 'You really shouldn't be talking to me, at all.'

'Have Kane and Edwards not talked to you?' Clayton enquires.

'Only this morning when I formally resigned from the board of Face Argent. They told me Readers, Friendship and McBrides want to reconsider their arrangement with Face Argent.'

'McBrides,' shouts Nigel.

'McBrides,' echoes Bitsa, slapping Phil so hard on the back, he spills his pint.

Claire walks over to Brian and kisses him full on the lips.

'We'd formally written to all three, stating our intentions,' Christine explains to Freddy, 'but we hadn't heard back from McBrides until just now.'

'I'd better kiss you, too,' Claire says to Paul. She kisses him and turns to Freddy. 'Paul wrote the proposal, his first and last act for G and W.'

'Last?'

'I'm joining Bros Brothers in New York.'

'We couldn't afford him, so,' explains Bitsa.

'Whoa, whoa, so if this all goes ahead, who will be who? Or whom?'

'Phil will be CD,' explains Cyn, 'Sergeant asked that Claire and I continue to work on the pet foods and we've done most of the Friendship work for next year already.'

'And McBrides?'

She shrugs. 'Freddy, we've put you in a bit of a compromising position, haven't we?'

'Not legally, have we?' enquires Nigel.

Freddy throws up his hands.

'As a final act, I said I'd call the clients and ask them why they haven't signed their contracts. And then, thinking about it, and the way they'd handled the whole shebang, and more, the way they'd treated my staff, I reneged. Withdrew my offer. It came back to me that many years ago, many, Marcus Welby impressed upon me that an agency isn't a bottom line, an agency is people.'

Freddy looks around his momentarily silenced audience. Clayton holds up a hand.

'Freddy, you asked us to meet you here. And in deference to you, there was no way we'd be economical with the truth. I apologise that, in our enthusiasm, we could have put you in a compromising position. Thank goodness we haven't. Also, you encouraged clients to speak to each other, so that their relationship with their agency was always open and—'

Freddy raises both hands in supplication.

'Yes, yes, OK Clayton, good point. And yes, I've always encouraged clients to talk to each other at agency get-togethers though it's a bit of a ploy, reasoning we'd have more clients happy with us than unhappy and they could influence those who were a bit off that week.'

'Backfired in the Crash era, Freddy.'

'Yes, Paul, it did but I still feel it's an honest policy.'

'Freddy, one thing,' Cyn takes Freddy by the elbow, 'you haven't heard about Claire and I.'

'The redundancy, Cynthia, redundant, it's such a dismissive word. Has a horrible finality to it.'

'We'd call it a firing. And I thought I'd better mention it because I've referred it to a lawyer.'

'A lawyer?' Freddy looks puzzled, then concerned.

'It was the nature of it. Kane told us we were being made redundant because Clair and I were in a relationship, and it was against company policy.'

'Eh?'

'He said the board had decided, determined, we're lesbian.'

'I assumed you were, Cynthia,' Freddy says straight-faced, and seeing her momentarily taken aback breaks into a broad grin. Cyn's face relaxes into a wry smile.

'Typical male.'

'Gotcha.' Freddy shrugs. 'Not that it's Face Argent's, mine, or anyone else's business.'

'Exactly, it's just that you were still on the board, Freddy, when it happened, but I'll tell my lawyer you were unaware, had absolutely no knowledge.'

Lawyer? Not that good looking lawyer who props up the front bar of the Nine Bells who's been chatting her up? whispers Paul sotto voce to Bitsa.

Bitsa nods, *Cyn does spend a lot of time in the front bar.*

Conversation is stilled for a moment as the atmosphere of giddy excitement subsides.

Clayton jumps in, 'then it falls to Christine and I to inform the clients you're no longer with Face Argent?'

'Please do, Clayton.'

'And Freddy, if they do happen to call you, you'll put in a good word for the new G&W?'

'Spoken like the consummate salesman, Brian.'

Freddy changes the subject, 'any other news?'

Jane seizes the moment.

'I'm pregnant,' she announces.

'Fantastic,' reacts Nigel.

'Yes fantastic, marvellous,' chime in others.

Freddy seizes her, then careful not to crush her, leans in and kisses her cheek. He then stands back, looking, hard and questioning at all the other men present, one by one. He finally settles on Phil and shakes his hand.

'Very funny, Freddy,' says Paul, the general mood lightening again.

Jane looks around her at the others, whose reactions were muted, or strangely forced.

'You all knew,' she says accusingly, in a hurt voice.

Claire puts down her drink and gently puts her arms around Jane.

'Felicity in accounts wasn't the only one who heard you puking. And she only mentioned it to a few G and W people.'

'And I have children, Jane,' says Christine quietly.

Freddy had gone to the bar, is leaning over it and pointing at the bar fridge. He holds up two fingers to Jimmy, who bends to open it.

'Oh no, not more focking jumping grape,' says Phil.

Chapter 100

It's the day before Paul takes off for New York. He's excited, apprehensive, just, he admits to himself, a little bit scared. Isn't worth doing if you're not, he tells himself as he enters Soho Square, skirting Cibber's statue of Charles the Second; something of a talisman throughout his career.

He'd walked past and stopped to read the plaque on the plinth on the way to the first morning in his first job as a copywriter. Lingering for a minute to collect his thoughts and calm himself before facing new colleagues, his first brief, and the dreaded blank page.

Two jobs later, he still hadn't strayed from Soho. He'd decided, for old times' sake, to take one more walk around the familiar streets, commit them to memory. But why, when there was going to be so much new in NYC to assail the senses?

Because, he said, because for him Soho was, as he'd discussed over several beers with Freddy; well, because it was, is, Soho. Their conversation had dwindled into silence, into a shared understanding as they'd stared deep into their fast dwindling pints.

Paul has decided upon a well-considered route. Down Greek St, along Old Compton, back up Frith, out of the side of Soho Square, into Dean Street and straight down and into the French at a leisurely pace.

"I'm going to stroll and gawp. Be a tourist." He stops suddenly, spins to look up at the façade of a building.

'Fuckin' tourist,' shouts a bike courier, swerving to avoid him.

Is it all in my head, thinks Paul, the magic, the knowing that Soho was the refuge, the haunt, gathering place of artists and bohemians, the disaffected, refugees, composers, writers, n'er do wells and misfits.

'Or even if you weren't aware, would it make you feel that? You feel it and understand,' Freddy, deep in his sentimental cups, had once suggested.

Paul ponders, if Freddy was right, would he have naturally gravitated here even if his career hadn't determined the move? Or would he have just walked through noting the neon, the mean, pinched buildings, few of architectural merit.

The tawdry, the tatty, the sleazy, interspersed with small businesses, small tradesmen and suppliers who in other districts, like New York's "Soho," have been forced out by flash fashion stores, the power of the brand.

Paul notes the new restaurants, bright, lively, optimistic, welcoming and already busy. Tables straggle onto narrow uneven pavement or hug the fronts of buildings with their worn, oft overpainted window frames.

But then Soho has always had its restaurants, its meeting places, introduced by those migrants, especially Italian and Greek, who'd created little corners of their homeland.

Contributing to Soho's enduring potion of tatt and treasure, sex and style, an oddly fascinating mixture. That's it, he thinks, it appeals to me, it appeals to me that it has existed in this way for centuries, the changes subtle, absorbed.

It appeals to me because I feel at home here, gravitate back to it whenever I feel melancholy, need a lift, and want to see a sardonically smiling, chagrined face of life. Stumbling out of Ronnie Scott's at 2am into dark drizzle, the sour taste of the hangover already in the mouth, the music still in the ears.

Or walking the streets, rain coated shoulders slowly getting chilly damp but feeling strangely exhilarated, drifting into a pub, knowing you'll hear a snatch of conversation, a turn of phrase to delight or disgust, surprise or crudely repel.

Seeing two famous actresses having a G and T on a dank low clouded day, pub already steamy, the fug of cigarette smoke lurking just under the ceiling, one actress perched on a bar stool pushing the other's large dog's probing nose away from under her bunched up skirt with her toe and saying casually, 'you can let him fuck you, darling, but he's not fucking me.'

The dark piss reeking doorways where he'd sheltered to light a cigarette; oh, for the days of Gauloises, Boyard Caporal, Morris's Egyptian; the aroma trapped in the damp wool of raised lapels.

'Tobacconist on a corner in Old Compton Street was where I bought them,' George once said, 'those oval Wills ciggies.'

The girlfriend who smoked Sobranie Black Russian who hadn't believed the Tiffany lighter Paul had given her was real. It was that doorway there where they'd stood and where she'd looked at the lighter, and him, suspiciously. She'd dropped him or was it vice versa, two days later.

He pauses at Locanda's dark doorway, suddenly realising he unconsciously memorises Soho every time he walks through it, however indifferent the buildings are to him. After all, they'd seen it all and would continue to do so.

Or was this realising just an excuse not to walk every street? His pace quickens as he reaches Old Compton, turns right, and right again as he moves into Frith Street. His feet take him into Bar Italia.

'Doppio espresso, please.'

He stands, facing the mirror as he always does. Finishes it in two slurps. Coming out of Bar Italia, Paul instinctively turns left, towards the French. Remembering his resolve to go right, then thinks what the hell and turns left again, oblivious to a passer-by doing a shuffling dance to avoid Paul's gyrations. Paul's seen it all before anyway.

'Oops sorry,' he mutters as he forces the man into the gutter, earning a reproachful glare.

He walks in the left hand door of The French and up to the bar as once he had so many years ago, intrigued by the worn brown woodwork, those proud posters on the wall, pronouncements of liberty by Charles de Gaulle and the Free French, long gone.

This'll be the last time for some time, he muses.

An aperitif, he decides, just as once I had my first one, was it so many years ago, a gauche junior copywriter from the suburbs, wondering what the elderly roué at the bar was sipping. And so plucked up courage and asked him, respectfully, much to the older man's amusement, and when he gently and graciously explained, bought him another. He was shyly tentative, again.

'Afternoon, it is just, isn't it Agnes, a Lillet I think, please.'

'And a bottle of Rose, you poncy flash git.'

Phil's bushy eyebrows twitch outside the window.

'You sentimental arsehole, 'scuse Agnes; Paul, you didn't think I was going to let you out of my sight today of all days, did you?'

Chapter 101

The next day Paul, Phil and Jane stand on the pavement outside Paul's old flat. A cab idles by the kerb. The driver picks Paul's suitcase, waves Paul aside, and hefts it in. Paul looks up at the place that had been his home, looks down the line of plane trees whose leaves languidly wave goodbye in the breeze.

Paul turns to look fondly at the couple he's passed his flat on to. Jane shrugs from under Phil's arm and steps forward. She puts her hand on Paul's shoulder for a moment then steps forward and hugs him, kissing him decisively on one cheek and then the other.

'You'll come back to see the babe, won't you? You'll bring Becs?'

She cocks her head at him.

'You've got to, seeing as you're his, her godfather.'

Paul nods. Jane steps aside for Phil. He steps forward and wraps his arms around Paul.

'Give us a hug, you soppy bastard.'

They wrap their arms around each other, slap each other on the back.

'You look after yourself, and her,' Paul mumbles into Phil's curly thatch.

'Yeh, ditto, go well, you know. I owe you a lot. Don't take any shit from the cockney brothers. Be Paul, you know. Be Paul.'

'Love to your mum. Have a pint in top club with Laurie for me.'

'A martini with Becs in that bar you go to.'

Paul's voice cracks as they disentangle themselves.

'Yeah well, love you both, bless you.'

Phil stands back, shakes his head like a big shaggy dog, putting his arm around Jane as Paul opens the cab door, pauses, looks back at the couple and salutes.

Jane pats her stomach. Phil suddenly smiles.

'Eh oop,' he gestures dismissively, 'now fook off.'

Postscript

Freddy Grimshaw pauses on the kerb in Broadwick Street, teetering for a moment, uncharacteristically prudent as a white van rushes by.

He looks around and up, affectionately, above the shopfronts and restaurants, above the hair salon being unlocked by a yawning assistant. Up at the worn, pitted, darkened brickwork and wonky windows of narrow Soho buildings that hide who knows how many generations of hopes and secrets.

Freddy, you're a romantic old fool.

He crosses the street and makes his way down towards Golden Square, to a nondescript, modern, dun fronted office building. Pausing on the steps, he looks around to see no one is watching and quickly rubs a sleeve over a brass plate neatly etched G&W in Bodoni Book.

He pushes open the glass door and turns right through another glass door into a modest reception area. He nods approvingly at the vase of fresh flowers on the desk, and notes receptionist Grace Selby has her long hair neatly pulled back and is wearing a severely cut black jacket and white shirt buttoned to the neck. She half rises from her seat.

'Boss man,' voice excited, 'Mr Grimshaw, where have you been?'

'Freddy,' says Freddy.

'Alright,' Grace smiles her familiar, wide, ingenuous smile, 'Now you're not bossman, you can be Freddy.'

'Thank you, Grace.' Freddy appraises her. 'Reader Industries not in today?'

'Yes, they are.'

Freddy cocks his head questioningly.

'Mr Sergeant took me aside at Christmas drinks and said the school uniform was a bit much, didn't do his, or my image any favours.'

'I said yes, it was probably time we both grew up a bit.'

'Grace,' said Freddy, 'very bold of you. A mature and perceptive observation.'

'He'd had a few by then. So had I, come to that. Where have you been, Mr Grimshaw, Freddy, if I may ask?'

'I was on a two-year exclusion clause, Grace, couldn't show my face anywhere near the agency.'

'Oh, I see. Ralph popped in the other day, looked very well, living in Paris now.'

'Jolly good.'

'Ooh, ooh and Jane's bringing Marion in today. Marion's the image of her mum.'

'Thank goodness for that.'

'Morning, Freddy.'

Freddy does a double take at the crop-haired, beardless, suited figure in front of him.

'Goodness gracious me, it's Philip. Thank goodness, the eyebrows still give you away.'

Phil steps forward with a broad smile and takes Freddy's proffered hand. Holding it, he turns his head and shouts, 'Eh oop you lot, look busy, chairman's in.'